FAMILIES, INTIMACY AND GLOBALIZATION

SOCIOLOGY FOR GLOBALIZING SOCIETIES

Responding directly to the globalization of society, this series combines survey, critique and original contribution, demonstrating what sociologists can bring to our global understanding of various areas of study. Individual volumes focus on the complex conditions of globalization in a particular sphere of human life, considering the philosophical, conceptual and methodological issues arising from globalization. Written by leading and emerging authors in their fields, each title simultaneously depicts the main contours of the area under investigation and offers a unique perspective on the matters at hand. In this way, readers are challenged to really think about – rather than passively accept – the issues under discussion.

Also published

GLOBAL HEALTH INEQUITIES
Fernando De Maio

SOCIAL MOVEMENTS AND GLOBALIZATION
Cristina Flesher Fominaya

HUMAN RIGHTS IN A GLOBALIZING WORLD
Darren J O'Byrne

FAMILIES, INTIMACY AND GLOBALIZATION

FLOATING TIES

RAELENE WILDING

First published 2018 by
RED GLOBE PRESS

Red Globe Press in the UK is an imprint of Springer Nature Limited, registered in England, company number 785998, of 4 Crinan Street, London N1 9XW.

Red Globe Press® is a registered trademark in the United States, the United Kingdom, Europe and other countries.

ISBN 978–1–137–33859–4 hardback
ISBN 978–1–137–33858–7 paperback

A catalogue record for this book is available from the British Library.

A catalog record for this book is available from the Library of Congress.

Contents

List of Illustrations   viii
Acknowledgements   ix

1 Families, Intimacy and Globalization: An Introduction   1
   Caring for parents from a distance   2
   Defining 'the family'   3
   Individualization and families   7
   Families in practice   11
   Globalization and migration: a story of turbulent homogeneity   12
   The complexities of global migration   13
   At the intersections: families, intimacy and globalization   16
   Structure of the book   18
   Conclusion   20

2 Transnational love and partnering   21
   Love and marriage in late modernity   21
   Romantic love and the pure relationship   23
   Marriage and family formation   26
   Love and marriage in globalization   28
   Marriage in a transnational community   28
   Marriage across national and cultural borders   33
   Transnational online dating   37
   Conclusion   39

3 Distant Couples   40
   A story of love, marriage, mobility and separation   40
   Marital relations and gender equality   42
   The trailing spouse   45
   Commuter couples   46
   LAT relationships   48
   FIFO relationships   50
   Transnational marriages   52
      Left-behind wives   52
      Left-behind husbands   55
   Conclusion   57

4 **Transnational Parents and Global Care Chains**   59
   The contradictory conditions of parenting   59
   Transforming parenting   60
   Global care chains and displaced mothering   65
   The global nanny   67
   Mothering from a distance   70
   Fathering from a distance   72
   The organization of childcare   74
   Conclusion   76

5 **Transnational Childhoods**   78
   Growing up in a non-traditional family   78
   Transforming childhood   79
   Children's experiences in the global care chain   81
   Migrating 'for the children'   86
   Forced return migration   88
   International adoption   92
   Conclusion   95

6 **Aged Care and Intergenerational Relations**   97
   A transnational care crisis   97
   Ageing populations and the care 'crisis'   98
   The 'left-behind' elderly   104
       Parents in Calcutta with children in the USA   105
       Parents 'left behind' in Albania   107
   Transnational aged care   108
   Transnational grandparenting   113
   Conclusion   114

7 **The Global Extended Family: Identities and Relatedness** 116
   A dispersed refugee family   116
   The nuclear and extended family   117
   Transnational families   120
   A Caribbean transnational family   123
   A Tongan transnational social field   128
   Indian transnational households   131
   Conclusion   134

8 **Beyond Heteronormative Relationships**   136
   The right to be a family   136
   Heterosexuality and the family   138
   Families of choice?   138
   The suffusion of families and friends   141
   Personal life and emotion work   142
   Queer migrations   144
   Transnational families of choice?   146
   Migration and the fluidity of sexual identities   149

Transnational friendships 151
Communication technologies and long-distance relationships 152
Conclusion 153

9 **Families, Intimacy and Globalization: Floating Ties** 155
Distant love? 157
The world 'family'? 159
Globalization of nuclear family ideology 161
From love to care 163
Nation-states, institutions and the world family 165
Floating ties 168

References 172
Index 197

List of Illustrations

Figures

1.1	Estimated proportions of 'nuclear families' (couple with children households) in select decades	4
1.2	Estimated proportion of single-person households	11
2.1	Crude divorce rates per 1000 population, 2011–14	25
4.1	Declining fertility in select nations around the world	61
9.1	Institutional, cultural and material constraints on perceived freedoms of the individual	166

In Focus

1.1	Nuclear family ideology	5
1.2	The reflexive self	8
1.3	Alternative readings of the individualization thesis	10
1.4	Creative responses to border closure: Turkish migrants in Germany	15
2.1	Heteronormativity and family formation	22
2.2	Sources of constraint in local marriage markets	27
2.3	National policies and international marriage	29
2.4	Mail-order brides and women as victims	34
3.1	Mobilities and mobile lives	44
3.2	Marriage as commitment to place and culture	53
4.1	Perspectives on parenting from Ghana	64
4.2	The national production of global care chains	66
5.1	Satellite babies	84
5.2	Unaccompanied refugee minors	89
6.1	The 'sandwich' generation	99
7.1	Family displays	121
7.2	Global householding	124
8.1	Suffusion and ideal types: family, friends and acquaintances	142

Acknowledgements

The research in this book has been supported by the Australian Research Council, La Trobe University Transforming Human Societies Research Focus Area, and La Trobe University Social Research Assistance Platform. No book is produced in isolation. This one is the result of many conversations and engagements with researchers and research participants, students and family members. I owe a debt to them all for inspiring my work and for helping me to think through the issues and examples that are explored and interrogated in the pages that follow. This book has benefited in particular from the close reading and excellent advice of a number of people, including: Loretta Baldassar, Cathrin Bernhardt, David de Vaus, Luke Gahan, Carolina Hernandez-Losada, Mary Holmes, Helen Lee, Makiko Nishitani, Wilasinee Pananakhonsab, Kerreen Reiger, Supriya Singh, Natcharee Suwannapat, Thanh Vu Thi, and the members of the Migration and Mobilities Research Group, convened by Val Colic-Peisker, who provided such insightful critiques at an early presentation of some of this work. I am particularly grateful to Shane Worrell for his assistance, and to the anonymous reviewers for their excellent advice. Thank you also to the dynamic, changing but always supportive team at Palgrave, in particular Tuur Driesser and Lloyd Langman. Of course, I take full and sole responsibility for the gaps and errors that remain in spite of their thoughtful suggestions.

Finally, no examination of families or intimacy is possible without reflecting on and situating that analysis in the context of ongoing experiences of caring and being cared for. I am grateful to the many people who consider me to be part of their family, and whom I consider to be part of mine, regardless of where they live around the world. This work would not have been possible without you.

Families, Intimacy and Globalization: An Introduction

The family is fundamental to human experience. Yet what is meant by the term is highly variable. For some, 'family' refers only to those who are related by bonds of birth or marriage that cannot be broken, even under conditions of violence and abuse. For others, 'family' refers only to people who share a committed, loving and caring relationship, regardless of the presence or absence of biological or legal connections. Cultural diversity adds to this already complex picture. What people mean by apparently simple terms that we all take for granted, such as 'marriage', 'parenthood', 'love' and 'care', can vary a great deal across national, cultural and linguistic borders. At the same time, people are crossing those borders at ever-increasing rates. The forces of globalization are contributing to unprecedented global population mobility, with many people travelling to other parts of the world for a range of reasons, including work, tourism, leisure, safety, or simply to be closer to their family and friends. Meanwhile, objects, ideas, images and media are circulated at incredible rates, transforming local cultural meanings and practices through their expression of visions and fantasies of how others are living out their lives elsewhere in the world.

This book is about the complex forms of families and intimacy that are being produced under contemporary conditions of globalization. I interrogate the ways in which intimately personal emotions and relationships are enmeshed in much larger forces of social and cultural change. These seem to create infinite possibilities for individual choice, yet national policy regimes, global economic inequalities and historical legacies continue to pattern individuals into narrow frames of moral obligations and structurally imposed requirements. My approach to investigating these complex relations is informed by an ethnographic sensibility, based on a firm belief that it is in the analysis of the micro encounters of everyday life that the larger-scale realities of national and transnational systems become evident, and that grand theories of social life must be tested. That is, the larger global transformations are evident in the small stories of how people interact with and care for each

1

other, and what they think and feel about their relationships. For that reason, I now turn to a brief story of family care, in order to begin teasing out the complexity of families and intimacy, migration and globalization. This leads to a more detailed discussion of the key concepts and debates that frame current knowledge of families under globalization, before I conclude the chapter with a brief outline of the chapters that follow.

Caring for parents from a distance

In early 2001 I was conducting an interview in Perth, Western Australia, with John, a man born and raised in Ireland, who for about 25 years had been living in Australia where he had married and raised his own children. The interview was for a project exploring how migrants care for their ageing parents across distance. During the interview, John described to me how he phoned his parents every Friday evening, visited them at least twice a year while in Europe on business, and had recently returned to Ireland for a few weeks to look after his father while his mother recovered after a short time spent in hospital. He explained that he shared the care of his parents with three siblings – two brothers who lived in Ireland, and a sister in the USA. This meant more phone calls, more visits in combination with business travel, and the occasional visit from family members to stay in his home in Australia. This was precisely the sort of intensive transnational activity the project was designed to capture, and the interview had been going well. Until, that is, I asked what I thought was a fairly innocuous question. 'Why do you do all of this?' I enquired, referring to the ongoing communications, visits and caregiving. He stopped, stared at me with an incredulous look on his face, and then responded: 'Because they're my mum and dad.'

For John, this answer was so self-evident that it seemed odd even saying it out loud. He phoned, visited and cared for his parents and siblings because they were his parents and siblings, with all of the assumptions about love, care, support and protection that this intimate family relationship entails. However, his simple response has remained with me over the years because it both answers everything and also almost nothing. After all, not all children want to care for their parents, ageing or otherwise. Neither do all people cooperate with their siblings. Some are disinterested, or too preoccupied with other parts of their lives, such as work, friends or children. Some have been abused, neglected or rejected by their parents as either children or adults and choose to live far away. Others have difficult relationships with siblings that they seek to escape. Sometimes, living at a distance from relatives can seem an easy solution to a difficult relationship, including when there are differences of opinion about lifestyle choices and sexual identities. By living in another country, it may be easier to reduce the expectations of being involved in each other's lives.

John's answer to my question helps to highlight some of the challenges that emerge in any effort to understand families and intimate life. There is a problem in generalizing about something that on the one hand seems to be universal and all-encompassing, while on the other hand is clearly contingent on an individual's own personal circumstances, family history and interpersonal relationships. This is the challenge that all researchers of family and intimacy have been required to grapple with, resulting in a long history of shifting approaches to defining both family and, more recently, intimacy.

Defining 'the family'

American anthropologist George Murdock (1965 [1949]: 1) argued that, while the term is admittedly ambiguous, 'family' can be usefully defined as:

> A social group characterized by common residence, economic cooperation and reproduction. It includes adults of both sexes, at least two of whom maintain a socially approved sexual relationship, and one or more children, own or adopted, of the sexually cohabiting adults.

In fact, rather than defining 'the family', what Murdock was actually defining was a much more limited social arrangement, 'the nuclear family', which he nevertheless contended was 'a universal human social grouping ... in every known society', successful and universal because it meets all of the necessary functions for human survival. Talcott Parsons (1955) extended this idea, by arguing that the nuclear family had evolved to meet the needs of 'modern man' in capitalist societies. It was mobile, efficient and fulfilled five necessary functions that were not accomplished elsewhere in a capitalist society: providing an appropriate site for approved sexual relationships; organizing economic cooperation by dividing tasks into male and female responsibilities; meeting the needs of reproduction by being the place for bearing and raising children; contributing to the socialization of both children and adults; and finally, of particular importance in the cold, uncertain context of modern society, providing a site of emotional support and psychological security.

Possibly informing their observations was the fact that, at the time Murdock and Parsons were writing their accounts of the family, they were surrounded by evidence of the triumphant dominance of the male-breadwinner nuclear family. In the 1950s, the UK, USA and other Anglophone nations such as Australia and New Zealand had larger numbers of nuclear families than any other household form, and more than had ever before been recorded (see Figure 1.1). In the USA, about two-thirds of households were nuclear families. However, unfortunately for Murdock and Parsons, this prevalence of the nuclear family was short-lived. By the twenty-first century, the nuclear family has become just one among many possible family forms, even in those nations where it briefly enjoyed ascendancy.

Accompanying the demographic dominance of the nuclear family in the middle of the twentieth century, there was also a widespread perception that the nuclear family was the most natural and normal family form. Other family types were considered dysfunctional and even pathological. However, by the 1960s it was becoming clear that divorce rates were high and rising,

	1950s	**1970s**	**2000s**
Australia	65%	44%	34%
United Kingdom	48%	43%	30%
United States of America	66%	40%	23%

Figure 1.1 Estimated proportions of 'nuclear families' (couple with children households) in select decades

Data compiled from ABS Census; Office for National Statistics 2015; Wetzel 1990; Hugo 2001; de Vaus 2004; Beaumont 2011; Cohen 2013; Vespa, Lewis & Kreider 2013.

there were increasing numbers of single-parent families and step-families, the age at first marriage was rising, there were increasing rates of cohabitation before or instead of marriage, and more people were having children without marrying (Cherlin 1981; McRae 1999; Hugo 2001; de Vaus 2004; Coontz 2005; Charles, Davies & Harris 2008). Indeed, as Jon Bernardes (1985) points out, a number of studies in the UK and the USA in the 1970s indicated that the so-called 'normal' nuclear family was not actually very common at all. How was this gap between the ideal social arrangement and actual social practices in nations around the world to be explained?

Many commentators at the time pointed to the social, political and economic turbulence they perceived around them, which they suggested was upsetting the 'normal' order of things. Some argued that this turbulence was placing the family in crisis and demanded that something be done (i.e. by governments) to fix it through legislation and policies that might protect the nuclear family. However, not everyone saw these changes as indicating a crisis. Feminist scholars, for example, argued that the nuclear family arrangement primarily benefited men and was largely detrimental to women (Reiger 1985; Waring 1988; Baker 1995; Bittman & Pixley 1997). As a social arrangement, it enabled men to earn an independent income, while women were economically dependent on their husbands or fathers and required to perform the unpaid and undervalued labour of housework, childcare, elder care and disability care. Moreover, the private traumas of the nuclear family were becoming public, exposing the family household as a potential site of sexual, physical and emotional abuse that women found difficult to escape without being stigmatized and forced into poverty.

Alongside these explanations of the apparent disjuncture between ideal and reality, another theory was also beginning to emerge: that, in fact, the family has always been highly variable, and so is likely to continue to be highly variable. As Jack Goody (2000: 1) argues, 'there is no end to the family; some kind of sexual coupling and child care is essential for the vast majority of humankind'. However, the particular arrangements that are used to organize both sexual coupling and the raising and care of children vary a great deal, shifting in response to the different constraints and opportunities created by diverse economic, political, religious, social and cultural contexts.

What emerges from this realization is that, in order to understand family life, it is necessary to take two distinct yet related approaches. First, it is necessary to investigate the ways in which people are organizing and living out the parts of their lives that are thought to be concerned with family: what David Morgan (1996, 2011) calls their 'family practices'. This includes the list provided by Murdock, of common residence, economic cooperation, sexual activity and childrearing. However, it can also be expanded beyond that list, to include things such as love, intimacy, affection, support, cultural maintenance, caregiving, power and social roles. Second, it is necessary to investigate the ways in which *ideas* about the family shape what people consider to be desirable and possible when it comes to organizing those parts of their lives. That is, while Murdock's account of the universality of the nuclear family may not have captured the *reality* of how people were living their lives, it certainly articulated a set of dominant assumptions about what family should or could be, rendering all other family forms relatively undesirable and problematic (Skolnick & Skolnick 1974). Murdock's definition reinforced the nuclear family ideology (see In Focus 1.1), the naturalized assumption that a breadwinning husband, caring wife and their dependent children are the family unit best able to provide for any person's economic, emotional and social needs, and to which all members of the society should aspire (Bernardes 1985).

The nuclear family ideology is in part successful because it provides a source of valued identities and personal goals (Bernardes 1985). Each individual within a family group is allocated roles in relation to each other member of the family, providing them with identities as a mother, son, sister and so on. This allocation of roles is also easily extended beyond biological connections. Marriage creates the roles of husband, wife and in-laws, while adoption and blended families create new roles such as stepsister, stepson, birth mother, half-brother and so on. Indeed, as new reproductive technologies

---

In Focus 1.1 Nuclear family ideology

Ideas and ideals regarding the family have enormous power. This is clear when we reflect on how family remains an overwhelmingly positive and desirable term, in spite of the evidence that families are often a site of violence, abuse and exploitation, as well as of love, affection and care. Family ideologies intersect with, reinforce and rely upon a range of other, related ideologies, such as those of femininity, wifehood and motherhood (Nava 1983), as well as of masculinity, fatherhood and husbandhood (Connell 1995). Indeed, it is the coexistence of these interlocking ideologies that provides 'the means by which contradictions and irrationalities are accommodated or rendered unapparent' (Bernardes 1985: 278). For example, gender ideologies make it possible for the care of children to be acceptable as unpaid work when it is defined as part of 'motherhood', even when the same activities performed by another person are defined as part of wage labour that requires payment in return.

create new relationships, new terms emerge to accommodate these, including donor father or womb mother, among others (Strathern 2005). Human creativity is not only evident in the names given to these roles and relationships, but also the association of particular sets of expectations, obligations and opportunities with each term. Thus, the ideology of motherhood provides women who are identified as mothers with an opportunity to access prestige, honour and value in return for their fulfilment of certain expectations about what is perceived as motherly behaviour directed towards her children (Reiger 1985; Hays 1996). These roles are both an opportunity for acquiring status and also an obligation. Not fulfilling the expectations associated with an assumed role can result in stigma, rejection and dishonour.

The expectations associated with particular roles within a family change over time, and are culturally specific. For example, in nations such as the USA, UK and Australia, both motherhood and fatherhood have undergone significant transformations in recent decades. The expectations of intensive motherhood now require women to invest more time and energy in their children, but motherhood has also expanded to accommodate 'working mothers' who are expected to contribute to the household income and provide a modern role model to their children through their participation in paid work (Reiger 1985; Hays 1996). Fatherhood, meanwhile, has shifted from men playing a largely authoritarian, relatively distant role towards greater expectations of emotional involvement with their children (Gerson 1994; Miller 2011). That is, ideologies of motherhood and fatherhood now encompass both emotional and hands-on caring roles in relation to children in addition to participation in paid work. This has contributed to a work-life collision, in which men and women struggle to meet the expectations of their roles in both family and paid work contexts (Pocock 2003).

Roles within a family carry the weight of obligation to fulfil certain tasks in relation to specific others within that family. In addition to being internalized as cultural models of practice, these obligations are also frequently enshrined in legislation and government policy. Thus, for example, laws in Australia oblige parents to provide economic support for their children, even when they are not co-resident in a nuclear family household (Child Support (Registration and Collection) Act 1988). Policies in Nordic countries encourage fathers as well as mothers to take parental leave soon after the birth of their child as part of a policy agenda to address ongoing gender inequalities in relation to caregiving and employment (Kjeldstad 2001; Haataja 2009). In the Philippines, couples are prevented from divorcing in order to emphasize the sacred qualities of the conjugal bond in a society dominated by Catholicism (Constable 2003b; Santos 2016). Meanwhile, the legal invisibility of same-sex parents in nations around the world leaves them vulnerable to the loss of their rights as a family unit and requires partners, parents and children to engage in additional relational work to feel socially legitimated as a family (Dalton & Bielby 2000). Governments around the world use the legislative and other tools available to them to not only support but also to actively produce the sorts of families that they consider to be normal, natural and effective. These laws and policies in turn institutionalize preferred modes of the family, with significant consequences for those who deviate from the assumed norm.

While national governments play an important role in institutionalizing particular family forms, it is important not to overlook the internalization of cultural models of the family by individuals themselves. Individuals care about fulfilling the roles they hold in relation to each other. Yet this concern about roles and the family is also subject to negotiation. In their study of family obligation in Britain, Janet Finch and Jennifer Mason identified that individuals perform their roles within family units not just through a sense of obligation imposed by cultural models or legal requirements, but also through a sense of commitment to each other (Finch & Mason 1993; Finch 1995). Moreover, this sense of commitment is the result of ongoing intersecting biographies of support, care and exchange that are perceived by individuals through the lens of culturally specific expectations of particular roles and relationships, as well as through the context of nation-specific policy and legal settings (Ikels 1993). Thus, the desire to provide daughterly care to an ageing parent will result in very different actions and behaviours, depending on the nature of the relationship between daughter and parent, and the national context of aged-care provision and policy (Baldassar, Baldock & Wilding 2007).

In this complex context of internalized cultural norms, shifting institutionalized models of the family, and social, economic and political change, it becomes possible to see the decline of the nuclear family in the second half of the twentieth century as somewhat inevitable. Rather than a crisis, the apparent demise of the nuclear family can thus be seen as the natural consequence of the gradual empowerment of women as part of broader patterns of economic, institutional and social change. The increase in divorce rates, for example, coincided with the introduction of legislation that made divorce easier for women to access, suggesting that many were in marriages that had already failed but were difficult to formally end. In addition, the high rates of people choosing to cohabit before marriage, not to marry at all, and to repartner after divorce all signalled a new capacity for women to earn independent incomes that enabled them to make choices about their intimate relationships that were based on factors other than economic necessity (Beck & Beck-Gernsheim 1995). Interestingly, in this new era of choice about marriage and family, many people still value marriage, choose to marry, and choose not to divorce. For example, the crude marriage rate in Australia increased slightly in 2014 to 5.2 per 1000 population, while the crude divorce rate dropped slightly in 2014 to 2.0 per 1000 population (ABS 2014). Moreover, many men and women who do get a divorce are also choosing to remarry and create new family households (Cherlin 2009; ABS 2014).

Individualization and families

In the late twentieth century, a new narrative began to replace the debate regarding the demise of the nuclear family. This new approach emphasized the emergence of a range of diverse ways of being or 'doing' families, which

German sociologists Ulrich Beck and Elisabeth Beck-Gernsheim (1995: 2) describe as including 'the negotiated family, the alternating family, the multiple family, new arrangements after divorce, remarriage, divorce again, new assortments from your, my, our children, our past and present families'. Rather than trying to understand the family as a particular social arrangement reinforcing hierarchies of gender and age, it was suggested that family might be best understood as a project designed by individuals to suit their preferences and circumstances. Family became perceived as something that people plan, negotiate and manage, rather than a set of binding rules and roles to be fulfilled and reproduced.

This understanding of relationships has been called the 'detraditionalization' or 'deinstitutionalization' of the family (Beck & Beck-Gernsheim 1995; Cherlin 2004), associated with what has become termed the 'individualization thesis'. As with debates about the nuclear family in the middle of the twentieth century, this perspective can also be approached in at least three ways. First, the individualization thesis is a narrative of late-modern social change. Under conditions of late modernity, it is suggested that individuals have become self-reflexive (see In Focus 1.2), engaged in a project of the self (Giddens 1991) and constructing a life of their own (Beck & Beck-Gernsheim 1995). The binding social identities of the past have been lost, with each person now responsible for constructing their own social arrangement and their own version of intimacy and family, as part of the project of the reflexive self.

It is not only the self that is subject to reflexive assessment, but also family and relationships. Under this regime of management of the self, people are not only required to reflect on what they 'feel' for other people, but also on whether other people are 'good' for them and will help them with their

---

In Focus 1.2 The reflexive self

An important development in scholarship of the self suggests that the self of late modernity is a product of reflexivity. This is quite different to how the self was understood at the start of the twentieth century, when it was assumed that the inner self was stable, true and could be known. Now, according to scholars like Anthony Giddens (1991), there is no distinctive 'self' that pre-exists self-reflexivity. The self is not a set of traits to be 'known' but is instead something that is produced in and through our reflection on our past and present, and our communication of our past and present to others. The self, then, is produced every day in the stories we tell ourselves and others about who we are, why we have done and are doing what we do, and what we hope to do in the future. But because this self does not already exist, it also creates anxiety about the self we are producing. So, for many people, self-help experts and counselling services become an essential part of everyday life, providing tools for navigating the options and developing a strategic life narrative. They help the individual to interpret their emotions and actions to help plan what comes next.

life narrative. This contributes to the emergence of what Anthony Giddens (1992: 58) has identified as the 'pure relationship', which he defines as:

> a situation where a social relation is entered into for its own sake, for what can be derived by each person from a sustained association with another; and which is continued only in so far as it is thought by both parties to deliver enough satisfactions for each individual to stay within it.

For the reflexive self, relationships and marriage have become increasingly contingent and are reliant upon ongoing satisfaction and compatibility with the construction of a 'life of their own' (Beck & Beck-Gernsheim 1995: 6). Instead of being closely tied to a nuclear family, as Parsons (1955) suggested, life in late modernity is instead argued to demand a specific type of individual: one that is always reflecting on the past and planning for the future and is able and willing to change as circumstances change. Unlike the modern nuclear family, which assumed longevity of the relationship, the late-modern individual is not willing to be tied to any relationship that is not meeting their current needs and expectations.

This is not to say that love, family and relationships have disappeared. Rather, as Beck and Beck-Gernsheim (1995: 3) argue, love and intimacy have become 'the new centre around which our detraditionalized life revolves'. Instead of turning to religion or tradition for answers about the meaning of life and how to live it, people now seek meaning and fulfilment in their lives by emphasizing love and the close emotional bonds they have with others. A good relationship is assumed to provoke intense and positive emotional states. So, emotions are constantly reviewed, interpreted and shared to test whether this particular relationship is indeed special and unique and a good fit for the narrative of the self (Lupton 1998; Illouz 2007).

Unfortunately, the high expectations associated with love, and the idealization of intimacy, mean that intimate relationships cannot possibly live up to expectations. It is simply not possible to remain swooningly in love while also managing work schedules, paying bills, looking after children and ageing parents and buying groceries. As a result, Zygmunt Bauman (2003: viii) declares, intimate relationships 'vacillate between sweet dream and nightmare'. At one and the same time they are highly prized and desired and yet, also, feared for the obligations and impositions they entail as well as the frustrations and disappointments they inevitably bring. The result is a persistent gap between the fantasy of love and its reality (Beck & Beck-Gernsheim 2002). Now, Bauman suggests, rather than actually seeking love and intimacy, the modern person is instead seeking connections and ties that might be enjoyed for the moment before being easily left behind without too much pain or complication. For Beck and Beck-Gernsheim (1995: 53), this emphasis on 'loose' rather than 'strong' ties is the inevitable consequence of the ceaseless decision making that is part of the contemporary life narrative.

As with Talcott Parsons' thesis regarding the nuclear family, so too the individualization thesis is able to draw on contemporary demographic data to support its claims. At the same time, what the data are interpreted to mean remains subject to debate and contestation (see In Focus 1.3). Families seem to be fluid and fragile, with divorce rates remaining high and individuals connecting and disconnecting in a range of household types and arrangements of care and support. This supports the notion that people are constructing a life of their own in response to emotional and economic opportunities and challenges. Moreover, in the same nations that have seen declining rates of nuclear family households since the 1950s, there has been a simultaneous trend towards single-person households (see Figure 1.2), seeming to support the notion that individuals are less reliant on and involved in interdependent households or families. Empirical research suggests that these are not lonely or isolated people. Indeed, there is evidence that people living alone maintain

---

In Focus 1.3 Alternative readings of the individualization thesis

In its most pessimistic reading, the tension between fulfilling the self and having an intimate relationship contributes to a situation in which love becomes yet another consumable in a society where a consumption ethos dominates all, with lovers desired, embraced and, inevitably, discarded when they no longer suit, so that it becomes possible to look for the next newer, better version of love. Thus, Bauman (2003: 12) equates love with the shiny new products in a shopping mall, with 'the fast arousal and quick extinction of wishes in mind, not the cumbersome and protracted breeding and grooming of desires'. In this version of the disposable society, it is fully expected that even goods that are perfectly satisfactory in the present moment will eventually be replaced. This is in part because, even as the new relationship is 'bought' or invested in, there is always a part of the self that keeps an eye open for the next opportunity. Relationships, although prized in general, are not necessarily valued in the particular, with the present version able to be easily disposed of and replaced at will.

Anthony Giddens (1992), in contrast, is more optimistic. He emphasizes that because people are no longer required to commit to the institution of marriage in order to have a relationship, they are able to demand more from their relationships. If their needs for intimacy are not being met, or their life narrative is being disrupted by their partner, then they are expected to find a partner who is more suited to their needs. This is a version of intimacy in which love and relationships are expected, and even required, to contribute to the development and fulfilment of the reflexive self, which is constantly considering how best to achieve its personal goals and desires. Where Parsons (1955) once saw the nuclear family as an ideal form for modern capitalism, it now seems that even this relatively small family unit is possibly too large and unwieldy, and too rigid, to enable the sort of flexibility and responsiveness that is necessary to satisfy both the labour market and the self of late modernity. In the pursuit of ever more meaningful intimate relationships, the family becomes a tool for temporarily organizing the sharing of emotions and resources, rather than a constraining institutional form that determines who might contribute what to the reproduction of a society and the raising of the next generation.

	1950s	1970s	2000s
Australia	9%	16%	24%
United Kingdom	12%	18%	29%
United States of America	10%	18%	27%

Figure 1.2 Estimated proportion of single-person households

Data compiled from ABS Census; Office for National Statistics 2015; Wetzel 1990; Hugo 2001; de Vaus 2004; Beaumont 2011; Cohen 2013; Vespa, Lewis & Kreider 2013.

very busy, demanding and rewarding social lives with those they are related to biologically as well as with networks of friends and others (McDonald 1995; Hughes 2013, 2015; de Vaus & Qu 2015a, 2015b). That is, they seek out multiple loose ties in order to construct conditions of intimacy that suit their flexible, fluid constructions of the self.

Nevertheless, there is reason to be cautious about the compelling case of the individualization thesis. As with the ideology of the family, so too the ideology of individualism has been critiqued for its emphasis on the needs and desires of a limited group of people and for universalizing a set of ideas and preferences that are limited, primarily, to relatively wealthy men and women who are able to delegate their caregiving requirements to others (Jamieson 1998). Just as the model of the nuclear family as a human universal failed to recognize the diversity of actual family forms, so too the notion of the self-reflexive individual able to pick and choose relationships according to personal need tends to overlook cultural diversity. It also tends to overlook the ongoing gendered division in care for children and other dependants, and the internalization of roles of responsibility, obligation, care and affection that bind individuals to each other. Rather than loose ties easily discarded like consumer objects, relationships are often experienced as binding and inevitable, embedded in roles that become part of self-identities, and in commitments that have been generated through years of exchange, support and intimacy.

Families in practice

An alternative to the individualization thesis lies in an argument that the family is not a particular form or structure, such as Parsons' nuclear family, or an individualized project of the self, but rather a way of interacting with others that is recognized as familial. This approach extends Goody's recognition that the family has always been, and will likely always be, diverse in its structures and organization. British sociologist David Morgan (1996, 2011) argues that families are the outcome of a range of relationship practices, which include such things as writing a will, celebrating Christmas or eating meals together on a daily basis. Thus, we have families because we participate in family practices that produce family relationships. To some extent, these practices can be identified as 'habits', which we perform because that is how we have always done things. In this sense, the family becomes a background set of assumptions that is reproduced without reflection, and reinforced by national laws and policies as well as ideologies of the family. However, there are other practices, which Morgan suggests are 'practices as action' rather than practices of habit. These practices are more reflective, selected from a range of possibilities, and aimed at constructing a particular form of relationship or a particular model of family. As will be explored in later chapters, it is perhaps this form of family practice that is likely to grow in significance under the conditions of globalization. This is because as more people, media and ideas become mobile and ideas of the family become deterritorialized, practices as habit arguably become more difficult to sustain. Novel situations become the norm, requiring an active response. It might be assumed, then, that families are increasingly the product of practices that are generated through reflection and reflexivity prompted by the intensification of global flows of people, ideas, media and objects. That is, rather than fulfilling a particular structure or set of functions, families are increasingly the product of people pursuing particular ideals and responding to changing circumstances and diverse social, political, economic, cultural and legal contexts. In order to better explore this argument, we must first outline some of the key features of globalization.

Globalization and migration: a story of turbulent homogeneity

Globalization emerged as a significant concept in the 1980s as a way of trying to make sense of how the world had been changing in preceding decades. The increased speed and ease with which people, capital, goods, media and ideas could travel and interact across the world had contributed to what David Harvey (1989) called 'time-space compression' and Anthony Giddens (1991) 'time-space distanciation'. It was clear that this process was having a significant impact on economies and cultures, as well as on social and political relations, but the precise nature, extent and consequences of that impact was (and still is) subject to debate. Some saw these transformations as producing new levels of homogeneity and uniformity across the world, captured by terms such as George Ritzer's (1993) 'McDonaldization'. This is the idea that modes of production can be rationalized by breaking them down into their smallest constituent parts, and then ensuring that each part is completed using the most efficient method possible. Predictability and control are key to these efficiencies, encouraging the reproduction of sameness without regard to local specificities. However, the result is arguably irrational, producing modes of work that trap people in repetitive mind-numbing tasks that dehumanize by removing all autonomy and creative potential.

Meanwhile, others point instead to the production of new modes of difference and heterogeneity or to a transcending of the homogeneity-heterogeneity divide. That is, the forces of sameness are counterbalanced by the ongoing production of uniquely local responses to globally circulating ideas, practices, norms and systems. It is this clash between forces pushing towards universality and differentiation at one and the same time that is captured in Arjun Appadurai's (1996) argument that the 'global' comprises various scapes, flows and disjunctures that rely on but also transcend the local, producing uneven terrains in which the global and the local intersect and interact. Roland Robertson (1995) offers the term 'glocalization' as a means of capturing the ways in which globalization is best understood not as a large-scale phenomenon that displaces the local, but rather as an intersection of the particular and the universal. Thus, even global chains such as McDonald's would necessarily accommodate elements of their product to the location in which they set up one of their restaurants, introducing locally appealing variations of their otherwise uniform menu and branding.

In simple terms, the 'global' is the product of many varied interactions and connections between people around the world, with globalization referring to that process of greater intensity of interconnectedness between people living in different locations. These interactions and connections are not even or balanced (Wallerstein 1974; Appelbaum & Robinson 2005). Rather, a range of asymmetries of power and both persistent and new inequalities contribute to benefiting some people over others. Thus, for example, many scholars argue that the digital divide is a new form of inequality that is layered on older modes of inequality as a result of uneven access to communication technologies (Amant & Olaniran 2011; Wilding & Gifford 2013). Other scholars argue that there are actually two sites of the global, referring to the 'global north' and the 'global south' as the relative beneficiaries and victims respectively of worldwide processes of interconnectedness (e.g. Gallas et al. 2016). In this formulation, the global north is not strictly geographical, and includes not only Northern Hemisphere societies such as Europe and North America, but also countries from south of the equator such as Australia and New Zealand. These are the nations that have historically benefited from the colonial era and, under postcolonialism, continue to be most able to accumulate wealth and wield influence on the global stage. Their citizens, too, are able to access the privilege of relatively free movement around the world (Torpey 2000; Neumayer 2006). Citizens of the global south, on the other hand, are relatively less able to extract benefit from the flows of wealth throughout the global economy and are also subject to constraints on their movement around the world. Rather than choosing to move somewhere else for lifestyle reasons, as is common among the elites of the global north, they are instead channelled into labour migration pathways that arguably continue to benefit those in the global north (e.g. Yeates 2005, 2009).

The complexities of global migration

The extraction of labour from poorer areas to benefit capital in wealthier parts of the world is not a new phenomenon. Indeed, much of early migration research was aimed at understanding precisely this phenomenon, whereby people from poorer areas (often rural, and often understood as more 'backward' or less 'modern') are 'pushed' out of their home towns or homelands and 'pulled' into the centres of capital and modernity (Cohen 1996). Thus, in the past (usually understood as the 1950s and before) the classic migrant story is of young men in rural Europe pushed to leave home by poverty and lack of employment opportunities. They were pulled into settler nations such as the USA, Canada, Australia and New Zealand where it was possible (although not likely) to make a fortune. These migrations were understood as economic strategies, with economic benefits flowing not only to the immigrant but also his former community – which would no longer have to support him and often received remittances – and the nation where he arrived, which benefited from his labour. Although these men often hoped to ultimately return to the home country, slightly older and wealthy enough to set up a family household with a farm or business, more commonly they would live out their lives in the new country.

This relatively simple story of movement from here to there became increasingly complicated towards the end of the twentieth and into the twenty-first century (King 2010; see also In Focus 1.4). In part, this growing complexity was the result of social scientists acknowledging that economic factors were not the only reasons people moved (e.g. Papastergiardis 2000; Baldassar, Baldock & Wilding 2007). Even the classic male migrants were often caught up in webs of family ties that continued to bind them to their hometowns. For example, men who arrived and found work would send letters or word-of-mouth messages back home, calling their brothers, sons, nephews and others to join them. Some of the men would also call on their parents to find them a wife in their hometown. After getting married by proxy, she would travel to the new country to set up a household and begin a family. She, too, might then call on sisters or other female kin to visit her, either to work or to consider meeting and marrying other young men from their hometown who had followed the paths of migration. These calls for more people generated chain and cluster migration patterns that sometimes saw entire communities created in the country of arrival that shared a common region or even a common hometown in the country of origin. Thus, while the dominant Australian population perceived only 'Italians', the arrivals from Italy readily identified each other as Veneto, Sicilian, and so on (Baldassar 2001).

The increased complexity of migration was also partly the result of migrants responding to shifting migration and settlement policies of receiving nations, which were adjusted on a regular basis in response to local and global economic, social and political contexts. For example, during periods of economic recession, such as the 1970s, some nations erected new and more stringent barriers in order to limit movement across national borders (Castles, de Haas & Miller 2013). These did not always have the desired effect of preventing migration, sometimes instead prompting new forms of movement across the borders that became even more difficult to manage.

Short-term contracts for overseas work have also been common across other parts of the world. For example, during the 1970s, many men from India, the Philippines and a number of other countries were recruited as

---

In Focus 1.4 Creative responses to border closure: Turkish migrants in Germany

The guest workers or 'gasterbeiter' were initially encouraged to enter Germany from Turkey to complete short-term work contracts of a few months or a year during the 1950s and 1960s (e.g. Mandel 1990, 2008; Jurgens 2001; Akgündüz 2008). This strategy was intended to benefit the German economy without importing a permanent ethnic minority: at the end of a contract, the men were expected to return to their homes and families in Turkey. Although formally short term, the contracts were also regularly renewed, so that many Turkish men lived most of the year in Germany, returning only briefly to Turkey to renew their visas and visit their wives and children. However, when the German economy slowed down, the visa system was tightened and it became more difficult to get a renewal that enabled a subsequent return. The German government's intention was to slow down the flow of foreign workers into Germany, so that Germans might have greater access to employment. However, instead of prompting the men to return to Turkey, the new visa regulations instead prompted more Turkish men to remain permanently in Germany where they could access work. Many began to bring their wives and children with them, creating precisely the ethnic community in Germany that the guest worker immigration system had initially been designed to avoid.

---

contract labourers in the Middle East, contributing vast amounts of money to their home countries in the form of remittances (Castles, de Haas & Miller 2013). But by the 1990s, demand for male labour had diminished significantly and been increasingly replaced by a demand for women who could work as domestic servants, nurses and carers of children and the elderly (Ehrenreich & Hochschild 2003; Asis 2005). Other changes were also occurring. Receiving nations began to perceive that they might shape their immigration programmes to attract highly skilled people and improve overall human capital in the nation. Increasingly, migrants were no longer primarily unskilled rural men, but also included those with a range of diverse skills and educational backgrounds, including medical professionals, mechanics, managers, IT professionals and engineers (Castles, de Haas & Miller 2013). Destination countries were becoming adept at changing their visa regulations, making it easier for some to enter their borders and almost impossible for others, producing both new formal but also new informal routes of migration, such as those between Mexico and the USA (Boehm 2012). Other forms of migration also became more significant, including the flows of international students – ostensibly temporary migrants, but often spending ten years or more in a host country while undertaking a combination of paid work and study (Vogl & Kell 2010; Brooks 2011). Political turmoil in numerous countries around the world also prompted massive flows of asylum seekers and refugees, forcibly displaced and often required to live in limbo inside or on the outskirts of large refugee camps while waiting for their home country to become safe to live in, or while hoping to receive one of the relatively small number of resettlement places made by signatories to the UNHCR Refugee Convention (e.g. Nolan 2006; Zetter 2007; Fiddian-Qasmiyeh et al. 2014).

By the early twenty-first century, it was clear that the patterns of migration had become increasingly complex and diverse, even as the number of people moving was rapidly growing. This contributed to what Stephen Castles and colleagues (2013) call 'The Age of Migration'. More people are migrating; more countries are becoming both countries of departure and of destination; women are no longer migrating only as spouses or family members, but also as employees; and migration is taking on multiple forms, including long term, short term, permanent, temporary, forced, voluntary, legal and illegal. The social and cultural effects of this transformation of migration patterns are felt everywhere, including by those who have never moved away from the place they were born. For example, countries such as Ireland and Italy have long histories of emigration, but have only recently been required to respond to ethnic and racial diversity within their borders. Indeed, across Europe concern is growing about how to manage the multiculturalism that is evident in streets, workplaces and schools, but which is in stark contrast with long-term histories of largely homogeneous populations. At the same time, increasing numbers of families are required to respond to the impact of migration on how they earn an income, create households, and provide care and support to each other. Of particular concern to some commentators is the recent feminization of migration (e.g. Piper 2003; Oishi 2005; see also Chapter 4). While male migrant labourers have often been required to spend long periods of time away from their families, this has rarely generated the sort of concern that has been expressed now that women are increasingly given opportunities to do the same thing. For some, the age of migration is also an age in which family connectedness has come under threat. That is, the demise of the nuclear family is secured by international migration, as is the prospect of individualized selves unmoored from intimate connections in response to labour market requirements.

At the intersections: families, intimacy and globalization

It is increasingly clear that migration is impacting on the ways in which people manage their relationships with spouses, children, parents, siblings, extended kin and friends. More people more often have to manage lives that are lived both 'here' and 'there'. However, it is the argument throughout this book that geographic dispersal of intimate ties does not necessarily lead to the conditions described by the individualization thesis. This is in part because, even as people are being separated by migration, new technologies are making it easier to manage and maintain intimate commitments across distance (Wilding 2006; Baldassar, Baldock & Wilding 2007). Once, communication around the world was only as fast as a ship, then as fast as an aeroplane, travelling primarily by letters or perhaps through messages carried by individuals moving between one place and another. Gradually, the telephone became more widespread, creating the relative miracle of synchronous communication across distance. Family members could hear the voices of their distant kin, albeit often with a slight delay, a crackle of interference, and an underlying fear of just how much the call would cost. Even so, distance still mattered, and was made evident through small incidents such as a phone line dropping out and being difficult to reconnect, or the exorbitant telephone bill having to be paid. Things are very different today. Now, family members living at a distance from each other – whether within the same country or spread across multiple places around the world – are able to share their lives with each other through text messages, phone calls, Facebook updates, Twitter, YouTube, Pinterest and any number of other options. The result is a clear increase in the frequency with which people communicate with their kin (Gubernskaya & Treas 2016).

This is the era of what Mirca Madianou and Daniel Miller (2012) have called 'polymedia', when people are able to sustain relationships at a distance through multiple, layered communication strategies. It is now possible to choose how to communicate a particular piece of information or a particular expression of affection so that it best carries the message to that particular person. Social lives can now be conducted virtually and transnationally, so that geographic distance seems to matter much less, even though moments of crisis such as illness or death quickly demonstrate that physical proximity – even if only occasional – remains essential (Wilding 2006). It seems that just as families and intimate relationships are being thought of by individualization theorists as at risk of collapsing under the weight of distance and movement, new technologies have stepped up to ensure that family and intimacy are carried on nevertheless.

The sorts of families and intimacies that are produced out of the global context of migration and new media require a new terminology, something that helps us to make sense of the ways in which individuals respond to the various national and global regimes of economic structures and opportunities, laws, policies, border control and cultural norms while engaging in the everyday practices that sustain their intimate lives and families. The term I propose is 'floating ties', a phrase that is neither completely solid nor entirely loose, but rather alludes to networks and connections that are flexible, adaptable and negotiable across national, cultural and social borders. People like John are making the most of these new conditions, which enable them to live in one country for lifestyle or economic reasons (John has a successful business in Australia) while also remaining involved with the lives of family members living on the other side of the world. His experience shows how families might become global while remaining intimate and caring. Relationships like his are being conducted in dialogue with the limits of borders, distance, bodies and place as well as in negotiation with their specific biographies of obligation and commitment.

The term 'floating ties' is also intended to capture another important dimension of families in a global world: the recognition that not only family practices, but also ideas about family and family roles are circulating across borders and space (Jayakody, Thornton & Axinn 2012). This includes ideas such as the nuclear family ideology and the individualization thesis, which provide individuals with models for their own family practices, but also inform the policies and laws that bind people to negotiating and responding to particular versions of the family. Thus, for example, Thornton (2001, 2005) documents how many of the less wealthy nations of the world are expected and compelled to reproduce nuclear family ideology as part of the funding for their development projects. Yet such ideas are never simply accepted and reproduced. They are adapted for and received by new audiences in complex ways that combine existing cultural understandings of family, intimacy, femininity, masculinity and love with new or alternative ideas.

It is also important to recognize that new ideas about families and intimacy are not simply imposed by governments and organizations. Global migration and the circulation of media and ideas ensure that individuals encounter a wide range of possibilities in their daily lives. As people travel more often across national borders for work, to avoid persecution or seek adventure, they are exposed to other ways of doing and being families. They see for themselves how families elsewhere are imagined and organized, creating opportunities to reflect on their own practices. Sometimes this can result in a reinforcement of ideas that are perceived as traditional, while at other times it produces new experiments in family life. At the same time, the mere fact of geographic distance within the family that is produced by members when they are living, working or travelling elsewhere requires the reorganization and reimagining of how they live their own family relationships in everyday life. New tools and different routines are created in order to maintain the family in response to new circumstances.

What is the impact of this new global context on how people meet their intimate partners, sustain their family relationships, and interact with those they care about and care for? What is the role of intimate relationships in shaping how people respond to the opportunities and consequences of the global flows of people, money and ideas? How do intimate family lives intersect with global migration and what is the impact on people's everyday lives and sense of self? These are the questions that drive this book. It is important to recognize that the terrain is vast, not least because globalization, migration, family and intimacy are themselves very diverse and contradictory processes. The approach I take to exploring these complex questions is to assume that many of the answers to them are best arrived at through quite detailed case studies of how specific men and women respond to their specific circumstances and opportunities, as will become clear in the discussions in the following chapters. However, alongside this attention to the details of intimacy, there is also recognition of the value of paying attention to the dominant, macro stories of globalization and intimacy, and their attempts to tell us something about what it means to be human in the twenty-first century.

Structure of the book

This book examines what happens to social relations when the turbulence of migration crashes into the transformation of intimacy on a global stage. How have families and relationships been transformed by the movement of people across multiple local and national spaces? What is the role of the family and intimacy in shaping the particular flows of people between one place and another? And what do the answers to these questions tell us about the nature of contemporary ties, networks, flows and spaces?

Chapter 2 considers the formation of couple relationships, by exploring how men and women find marriage partners across national borders. Communication technologies play an important role, providing access to potential partners who once existed only in the realm of fantasy. Yet the continuing presence of fantasies of intimate relations with 'exotic' or 'modern' Others shapes the ways that people respond to that potential, sometimes with heartbreaking results. In Chapter 3, I explore what happens to couples who are trying to maintain a relationship while living in unconventional households. These include couples with 'trailing spouses', 'living apart together' relationships, and commuter relationships. The stretching of the couple household highlights the gendered inequalities that persist in many couple relationships, and the ways in which men and women negotiate, transform and resist those inequalities.

In Chapter 4, I move from couple intimacy to intergenerational care, by examining the ways in which families care for children. The phenomenon of 'global care chains' is introduced as a new, globalized mode of providing care to children. In Chapter 5, I explore global parenting from the perspective of children who are moved across national borders for formal or informal education, or as part of international adoption.

In Chapter 6, I look to the other end of the life cycle, by considering how families organize care of older people. In contrast with the individualization thesis, the efforts men and women undertake in order to achieve what they consider to be 'good' aged care demonstrate that family ties are strong, even if they are less grounded in local sites. This is further emphasized in Chapter 7, where I explore the continuation of the extended family network. Research is clearly demonstrating that the apparent dominance of the nuclear family and of individualization processes have not resulted in the end of the extended family network. Indeed, some argue that sustaining these extensive, loose ties to kin is potentially useful in managing the insecurities and opportunities of late modernity. In Chapter 8, I then consider the 'family' as including 'family-like' relationships. For the individualization theorists, friends are the model of contemporary relationships – intense while they last, but easy to dispose of when they no longer satisfy. Relationships are presumed to be equal, undemanding and disposable. However, the phenomenon of online friends and social networks suggests that new communication tools create new types of friends with different sets of obligations, including in the spheres of online gaming and networking. Furthermore, the research evidence indicates that such relationships are not necessarily at the expense of face-to-face relationships and personal communities. Rather, they tend to supplement and intersect with offline social networks of relationships and support.

Finally, in Chapter 9 I return to the questions that drive the book, asking how intimacy and family have transformed and been transformed by globalization and migration. The concept proposed to support this analysis is 'floating ties'. For many, the term 'floating' will evoke an image of a vessel bobbing on water, perhaps a raft on which the members of a family or of a kinship network are more or less precariously balanced, always at risk of plunging into the depths of the ocean beneath them if they let go of each other or of the raft. Indeed, this image captures well the sense of transformation of the family, with the raft all that remains after the solid structures of tradition have disintegrated. My intention, however, is to use floating to refer instead to a sense of being light and airborne, perhaps like a spider's web or perhaps even a mode of flying. Thus, what the concluding chapter aims to make sense of are the ways in which people construct apparently stable, durable structures – families – that are nevertheless flexible enough to sway with and adapt to the familial, life-course, national and global winds of change. The floating ties, then, are perhaps best understood as the simultaneously intangible and binding forces that tie people together, in spite of the pressures of separation and individualization that are seen to be constantly threatening to pull them apart.

Conclusion

The grand narratives that have been rehearsed above are necessarily simplified accounts of some of the dominant stories about how the world works in the twenty-first century. They also present some important contradictions to resolve. On the one hand, it seems that the family is becoming less significant as a social institution, with individuals making more choices based on their own individual preferences and desires, and their own life narrative, rather than on established expectations of marriage and family. Yet, as the story of John demonstrates and migration research tells us, families remain very significant: people follow family members along migration routes, bring family members with them when possible, and use a range of communication devices to connect with family members living elsewhere when they are not able to be in the same space at the same time. Are these examples of pure relationships, in which each individual is getting sufficient satisfaction to continue the relationship? Or is something else at stake? It is difficult to reconcile the flimsy fantasies of love and intimacy as loose ties produced by momentary pleasure, on the one hand, with, on the other hand, the amount of effort that many people put into remaining connected to and exchanging support with those people they recognize as belonging to their families. It is these contradictory experiences that are the focus of the chapters that follow.

Transnational love and partnering

If Hollywood is to be believed, romantic love is the only worthwhile reason for creating a couple relationship or entering a marriage. However, anthropologists and historians also tell us that the rules of partnering are diverse, with romantic love playing a relatively new and limited role. This is not to say that romance and love are recent inventions. Rather, marriage and partnering have long been thought of as too important to leave to the fickle chance of unreliable emotions that are prone to shift when a new source of attraction arrives on the scene. In many social and cultural contexts around the world, the production of the new generation and the intergenerational transfer of property, status, knowledge and authority associated with marriage have demanded that parents and extended kin become involved in any decisions made about partnering. Yet, if we are to believe the individualization theorists, these roles and traditions no longer hold the significance they once did. How are the rules of love and partnering changing as a result of new pressures to live a life of one's own? Then again, just how widespread are these new pressures? What other rules, roles and expectations shape the decisions people make about whether, whom and when they partner? In this chapter, I explore some of the global variability of heteronormative love, partnering and marriage as they are conducted across national and cultural borders (see In Focus 2.1; for a discussion of non-heteronormative relationships and experiences, see Chapter 8).

Love and marriage in late modernity

The hit Chinese television programme *If You Are The One (Fei Cheng Wu Rao)* is not just a dating show, it is a popular culture phenomenon. Episodes are avidly watched by large audiences in China and around the world, who also contact the contestants on the dedicated social media platform and share comments with each other about marriage and falling in love. Each episode

---

In Focus 2.1 Heteronormativity and family formation

An often unacknowledged aspect of the ideology of the family (see Chapter 1) is its foundations in heteronormativity. This is the assumption that the only natural and normal form of human sexuality is attraction between a man and a woman. Yet this is in conflict with the fact that human beings have a wide range of possible sexual orientations, practices and identities. Indeed, normal human biological variation includes a small percentage of people who are born without a clear identity as either male or female, but rather with characteristics of both. Across English-speaking nations, such variations have historically been medicalized and subject to surgical and/or medical 'cures'. In some other cultural contexts these identities are recognized by additional gender labels (neither male nor female) that are sometimes associated with a special social status (e.g. Nanda 1996; Jacobs, Thomas & Lang 1997).

An important part of the social transformations captured by the individualization thesis is the challenging of heteronormative assumptions and traditions about partnering, marriage and love. For Giddens (1992), same-sex relationships represent the vanguard of the pure relationship because the lack of gendered norms requires the ongoing negotiation of roles and norms of intimacy within the couple. Other scholars have sought to decentre the couple relationship altogether, arguing that non-heterosexuals create 'families of choice' in which roles and identities are not constrained by gendered heterosexual ideologies of the family (e.g. Weeks, Heaphy & Donovan 2001; Weston 1991). In the second half of the twentieth century, widespread activism achieved significant political advances around the world in the legal recognition of non-heteronormative identities and families and the removal of harsh penalties for those engaging in non-heterosexual relationships (e.g. Altman 1993, 2013). This now includes legal recognition of the rights of same-sex couples to register their unions and to bear and raise children. However, it was not until 2001 that the Netherlands became the first nation to legally remove any distinction between heterosexual and non-heterosexual marriage. While many governments across the world, particularly in Europe, South America and North America, have now followed this lead, many others maintain marriage as a right preserved only for heterosexual couples. The implications of these divides for families and relationships are explored in more detail in Chapter 8.

---

begins in the same way. As the pop theme tune throbs, 24 young women stride out to stand behind the individual podiums set out in a semi-circle along the back of the stage. They are greeted by the host, Meng Fei, who also introduces his one or two special guests, people who play an important role as fictive aunts and uncles, ready and available to provide sage advice to the contestants about choosing a suitable match. Meng Fei invites the young women to turn on their lights by pressing a button on the top of their podium, signifying they are ready to find love. Moments later, the first male contestant arrives on the stage to a whoop of response from the gathered studio audience. After he exchanges greetings with Meng Fei, he is asked to identify his favourite female contestant, in secret, on an electronic keypad. The women are then given their opportunity to assess their first response to him. Already, some have decided that he is not the one for them, and turn off their podium light. For the others, a series of short, pre-recorded videos provide them with an opportunity to learn more about the male contestant as he describes his work, his interests, his past relationships and his family and friends. Between each video, the women ask him questions, flirt and share some of their own ideas about love and marriage. By the end of these exchanges, the man is able to choose his favourites from the women whose lights are still turned on. Occasionally, one of these is his first choice, and the romantic love narrative is completed by the couple leaving the stage hand in hand. Sometimes, he changes his mind and leaves with another woman who has convinced him through their interactions that she is right for him. More often, he leaves alone, hoping to find a match when his social media profile is displayed on the programme and associated website. This is heteronormative partnering in a modern style.

There are numerous dating shows around the world that seek to tap into the drama of romantic love and attraction by encouraging men and women to meet each other on national or sometimes international television. In many respects, *If You Are The One* is simply another iteration of these programmes. However, it also differs from those other programmes in significant ways. Dating shows that have been aired in the US, UK and Australia such as *Blind Date*, *Perfect Match* and *Naked Attraction* tend to emphasize sexual attraction as an important component of romantic love. The goal in these programmes seems to be to find someone to date, in the full knowledge and expectation that the relationship is unlikely to last for any great length of time. In contrast, the contestants in *If You Are The One* present themselves as seeking a partner for marriage. Their goal is more complicated than simply identifying someone they are willing to go out with for dinner a few times. Within the framework of the programme, the hosts and producers are encouraging contestants to look for 'the one', a lifelong partner with whom to spend their life and create a family. Alongside the acknowledgement of romantic love, they are being asked to identify a suitable marriage prospect. In spite of the Hollywood message that love and marriage go hand in hand, the reality is that the two goals often pull in opposite directions, representing two different narratives about love and partnering. Romantic love is generally associated with intense but short-term intimacy, a counterpoint to the long-term, less passionate love that is more commonly associated with marriage.

Romantic love and the pure relationship

Romantic love is an 'intense attraction involving the idealization of the other' (Jankowiak 1995: 4). This idealizing includes imagining that there is only one person, somewhere in the world, who is a perfect match, a soulmate who is able to provide lifelong happiness. It is recognizable in the exciting 'butterflies-in-the-stomach' recognition that someone is special, and especially desirable. This is what the contestants in *If You Are The One* are initially looking for when they assess each other on the stage. Does he make my heart race? Does she look like my type? Romantic love is associated with an intense experience of attraction that idealizes its object, and provokes an overwhelming desire for intimacy with that person (Jankowiak 1995). In contemporary Western societies, the emotions of romantic love are presented as an almost spiritual experience of transcendence and pleasure (Lindholm 1995), which has also become an essential part of the narrative of marriage and even a necessary precondition for the decision to marry (Wilding 2003).

This emphasis on inner emotions as the basis of partnering is associated with a broader set of transformations that are suggested to have reduced external constraints on partnering. It is argued that, in contrast with the past, there are fewer social bonds limiting the individual's choices of an intimate partner. Some of the factors that are identified include that non-familial institutions have become more important for education and production, kin are more dispersed and thus their demands less binding, and couples are having fewer children who are living for longer periods of time and this is contributing to changing attitudes towards both marital partners and offspring (Goody 1983: 1). According to some theorists (e.g. Beck & Beck-Gernsheim 1995, 2002), an important result of these transformations is that individuals became less tied to the social contexts and social identities into which they were born. They are individualized and detraditionalized. This can be reflected in more people moving away from their family of origin and pursuing work and life opportunities elsewhere, either through rural–urban migration or international migration. The separation from local communities and family ties brings with it a greater sense of freedom when finding a marriage partner. At the same, it also makes it necessary to develop new ways of finding potential partners.

An important part of this transformation has been the emergence of romantic love as the most acceptable basis of marriage. Eva Illouz (1997) documents the emergence of a romantic imaginary in the USA that produced new rules of meeting, dating, partnering and marriage that rely on the interpretation and expression of emotions of romantic love within the confines of consumer culture. This does not mean that the physiological feelings of romantic love did not previously exist (but see Aries 1962). Rather, as Illouz (1997) points out, the cultural values of capitalism now stipulate how the feelings that we experience and label as 'romantic love' should be interpreted, and what sorts of actions those feelings should motivate. Moreover, increasingly, 'the one' is sought among not only local social networks of potential partners, but also from the many millions of imagined possibilities from around the world who participate in online dating sites (Illouz 2007). Thanks to new technologies of finding and meeting potential partners, love is no longer strictly limited by geographic location or even a shared culture or language. Rather, the ideal partner can be imagined as living in some remote location, simply waiting for a serendipitous event to initiate a meeting that was always destined to occur. It is this moment that the contestants and audiences on *If You Are The One* are waiting for, producing a sense of achievement when a couple identify each other as their favourite and leave the programme apparently to live happily ever after. At the same time, romantic love and the pure relationship are not recognized as a particularly robust mode of partnering for the long term. This is because the emotions that gave rise to the sense that this person is 'the one' are easily transferred to another object of affection. Indeed, according to Anthony Giddens (1992), the reflexive self requires that each person in the relationship continually reflect on and review their choice of partner.

Men and women expect to find and enjoy a satisfying 'pure relationship' with another person (see also Chapter 1), in which each person remains only for as long as they receive satisfaction from that relationship. Unlike the bonds of marriage that require a couple to remain together until death separates them, the pure relationship entails an obligation to end the relationship when it no longer delivers the emotional and other satisfactions that are a requirement of accomplishing the project of the self. This is not perceived as a failure of romantic love. On the contrary, when the relationship fails, it is because that person was not actually 'the one'. Thus, the search must continue.

High divorce rates are often identified as evidence of the relatively fickle approach to partnering that relies on romantic love and the pure relationship as its foundation. Yet it is also clear that globalization has not resulted in a uniform experience of divorce around the world. While crude divorce rates (number of divorces per 1000 population) in some nations are rising (e.g. Croatia, Egypt), divorce rates in other nations are falling (e.g. Germany, Japan) (see Figure 2.1). Meanwhile, there are also significant disparities in some nations between urban and rural divorce rates. For example, Mexico's national rate of 0.9 divorces in 2014 is comprised of a rate of 1.2 in urban locations and only 0.2 in rural contexts. While this might easily be interpreted as an indicator of the denser social relations and more conservative or

	2011	2014
Australia	2.2	2.0
China	1.6	Not available
Croatia	1.3	1.6
Czech Republic	2.7	2.5
Denmark	2.6	3.4
Egypt	1.9	2.1
Germany	2.3	2.1
Ireland	0.6	0.6
Italy	0.9	0.9
Japan	1.8	1.7
Mexico	0.8	0.9
New Zealand	2.0	1.8
Peru	0.2	0.4
Singapore	1.9	1.8
Turkey	1.6	1.7
United Kingdom	2.1	Not available
United States of America	2.8	Not available

Figure 2.1 Crude divorce rates per 1000 population, 2011–14

Data from UN 2015 Demographic Yearbook, available at: https://unstats.un.org/Unsd/demographic/products/dyb/dyb2015/Table25.pdf.

traditional social norms in rural rather than urban contexts, such an explanation does not easily account for the declining divorce rates in nations such as Germany or Australia. The realities of partnering, divorce and repartnering are likely to be much more complex and nuanced than individualization theory alone can explain.

Marriage and family formation

Alongside claims that marriage has become less important, less structured and less binding in late modernity, there is also an alternative story about partnering. This story is less one of personal fulfilment, and more a narrative of individuals seeking a stable long-term partner within the confines of the local marriage market. Rather than emphasizing romantic passion, this narrative is focused on love that is stable, long lasting and incremental (Collins & Gregor 1995), based on mutual support and exchange that helps each partner to achieve their goals of family formation. It is this narrative that is emphasized in accounts of arranged marriages. Rather than couples forming a partnership based on romantic passion, elders in the community identify a suitable match based on a range of factors associated with a greater potential for compatibility. These include similar family backgrounds and values, similar or compatible educational and occupational ambitions, and in some cases a similar class, caste or ethnic background.

The narrative of longevity as a goal of partnering is evident in *If You Are The One* when contestants ask questions about each other's values and expectations regarding aged care, plans regarding having and raising children, or their ambitions in terms of geographic location and economic prospects. Their immediate response to the thrill of romantic attraction is mediated by expectations that their selected partner must be able to provide the prospect of a long-term partnership that meets a range of practical needs and familial expectations. Indeed, the fictive aunts and uncles in the programme play an important role in encouraging contestants to only invest in a relationship that is likely to satisfy both their existing familial obligations and those they anticipate or hope to have in the future.

The continued concerns about relationship failure indicate that even when there is an apparent freedom to marry 'anyone', this is also accompanied by a sense that not just 'anyone' will do. As Teresita del Rosario (2005: 266) argues, a long-term partnership such as marriage 'is not restricted to two individuals; rather, it encompasses entire social networks in which the two marrying individuals are located. With this comes the responsibility among partners to care for and look after the communities they inherited vis-à-vis marriage'. Personal satisfaction, then, is not entirely the province of the individual. Rather, it becomes a negotiation of individual desires and the positioning of those desires within broader social and cultural contexts and interpersonal roles and obligations. These include family formation and status as well as feelings of love and passion.

There is also another set of constraints on marriage, evident in the research on homogamy and hypergamy (e.g. Lichter, Anderson & Hayward 1995;

Blackwell & Lichter 2004; Schwartz 2013). Homogamy refers to the tendency for people to choose marriage partners who are similar to them, often measured in terms of factors such as their education, occupation, family background, ethnicity and geographic location. In combination with homogamy is a patterned preference for hypergamy, referring to the tendency for women in particular to seek partners who have a higher status than them in terms of factors such as their education, occupation, wealth, social status and even with reference to physical features such as their height. Thus, in spite of the perception that online dating sites and international mobility provide individuals with potentially limitless options to identify a partner and locate 'the one', in fact the range of potential partners is typically very narrow. Some researchers argue that specific groups of people are pushed out of the marriage market altogether by shifts they have no control over, such as changing education patterns and demographic transformations (see In Focus 2.2).

In Focus 2.2 Sources of constraint in local marriage markets

In recent decades, many nations across Asia have seen a significant transformation in marriage patterns in spite of the continued expectation and desire to marry. This is typically attributed to the effects of broader social, cultural and economic transformations, including urbanization, universal education for both girls and boys, and the increasing participation of women in paid employment (Jones 2012a). The result is a significant increase in people who remain unmarried as well as a notable increase in the age at first marriage. For example, in 1970 marriage was almost universal in nations such as Hong Kong, Thailand, Singapore and Japan, with approximately 5 per cent of women remaining unmarried at 35 to 39 years old. By 2005, this figure had increased to between 15 and 20 per cent (Jones 2010). In the same countries, the age at first marriage has increased by up to 5 years between 1970 and 2010. For example, in Japan women were marrying at 24 years old but are now marrying at 29, while men who used to marry at 27 now wait until they are 31 (Jones & Yeung 2014).

The marriage rates are not the same for all parts of the population. Marriage rates are higher in rural than in urban locations (Jones 2005). Education also seems to play a significant role. In Thailand, for example, 23 per cent of women aged 35 to 39 with a tertiary education remain unmarried, compared to only 7 per cent for those with primary education or less (Jones 2010). In contrast, men with higher education are more likely to be married than those with lower levels of education. This is contributing to what has been called a 'marriage squeeze', whereby 'imbalances may not always be in terms of absolute numbers in the potentially marrying ages but rather in terms of numbers in the groups that the society considers as having the potential to marry each other' (Jones & Yeung 2014: 1579). Homogamy and hypergamy are significant in understanding this mismatch. Men with low levels of education are unlikely to want to marry women with higher levels of education and highly educated women are unlikely to want to marry less educated men; meanwhile, highly educated men are less likely to consider it an obstacle if their partner is less well educated than themselves (Jones 2012b). One of the consequences is a greater tendency for men and women in nations experiencing a 'marriage squeeze' to seek marriage partners from outside the nation through international and online matchmaking agencies. This phenomenon, known as 'global hypergamy', is discussed later in this chapter.

Love and marriage in globalization

The field or marriage market within which the search for 'the one' takes place is becoming increasingly global and international (Niedomysl, Osth & van Ham 2010). This creates the distinct possibility that marriage partners will misunderstand each other's goals and aspirations. They might idealize their romantic other from their own social and cultural position on the world stage, possibly failing to see the ways in which the person they have idealized is both more and less than that fantasy. In a globalized context of dating, love and marriage, desires become stretched across larger distances and more complex cross-cultural and cross-national contexts (Williams 2010). How do people navigate the new possibilities of love and partnering in an era of migration, travel and communication technologies?

There are two quite different models of global love and partnering that help to explore this question. The first is a pattern of marriage partnering that relies on existing social networks that support arranged marriage but extends these transnationally. In this model, family and community networks play an important role in ensuring the success of the marriage, but the individuals getting married have less agency in their choice of a partner. This strategy produces marriages between people who live in different countries, but who share a common cultural background and social network. The second pattern is a form of marriage that more closely resembles the individualized freedoms commonly associated with late-modern unions. A growing number of men and women expand their marriage options by using the internet and online matchmaking services to connect with people living in different countries who are also from different cultural backgrounds. These couples have no overlapping social networks and create a union as autonomous individuals. However, even in this form of marriage, social networks and cultural contexts play an important role in narrowing down the millions of possible partners to a select handful of potential partners, before making that important decision about 'the one'.

Marriage in a transnational community

Britain is home to many large and vibrant migrant communities. For example, Katherine Charsley (2005a, 2005b) describes the community of men and women who have been migrating from Pakistan as post-war labour migrants. The original wave of predominantly male migrants tended to bring a wife from Pakistan when they were settled in Britain. It was generally expected that their own British-born children would most likely marry local members of the community. This is indeed the case for some of the second generation. But for the majority, it is now more likely that they will source their marriage partners from their parents' homeland, Pakistan (Charsley 2005a: 382).

A number of factors contribute to this trend to marry partners from overseas. First, there is a preference in the local community for arranged marriages between first cousins. In many cases, the majority of the migrant's siblings remain in Pakistan, meaning that the preferred marriage partners – the children of those siblings – are also predominantly in Pakistan. Second, at the same time, migration remains a valued economic strategy for kin in Pakistan, but is not one that is easily achieved. This is because, third, the national policy and legislative context shapes the opportunities for both migration and marriage of specific social groups (see also In Focus 2.3). In recent years, opportunities for migration from Pakistan to Britain have been reduced by tighter migration regulations. Indeed, one of the few options still readily available is spousal migration. This means that cousin marriage

---

In Focus 2.3 National policies and international marriage

Nations adopt policies and laws that support local social and cultural norms regarding partnering and family formation. However, such norms are highly variable around the world. This creates a complex terrain for migrants, who are often required to negotiate contradictions between their own cultural expectations and those enshrined in the laws and practices of the nations where they live.

One clear example of these contradictions is in relation to polygamy, the practice of having more than one spouse simultaneously. Polygamy is considered deviant and is illegal in most Anglophone and European societies, but is widely practised in other nations. In some cases, transnational migration can prevent and disrupt polygamous unions, whereas in other cases polygamy is a strategy for migration. For example, many people forced to flee their home countries due to violence and persecution find that their polygamous families are not recognized by settlement countries across Europe, North America and in Australia. In such cases, families are reconfigured and dispersed in response to the bureaucratic requirements of resettlement. In other instances, informal polygamy becomes a strategy for negotiating the long periods of family separation produced by some forms of international labour migration. For example, men from China working in Hong Kong for extended periods of time sometimes establish a second family in their place of work while continuing to maintain an ongoing relationship with the first family (Lang & Smart 2002). In other cases, polygamy becomes a strategy for migration. This was the case of a Turkish man who already had a wife from a religious marriage in Turkey when he fled alone to Denmark to seek asylum as a political refugee. Once there, he married a Danish woman in order to acquire a residency permit. Some years later he divorced his Danish wife before returning to Turkey to bring his original wife and children to live in Denmark (Charsley & Liversage 2013).

Using marriage as a strategy for negotiating migration obstacles and requirements is viewed with suspicion and condemnation by many destination countries. For example, the so-called 'Turkish trick' described above has since been identified and limited by new laws in Denmark that now make spousal migration much more difficult (Charsley & Liversage 2013). Policies regarding transnational marriages are also used by nations to shape migration flows and to manage the diverse populations produced by immigration. This can include limits on marriage migration from particular nations in the interests of integration as well as requirements regarding age differences, economic conditions and evidence of a romantic relationship prior to marriage, not all of which fit with migrants' expectations of their marital relationships (Williams 2010).

is an important resource within the family network, opening opportunities for migration of other members of the family who might otherwise be unable to migrate.

However, these practical explanations do not account for the full picture. Also at play are perceptions of cultural identity and ties of affection to kin. While they live their lives in Britain, people in the Pakistani community in Britain are also closely tied to Pakistan. They identify strongly with the cultural traditions and religious practices of their homeland, and also maintain active and ongoing communications, visits and exchanges with their extended kin in Pakistan. Marriage between their own children and young people in Pakistan provides another important opportunity to reinforce those connections and that social and cultural identity.

This point is further reinforced in Katy Gardner's (2008) research on transnational marriages arranged within kin networks that span Bangladesh and Britain. In Bangladesh, migration is one of the few avenues for pursuing economic security and wellbeing. However, different types of migration have varying levels of success. The two most common forms of migration are labour migration to the Middle East and spousal migration to Britain. Spousal migration is the preferred pathway, because it tends to have the most successful outcomes (although success is never guaranteed). Labour migrants to the Middle East must rely on strangers as agents to facilitate their movement across borders, and often have to engage in risky and illegal activities in order to gain overseas employment. Operating outside of their kin networks, they are relatively insecure and at risk of exploitation. In contrast, spousal migrants to Britain are enmeshed in kin networks that are known, trusted and able to offer support such as accommodation, employment and advice in the host country. Spousal migrants also benefit from being able to become integrated into an existing settled community network of Bangladeshis in Britain, which provides a variety of ethnic-specific services and institutions.

The transnational arranged marriages Charsley and Gardner describe rely heavily on social networks, and are made possible by the ongoing flow of resources that sustain transnational family life. In this context, maintaining good reputations within the family network and community become vital. Importantly, a good marriage reputation has to be directed not just towards potential partners and their families in the local area, but also towards being perceived as marriageable across national borders. This has an impact on the social and cultural norms of behaviour that young people are expected to follow. British-born men and women are expected to behave in accordance with Bangladeshi moral expectations, while Bangladesh-based young people are expected to demonstrate their ability to engage with British cosmopolitan attitudes, employment and practices, including working in business rather than agriculture. Their family networks observe them closely, making sure that they are meeting expectations that would make them good potential marriage partners. Every time they visit each other, or communicate by phone or online, they are also assessing their reputations within the family and community network. Sometimes, individuals might need a bit of help to build their reputation. So, for example, kin in Britain might send money to support young people in Bangladesh in a small business, not in the hope of making a profit from the business, but rather in the hope of demonstrating that they are potential spouses in Britain.

One of the risks of transnational marriage, even within a kin network, is that the geographic distances make it easier to deceive or be deceived. This becomes even more of a risk when marriages are not arranged within the kin network. In a study of middle-class Tamil Brahman transnational marriage practices, Kalpagam (2005) explores the preference for 'America *varan*', a marriage alliance with an Indian resident in North America. She notes that close kin marriages such as cousin marriage are not the preference among this social group. This means that personal networks are less likely to provide sufficient options for America *varan* matches. Instead, young people's horoscopes are circulated through the community or through the temple network in the hope that a good match will be identified. In addition, some people post advertisements in selected newspapers, magazines and on the internet. However, these are seen as less 'traditional' means of identifying partners, and thus as more risky than using temple or personal networks. Once horoscopes have been matched, the families then try to establish the suitability of the couple on other grounds: are they of appropriate social status, what is their family background, do they have any hidden girlfriends/boyfriends, are they of good character, and so on. In answering these questions, the personal and kin networks of the potential spouses can be helpful. For example, a cousin living in North America might be asked to telephone or meet with a prospective partner before a decision is made on whether to pursue the relationship.

In all of these examples, the risks associated with choosing a marriage partner is managed and decreased by placing an emphasis on 'tradition', something that is associated with stability and security. For the *varan* matches, tradition is signified by the reliance on the temple as the appropriate space for identifying appropriate partners. In the case of Pakistani and Bangladeshi transnational marriages with partners in the UK, the tradition of cousin marriage is relied on to manage the potential for failure.

Tradition is also used, albeit in a different way, as the basis of cross-border marriages in South Korea. Caren Freeman (2011) explains that, in South Korea, an estimated 27 per cent of rural and nearly 12 per cent of all marriages are between a South Korean man and a foreign bride, typically someone who is Chosŏnjok, an ethnic Korean living in China. This practice is traced back to government-sponsored industrial development in the 1960s, which contributed to the depopulation of rural areas. South Korean women, in particular, were encouraged by their mothers to escape to the relatively wealthier urban centres for work and marriage in order to avoid the comparative poverty of rural married life. Eldest sons, on the other hand, remained subject to cultural expectations that they would remain on the farm and care for their ageing parents. The result was a growing problem of 'bachelor farmers', unable to fulfil cultural expectations of masculinity because of the lack of women available and willing to marry them (Freeman 2011: 37). The government recognized this as a national crisis that was putting the viability of its farming and food production sector at risk of disappearing altogether.

The South Korean government responded by funding matchmaking programmes. At first, these sought to bring brides from urban centres into rural areas. Then, an effort was made to match marital partners across rural towns. Both of these initiatives were initially successful but rapidly dwindled in popularity. It was only as diplomatic relations improved with China in the late 1980s and early 1990s that a new, more successful programme was developed: 'in addition to the agricultural goods and capital that had been given clearance to enter the nation from abroad, the state added Chosŏnjok brides to the list of acceptable foreign imports' (Freeman 2011: 41). Marriages between South Korean bachelor farmers and Chosŏnjok brides – ethnic Koreans living in China – were organized during government-funded four-day marriage tours to North Eastern China.

The scheme proved popular, and by 2011 there were more than 1250 international marriage agencies registered in South Korea as well as an unknown number of unregistered brokers. The marriage tours were perceived as contributing to a larger national project of reunification of Chosŏnjok in South Korea, which resonated with nationalistic desires for a reunification with North Korea. For rural South Korean men, Chosŏnjok women seemed to create a link back to an earlier era in which Korea was united. The women were imagined as 'unspoiled' compared to South Korean women, 'occupying a space and time untouched by modernizing influences', and fulfilling feminine virtues of purity and obedience (Freeman 2011: 42). However, when some of the migrant brides failed to live up to these idealized expectations, Chosŏnjok women became increasingly subject to hostility and suspicion. This resulted in a growing number of people seeking brides from South East Asia, perceived as both '"cheaper" and "more compliant"' (Freeman 2011: 48).

The Chosŏnjok women, too, were open to the opportunity for marriage migration, but not because it facilitated some notion of a return to tradition. Rather, they were frustrated by the lack of local employment opportunities and future prospects and attracted to South Korea's reputation as a modern nation. A primary advantage of marrying a man in South Korea was that it could open up a range of employment opportunities for women, in roles such as nannies, factory workers or bilingual service workers, or as entrepreneurs (Freeman 2011: 147). Indeed, some of the women used their experience of international marriage and the resulting cross-border networks and knowledge to earn incomes and create businesses themselves as matchmakers. This was an extension of a standard practice, in which many women who migrated as brides would in any case be asked to help find a suitable match for family, friends and neighbours both in South Korea and in China. Some women combined regular visits to their home town with marriage tours, bringing farmer bachelors with them to meet eligible women. In other cases, Chosŏnjok men would travel to South Korea to meet with distant kin in the hope of finding a suitable marriage partner for a daughter or sister. For many people – as had been the case in the past – matchmaking was an activity done 'on the side', rather than a full-time occupation.

In all of these examples of transnational marriage, men and women seek to marry across national borders, but to do so within ethnic communities.

This appears to provide a greater guarantee for the success of the marriage, because it is more likely that there will be shared expectations of how a marriage should function and what roles the men and women should play. Their goal is to reproduce past expectations of marriage and relationships, rather than generate new modes of interaction. This is made possible by couples already being part of the same kinship network, religion and transnational community.

The possibility of a shared experience is also undermined by the fact that the union is transnational. The men and women have different experiences to draw on as a result of having lived their lives in different locations prior to marriage, being exposed to different education systems, media, government policies and non-familial social structures. The gender inequalities that shape how a couple conducts their marriage are further overlaid by other global inequalities, including those between Western and non-Western nations, and those between migrants and non-migrants.

The intersections of these layers of inequality can result in very different outcomes for any particular marriage. For example, a British-born woman married to a Bangladesh-born man might have more social and cultural capital in Britain than her husband, and be able to use this to influence the level of equality and affection in her marriage. In contrast, a woman from Pakistan migrating to marry a British-born man may be required to live up to his expectations of marriage, rather than assert her own. Importantly, this relative power can itself have very different outcomes in any particular marriage. For example, the relative structural power of the British-born wife might be used by her to assert a less equal division of labour within the household, if she prefers to maintain a strong gendered distinction between homemaker and income earner. Similarly, the British-born man might seek to impose a more equal gender relation on his Pakistan-born wife than she feels is desirable.

Marriage across national and cultural borders

While all marriage entails some risk of a poor match, a transnational marriage that crosses cultural and ethnic as well as national borders is seen as particularly risky. Indeed, matchmaking that is conducted outside of social networks can be seen as a thinly disguised form of human trafficking, in which women are sexually exploited as a result of their global economic vulnerability (see In Focus 2.4). This critique of transnational marriages draws in part on the assumption that love and money should be kept separate. It also draws on a critique of global inequalities, which further exacerbate the unequal status of men and women. Yet it is also clear that men and women often turn to marriage across national and cultural borders as a response to the effects of global and local inequalities on their lives and opportunities.

Commercial matchmaking has become a common practice in many parts of the world. For men in Singapore who earn low wages in low-skilled jobs, these services provide a solution to the problems they face in finding a

---

In Focus 2.4 Mail-order brides and women as victims

Not all research on transnational marriage recognizes women as agents able to make choices about marriage. The discussions of 'mail-order brides', in particular, identify women as passive and powerless victims in the global process of their commoditization and exploitation (e.g. Hughes 2000). These accounts critique websites offering international marriage for their positioning of women as 'products' sold to Western men, a progression from the past era of printed catalogues. For example, Leonora Angeles and Sirjit Sunanta (2007) discuss Western-Thai and Western-Filipino intermarriage websites as spaces in which women are represented as objects of 'exotic love' that men can choose, purchase and act upon. The women are presented as 'traditional … respectable, trustworthy, honourable, sensitive, and caring' (p. 14), as well as 'beautiful, petite, feminine, affectionate, sexy' (pp. 16–17). Globally circulating assumptions that Thai women are more 'traditional' than their Western counterparts are drawn upon to claim that Thai women are 'naturally' positioned and culturally predisposed to be ideal wives. Similarly, Filipinas are presented by Filipinaladies.com in the following way: 'Devotion to one's husband is part of Filipino culture so they are affectionate and supportive at all times. They love children and give much of their time and effort to raising a happy family.' (p. 18)

For scholars such as Angeles and Sunanta (2007; see also Sciachitano 2000), these claims about the cultural characteristics of Asian women serve to essentialize them as the exotic and desirable 'other'. In the process, they both draw upon and reinforce sexist, racist and colonial views that have 'contributed to intensifying violence against Third World women in general, and Thai and Filipino women in particular' (p. 7) by facilitating the commodification of women and normalizing their violation (see also Tolentino 1996). At the same time, Western women are essentialized as the opposite of the desirable Asian woman. Unlike the 'traditional' and 'caring' women being offered on the websites, Western women are described as uncaring and unappreciative of men and their needs, if not actually man-haters. Thus, according to WorldClassService.com, 'There seems to be a near-perfect match between the Western men, who are unappreciated and get no respect in their own countries, and the Filipinas, who would be happy to find someone who simply does his job and hopes to come home to a pleasant family life after work' (Angeles & Sunanta 2007: 19).

---

marriage partner. In 2010, marriages between Singaporean citizens and foreign spouses accounted for nearly 41 per cent of all marriages in Singapore, most of which were between Singaporean men and foreign women. In explaining this rapid increase in international marriages, Yeoh, Chee and Vu (2013: 286) point to a

> growing mismatch in marriage expectations between the two largest groups of singles: on the one hand, independent-minded, financially well-resourced graduate women with sophisticated expectations of marriage partners, and on the other, Chinese-speaking blue-collar male workers with low levels of education with a preference for women willing to uphold traditional gender roles and values.

It is this latter group of men who have increasingly turned to commercial matchmaking services in Singapore to find brides overseas, hoping to appeal to women from poorer countries as prospective marriage partners.

Nicole Constable (2003a: 146) calls this phenomenon 'global hypergamy', meaning that the 'expectation that women will marry up and out of their own social or economic group' has now become shaped by global social and economic groupings. In the case of global hypergamy, women want to marry up and out of their own *national* economic group, not just up and out of their own local social or economic group. Thus, men who occupy a low social and economic status in their own country might be able to use their position as members of a wealthier country to attract brides from poorer countries. This does not mean that all women in poorer countries wish to marry men in richer countries, or that all men in richer countries are desirable marriage material, even for women in poorer countries. As Constable (2003a: 146) explains, women do not '"settle" for just any western man'. They have expectations that go beyond the country of residence of their marriage partners, including such things as shared education levels and common interests, and shared expectations regarding having children and being able to work and earn an income.

Kathryn Robinson (2007) argues that the desire for 'traditional' brides is linked to a common male experience of modern postindustrial economies, in which men have been economically as well as socially and culturally marginalized compared with their fathers. Finding a traditional bride is one way of resisting the decline of a patriarchal gender order that once rewarded them in status in spite of their relative lack of economic power. By tapping into larger discourses of progress, in which poorer nations on the global stage are perceived as 'lagging behind' the developed world, they turn to women from poorer nations as a way of accessing a past way of life, in which it might be possible to continue to uphold the forms of masculinity, femininity and gender relations that they were raised to consider desirable.

While tradition might operate as a source of security and comfort for men, it plays a less straightforward role for the women. On the one hand, women often seek to fulfil 'traditional' expectations that they marry and have children. The motivation to be a mother and a wife is strong, and is not simply felt as external social pressure but also as an internal desire. When women encounter obstacles to fulfilling these desires in their local community, they are sometimes prompted to explore opportunities to find marriage partners overseas. So, for example, when Wilasinee Pananakhonsab (2016) interviewed Thai women and asked them why they decided to use cross-cultural internet dating sites, many explained that they were looking for a pathway to marriage and motherhood that was closed off to them in Thailand. One woman described her decision thus:

> I was married to my first ex-husband for six years. He left me for another woman when I was pregnant with my second child. I chose to divorce him. I met my second ex-husband because he was my customer [in a small business]. He never looked for another woman, but he asked me

many times about my sexual experiences with the first ex-husband after we got married. When I would not answer him, he would get angry with me. I couldn't understand why he was like that. It was so weird. He knew I was a divorced woman before he was in a relationship with me. I decided to marry him because I thought that he could accept my status as a divorcee. But after we lived together, I realized he couldn't. I asked myself why I had remarried with a Thai man if he couldn't accept my past. I couldn't change it *(my past experiences)*. I felt as if I was nothing and worthless when I was with him. I decided to divorce again.

When she decided to look for a *farang* man on a cross-cultural dating site, she was trying to avoid the stigma associated with divorce in traditional Thai gender roles and expectations. She, and other women like her, believed that Western men were more 'modern'. This meant that they were likely to be more accepting of women who had experienced previous sexual partners and marriages, less likely to be influenced by local expectations that older women are not good for marriage, and more likely to be sexually faithful to their wife (e.g. Kojima 2001; del Rosario 2005).

It is in this way that transnational matchmaking sites produce an interesting contradiction. As Minervini and McAndrew (2006: 115) argue, they 'may be in the perverse position of attempting to match independent, non-traditional women with very traditional Western men'. Both the men and women have expectations about how husbands and wives should behave, which are shaped by their own local cultural assumptions, but also by globally circulating ideas about the cultural practices and beliefs of others. The women, for example, will have been exposed to ideas about gender equality and women's rights that are circulated through international popular media as well as through government and non-governmental organization (NGO) policies and campaigns. They have also encountered ideas of romantic love in the same way. These will intersect in complex ways with their desire for marriage and their locally produced expectations of what marriage entails.

What this tells us is that sexual and marital subjectivities – what it means to be a wife, a mother, or a woman – are constituted in different ways in different social and cultural contexts (Palriwala & Uberoi 2005; Robinson 2007). For example, in contrast to dominant discourses in Western nations, it is not necessarily appropriate to assume that sex and love must be separated from money and financial security. Thus, in Thailand, a good husband can be perceived as a man who gives his wife regular monetary payments, even when she is earning her own income, because this is an accepted way of expressing intimacy, care and affection (Suwannapat 2014). Meanwhile, men from Western backgrounds often find it confronting when their Thai girlfriends or wives expect to receive money that they can send to their parents and extended kin. Men often see these requests as a sign that their partner is not really in love with them but is, rather, only interested in the financial support they can offer (Pananakhonsab 2016).

The mail-order bride websites contribute to the potential for misunderstanding, by tapping into the fantasies their male clients have regarding submissive, affectionate, caring women, without simultaneously alerting men to the potential for different understandings of the intersections of romantic love and financial support in the relationship. In the context of gendered, economic and global inequalities, this can result in women being required to fulfil the expectations held by their husbands without having their own expectations fully met. In some cases, this can contribute to conflict-ridden relationships and tragic incidences of domestic violence and spousal abuse.

The exchange of money does not necessarily mean that there is a lack of intimacy. The problem does not lie with the relationship between love and money, but rather with the capacity for autonomy. This is made clear in Therese Blanchet's (2005) account of how young Bangladeshi women are sold into marriage in ways that clearly resemble slavery, and which provide them with few opportunities for resistance or autonomy. The problem here is not the presence or absence of money, but rather the capacity for women to assert their needs, desires and expectations and to have autonomy over their bodies and choices in their relationships. In this respect, not all online or commercial matchmaking services are equal. Rather, while some commercially arranged marriages – both transnational and intranational – are sites for the enslavement and exploitation of women, others provide a source of pleasure, satisfaction and reward for both men and women.

Transnational online dating

The recent expansion of internet dating sites provide women as well as men with an opportunity to be highly selective about whom they consider for marriage. People using these services are able to control whom they communicate with, when, for how long, and whether and when they want to cease communication (Illouz 2007; Pananakhonsab 2016). Far from the depiction of internet brides as being submissive victims of male fantasies, these are women who are finding ways of being more assertive and autonomous in their relationships. They are able to use internet dating to avoid relying on social networks for introductions to men, instead being able to find prospective partners on their own. The internet, for many women, is a tool for increasing autonomy and independence, and for avoiding local gendered constraints in favour of individualized freedoms.

Internet dating sites allow men and women to seek partners from around the world according to a list of objective criteria. They are also able to present themselves to millions of people simultaneously, expanding the chances that they will find 'the one' among the many possibilities (Illouz 2007). When they identify a possible match, they can get to know them a little better online without creating any sense of obligation. Messages can be exchanged in which the act of typing out provides a sense of control over what is said and how it is said. The potential social awkwardness of a first date is sanitized into a carefully choreographed exchange, even as the authors of the messages feel that they are able to express their innermost thoughts and feelings and convey their 'true' and 'authentic' selves (Ellison, Heino & Gibbs 2006).

This seems to be romantic love par excellence, with its emphasis on constructing a fantasy of intimacy in which each partner is able to present their perfect and ideal self (Illouz 2007). The internet allows for the erasing of all of the minor and major frustrations and limitations of everyday life. The incompatibilities of work schedules and childcare, bodily flaws and faults, annoying habits or difficult personalities, incompatible friends and so on are erased in the online sharing of an innermost self with another. In the online environment, the ideal self can be carefully projected, and the various everyday frictions that constantly undermine that ideal self in the offline world can be ignored and put aside.

In reality, normative models of femininity and masculinity continue to prevail (Jagger 2001, 2005). Women find it particularly difficult to step outside of stereotypes of femininity when displaying themselves in online dating sites, tending to emphasize female characteristics such as physical attractiveness, their capacity to be 'warm' and caring, and their ability to listen (Jagger 2001: 47). In contrast, men do seem to have a greater capacity to enact a wider range of modes of masculinity in their profiles. Women from South East Asia are likely to find themselves trapped into presenting themselves as ideal, traditional, feminine prospective brides in order to attract potential partners to their online profiles (Sciachitano 2000). The goal of online dating requires a balance between the need to be relatively honest (and so not disappoint a potential partner when they do finally meet) and the need to attract interest to a profile in order to have a chance of locating a potential partner. In practice, this tends to translate into online profiles oriented towards presenting the person as closer to the perceived ideals of femininity and masculinity than they are in the offline world (Minervini & McAndrew 2006; Brand et al. 2012; Bridges 2012). Thus, even as women are using the internet to escape the constraints of local gendered norms and expectations, they are also coaxed into reproducing and standardizing gendered norms and expectations of representing women on a global scale.

For this reason, the representation of women in international online dating sites is not a simple exchange between two individuals who are seeking a romantic partner. Rather, the representations of women online have implications for all women, and particularly for all non-white women, who are symbolically objectifying themselves as commodities subject to the Western male gaze. The autonomy that women seek by engaging in online dating is not simple to achieve. Even as they assert their agency, they are also at risk of reinforcing global gendered and national inequalities.

While the internet appears to be a tool allowing unfettered freedom to marry just 'anyone' from 'anywhere' on your own terms, it is important to recognize that online meeting and dating are not random acts of 'love'. Rather, they are shaped by both the limitations of online profiles as reinforcing existing inequalities such as gender and age, as well as by what Nicole Constable (2003a) has called the 'cultural logics of desire'. That is, online dating and transnational marriages continue to be structured by larger frames of inequality and dominant cultural models. Even as women might escape local forms of kinship-based power or particular forms of cultural constraints, they are simultaneously implicated in other power dynamics, which require them to resist again, and in different ways, the gendered norms and assumptions that circulate at a global level.

Conclusion

Marriage is a complex negotiation of gendered norms and expectations. Even though it has often been argued that marriage is not good for women, because it reinforces their subordination to men, marriage remains a desirable goal for both women and men. This is true even when marriage is no longer a requirement for economic security. People continue to value and desire long-term, formalized intimate relationships, in which to have and raise children, share a household and build economic security. Yet the transformation of the social and economic conditions throughout nations around the world has necessarily changed the context within which marriages are organized.

It is easy to slip into an assumption that all marriages are now based on romantic love, which places the emotional intensity of attraction to the forefront of decisions about relationships (Beck & Beck-Gernsheim 2013). However, this would fail to account for the complex ways in which people use kinship networks and the internet to find possible marriage partners. As the contestants in *If You Are The One* know only too well, attraction is only part of the equation. It is also important to find a marriage partner who is a good match in terms of meeting economic ambitions, family expectations and helping the individual to fulfil their sense of being a 'good' man or woman, as well as a good husband or wife. For British-born Bangladeshis, an attractive spouse might be someone who has been running a business in Bangladesh. For a man in Pakistan, it might be a cousin in Britain who his family know to be modest and sufficiently traditional. For a Thai woman, it might be an Australian man who is able to accept her as a wife in spite of her past marriages and divorces.

There is also, importantly, a desire to enter a marriage that is likely to last. The search for tradition seems to play a role in fulfilling this desire. Yes, relationships are increasingly contingent and yes, this provides the opportunity to renegotiate gendered relations and expectations within a relationship. However, the desirability of a long-term relationship is itself an important source of satisfaction, and one for which other forms of satisfaction are readily sacrificed. Indeed, the forms and degrees of sacrifice that people are willing to endure become more evident in the next chapter, in which we examine the ways in which couples manage their marriages across long distances and national borders. These stories provide a clear sense of what some people will endure in order to sustain their marriages.

Distant Couples

In spite of global variations in partnering, in Western nations the dominant model for family formation remains that of the heterosexual monogamous couple. However, even this model has undergone significant transformation in recent decades. Terms such as 'serial monogamy' seek to capture the making, unmaking and remaking of couple relationships that has now become more accepted as the norm of intimate lives (see also Chapter 2). Also, couple relationships are no longer assumed to be only heterosexual, with growing evidence of Western nations accepting same-sex unions, if not same-sex marriage (see also Chapter 8). In this chapter, I focus on another source of transformation of the couple relationship that is a product of not just the increasing incidence of international migration, but also the growing significance of mobilities in everyday life. Ulrich Beck and Elisabeth Beck-Gernsheim (1995) argue that the demands of the labour market are making it more difficult for couples to remain together, provoking the unmaking and remaking of intimate ties that suit the requirement that employees are flexible and mobile. In this chapter, I explore the ways in which couples maintain their relationships across time and distance in spite of these demands for flexibility and geographic mobility. Through accounts of trailing spouses, living apart together (LAT) relationships and fly-in-fly-out (FIFO) families, I argue that people adopt many creative approaches to maintaining committed couple relationships of love, care and support, challenging claims that the breakdown of relationships has become a late-modern norm.

A story of love, marriage, mobility and separation

I was interviewing participants for a research project about weddings when Elise and Trent invited me to their home for an evening meal. Both were information technology professionals, Elise working in the public service and Trent for a private company. Their hours were long, but the pay was good and they both enjoyed their work and the challenges it presented. This Thursday night was the best opportunity for them to contribute to my research, an exploration of weddings and marriage. Elise had prepared a soup and roast, Trent had bought some wine, and I brought a cake for dessert. We talked, laughed and ate, and both Elise and Trent were clearly enjoying the prospect of their wedding, although I noted some tension in their exchange.

'Trent just isn't that interested in the menu, or the flowers, or the colour coordination of the clothing', Elise explained. Trent responded: 'I just don't have the same ideas as she does, the same tastes, so it's better to stay out of it. I'm in charge of the music for the reception.' Elise looked at him intently: 'Have you called that DJ yet?' He looked at me, then turned back to her, 'No, I'll try to call him tomorrow.' Elise sighed, rolling her eyes and explaining to me, 'It's the only thing he has to do, and it's been over three weeks now. Still no DJ. This is what it's like!'

When I asked Elise and Trent why they were getting married, they explained that they were in love. This was a typical response to my question, and reflected the strong assumption that love is the foundation of a marriage in Western societies (see also Chapter 2). However, the connection between love and marriage is never straightforward or automatic. Elise and Trent had bought a house together two years earlier, and had been cohabiting since. Their families and friends had almost given up asking when 'the big day' would come, assuming that they would remain a de facto couple. Then, a few months before our meeting, Elise's grandfather had been hospitalized with an illness. Although he had recovered well, it had been a significant moment in their decision to marry. Her grandfather had always hoped to walk Elise down the aisle, as her own father had left the family and gone overseas when Elise was young. She decided she wanted to make sure that his hope could be fulfilled, something that suddenly seemed more urgent after this reminder of her grandfather's mortality. When she discussed this with Trent, he was eager to agree – he had long wanted to marry, but was aware that Elise was resistant to the idea for what he considered to be 'mysterious reasons of her own'. He organized a romantic proposal over candlelight, and they set a date.

Elise was not unusual in having strong ideas about her wedding. This was her opportunity to express her individual taste to her family and friends (Goldstein-Gidoni 1997; Boden 2003; Otnes & Pleck 2003). She knew that she wanted the wedding to be solemn with a nod to religious symbolism, but also a fun party that would celebrate their love for each other. She enjoyed setting up the gift registry and filling it with desirable things, and shopping for a dress that fulfilled her idea of herself as a bride. She drew on the shopping, decorative and fashion expertise of her mother, sister and girlfriends to make sure that everything from the cake to the invitations was just right.

Trent's experience was also fairly typical. When he made suggestions about venue, food or clothing for the event, he was usually dismissed as not understanding what a wedding should be like. He accepted this, declaring that it was not really his strong point. Most men find themselves unable to make significant contributions. At best, they might be asked for their opinion on the music for the reception, the selection of a videographer, or the menu.

This was in spite of the fact that couples such as Elise and Trent asserted that their relationship was egalitarian; they shared decisions about household purchases, they each contributed to housework and they each earned a similar income. At the same time, their divisions of labour were also oriented to their personal preferences. Elise preferred to take responsibility for the cooking and cleaning, while Trent preferred to take care of the garden and rubbish. They both pointed out, too, that Trent's sporting commitments meant that he didn't have as much time for housework as Elise. In any case, she didn't trust him to meet her high standards. So, while she tended to contribute more, the arrangement was one they both agreed to and were satisfied with.

Two years after their wedding day, Elise informed me that she and Trent were separating. He had been offered an excellent position in Singapore by his employer, and was keen to pursue the opportunity. Her own career in the public service was progressing well, but required her to continue living in the same city. She had no intention of leaving. More importantly, she explained, they just didn't seem to be able to agree on anything anymore. As her responsibilities at work were increasing, she was hoping that Trent would take on more of the housework, but this was something that he seemed incapable of doing. He suggested she employ a cleaner, but she was concerned this would just give her another person to manage when she was already busy. They also argued about having children. Trent wanted her to take time off work to have at least two children. She wasn't willing to sacrifice her career, and couldn't see how Trent would step up to take on some of the load if children were added to the mix. Though painful, it seemed that the best solution was to separate, a decision they had taken several months of arguments to reach.

Marital relations and gender equality

Elise and Trent are not an unusual couple. Their hopes, dreams and obstacles are the same as those of many couples in contemporary Western societies. Women are acquiring education, entering professions and participating in the paid workforce at unprecedented rates. At the same time, they are maintaining responsibility for the household and for childcare, with men failing to take up domestic responsibilities at the same rate. The result is a double burden for women, who balance both paid and unpaid work, as well as a growing care deficit that impacts on dependants such as children and the elderly (Beck & Beck-Gernsheim 1995). In spite of clear advancements in gender equality in the context of paid employment, the model of gender relations that Talcott Parsons (1943, 1955) assumed to be functional in the nuclear family unit is remarkably persistent, with responsibilities for the home and for care remaining strongly gendered (Baxter 1997; Baxter, Hewitt & Western 2005).

Elise and Trent recognized that they performed different roles in the family home, but were unwilling to see this as a form of inequality. Rather, at least in the earlier stages of their relationship, they defined it as a consequence of personal choices and preferences. That is, women are not forced to do more domestic labour, but choose to spend more of their time in this way.

This helps to explain one of the trends in domestic labour – that women are reporting spending less time doing unpaid work, while men are not reporting spending any more time to fill the gap (Bittman & Pixley 1997; Baxter 2002; Pocock 2003). Women are reducing their standards and expectations, increasing their efficiency, or paying other women to do the work for them.

The transition into parenthood provides a key moment in reinforcing these inequalities. Analysis of survey data by Baxter and colleagues (2008) demonstrates that women take on much larger proportions of household labour when they have children, whereas men's participation remains relatively steady. Yet surveys also demonstrate that most women and men consider their division of domestic work to be fair; even when the division of labour is unequal, they state that their relationships are egalitarian and they believe that egalitarianism is important to them in their relationship (Baxter & Western 1998; Lindsay 1999).

In order to understand this apparent paradox, it is necessary to recognize the role of gendered subjectivities in shaping how people perceive their relationships and what they do within them. In their classic account of gender, Candace West and Don Zimmerman (1987) argue that gender is not something we are born with, but rather something that we 'do'. Through our interactions with others on a daily basis, we both produce our own gendered identities and shape the gendered identities of others. These are not random productions. Rather, they are produced according to sets of gendered scripts, including what Connell (2002, 2005) terms 'hegemonic' masculinities and femininities. These are powerful models regarding what it means to be a good woman or a good man, which shape not only how people present themselves and how they behave, but also how they feel about themselves. That is, our gendered identities are not simply imposed on us by external expectations, but come to be internalized, producing and produced by our emotions.

The cultural models of gender norms and roles vary significantly around the world. However, as will become clear in this chapter, there is a strong global tendency to attribute income-earning activities as masculine and caregiving activities as feminine. The dominant model of capitalism that Parsons identified in the mid-twentieth century is persistent. This is not to say that people are unable to resist or negotiate these norms. In diverse nations around the world, culturally specific traditions regarding masculine and feminine behaviours and identities provide alternatives. In modern Western nations, the emergence of cultural expectations regarding gender equality and individualization provide another set of alternatives. Anthony Giddens (1992) explains that we are entering a new era of democratic intimacy, in which men and women only remain in a relationship as long as it meets their expectations and enables them to fulfil their life narrative.

It is clear from the case of Elise and Trent that the life one makes for oneself entails negotiating contradictions and dealing with the limits of choice. The demands of labour market mobilities make this even more challenging. In addition to permanent migration, there is an increasing pressure for people to be highly mobile in order to sustain their careers (see In Focus 3.1). As a result

---

In Focus 3.1 Mobilities and mobile lives

Historically, migration studies have focused on understanding the reasons people leave one place, the reasons they choose to move to another place, and the impact of their settlement on those new places or the impact of their departure on the places and communities they leave behind. This approach gained further complexity in the 1990s with attention to transnational social fields, the meaningful connections maintained by migrants between the places they leave and the places in which they settle (Glick Schiller, Basch & Blanc-Szanton 1992).

More recently, John Urry (2000, 2007) has become a key figure in what is now known as the 'mobilities turn' or 'mobilities paradigm' (Sheller & Urry 2006). The mobilities approach looks beyond migration, to consider the ways in which new technologies of transport and communication have transformed everyday lives in the twenty-first century. It draws attention to the fact that not only migrants, but also tourists, commuters, delivery drivers, cruise ship personnel, transport staff, airline pilots and others are increasingly organizing their lives around continual, persistent movement. Moreover, the internet and mobile telephones are producing new means of connectivity that transform experiences of movement, distance and proximity.

There is a certain lightness and sense of freedom associated with the idea that everyone, everywhere seems to be on the move – a perception captured in the idea of 'liquid modernity' (Bauman 2000). However, on closer inspection it becomes quickly apparent that this is not entirely true. Mobilities are not evenly distributed across the globe, nor are they always to be celebrated. Some people have mobilities forced upon them when they would prefer to remain in place, as is the case with those who are forced to migrate due to persecution, war or violence, or those who are required to move and make way for major development projects such as dams in India and China. For others, immobilities are the norm, the capacity to move limited to those who have access to passports or the economic resources necessary to participate in moving between here and there. Indeed, some argue that a mobile subjectivity is necessarily a bourgeois, masculine subjectivity (Skeggs 2004), while others argue for attention to the 'constellations of mobility' produced by uneven representations and practices (Cresswell 2010). These critiques provide an important background for an analysis of how couples and families respond in gendered, classed ways to the demands, opportunities and challenges of movement, separation and connection, as is discussed in this and later chapters.

---

of these pressures, Elise found that it is difficult to be a wife and mother and a career woman. Trent found that it is difficult to be both a supportive husband and a transnational employee. In their case, the decision was made to end the relationship in order to protect their careers and manage their disagreements. Yet many couples find other strategies for managing similar problems produced by the demands of mobile lives. It is these strategies that are the focus of the following discussions in this chapter, including an examination of the 'trailing spouse', the 'commuter couple', 'LAT' and 'FIFO' relationships and transnational marriage.

The trailing spouse

Diplomats, executives and military personnel are among the many employees who are routinely required to relocate for extended periods of time and live in other countries in order to perform their work. When they do so, it is generally expected that their spouse and children will follow, but not extended kin such as parents. This model both assumes and reproduces the nuclear family, with the employee usually male and the 'trailing spouse' or 'tied migrant' usually his wife (Harvey & Wiese 2007). These families are required to be agile, mobile and responsive to work opportunities, often at the expense of ongoing social networks based in particular places. Uprooted from their own support networks, trailing spouses are nevertheless expected to provide emotional support and a loving family environment for their working spouse and to raise any children the couple might have (Makela, Suutari & Mayerhofer 2011; McNulty 2012: 418). However, they adopt this role in an unfamiliar environment and without established social support networks, or even the institutional support that their employee spouses tend to receive as part of their relocation (Harvey & Weise 2007: 364). The result, argues Bandana Purkayastha (2005), is a 'cumulative disadvantage' in which the careers and wellbeing of wives are undermined in order to support the careers and wellbeing of their husbands (Cooke & Spiers 2005).

There are a number of factors contributing to this accumulation of disadvantage. One is the lack of support provided by employers to the trailing spouses of their employees, who are expected to relocate at short notice and recreate their family household in a new culture and society (e.g. Miller 2013). Another, and one of the biggest problems reported by tied migrants, is the lack of opportunities to build their own career (Harvey & Weise 2007). In some cases, visas limit their working rights and produce dependency. In other cases, language obstacles or local lack of skills recognition lead to unemployment or underemployment.

Trailing spouses with children, sometimes called 'trailing parents', face particular obstacles (Ryan & Mulholland 2014). For example, in both India and China, professional women typically continue to work after having children, supported by extended kin or even extended family households who are able to provide childcare and support for domestic tasks. This enables women to meet the expectations that 'family comes first' and that the husband's career is most important, without having to relinquish their own employment opportunities. However, as trailing spouses they are unable to replicate these support structures. As a result, highly skilled professional women are either required to remain in the home caring for children and their husband, or are underemployed in low-wage, low-status or part-time positions (Cooke 2001, 2007; Jagganath 2015). The cultural norms that produce greater gender equality in the home country are reversed by the particular arrangements of the trailing spouse, which reinforce and in some cases require the reproduction of a nuclear family household in which it is typically (though not always) the man earning the income and the woman who is the dependent caregiver.

While the male breadwinner model of the nuclear family is common among families with trailing spouses, it is not the only possible outcome. Indeed, in some cases, the trailing spouse is male and the employee is female. Male trailing spouses remain a minority, but have been a growing minority since before the 1990s. In 2001, *The Wall Street Journal* estimated that approximately 13 per cent of expat workers were female (Jordan 2001), and in 2013 the *Financial Times* suggested this had grown to nearly 25 per cent (Clegg 2013). In these cases, it is the trailing husband who faces the problems experienced by trailing partners and whose career and social networks are impeded by the relocation. In addition, trailing husbands – being in a minority – report problems with accessing the social networks produced by trailing wives, which tend to assume the femininity of their members.

While most cases of trailing spouses describe the negative outcomes for gender relations and for the employment prospects of the tied migrant, there are also some examples of trailing spouses experiencing an improvement in gender relations. For example, Akiko Yasuike (2011) explored the experiences of trailing wives of Japanese businessmen temporarily located in the USA. She found that the dominance of the masculine corporate culture in Japan became diluted in the American context. In Japan, male corporate employees were defined as efficient and effective if they were able to dedicate time to their employment to the exclusion of their family, evidenced through long working hours, after-work drinking with the boss and attendance at weekend golf. However, once in the USA, Japanese men became more aware of American norms of fatherhood and marital life, and some started to spend more time with their children and partner. Whereas in Japan a husband might be ridiculed for coming home early on a wedding anniversary, or spending time shopping with their wife, in America these became newly defined as desirable and expected activities. Indeed, wives reported that in some cases it was the return to Japan that created the biggest problem, especially for children who had become accustomed to a father being present in the USA and had to adjust to his absence in Japan.

Commuter couples

Not all couples choose to relocate the entire family in order to manage the demands of employment and careers. Another option, which is potentially less damaging to gender equality, is for the employee to undertake long-distance commuting, while their spouse remains and maintains the couple's home and social networks. The advantage of this option is that this partner is not required to migrate, and so does not need to give up their employment opportunities or negotiate a new home, social network, language or culture (van der Klis 2008). Instead, they are able to continue their lives, albeit with the regular and routinized absence of the employee partner.

Naomi Gerstel and H. Gross (1982) were among the first to identify commuting as a response to the emergence of the dual-career family. They argued that commuter marriages were a characteristic of more egalitarian couples who recognized that both men and women should be supported in their careers. As professionals, both men and women consider their careers as an important source of identity and self-worth. Being highly paid, they are also better able to sustain the costs of frequent long-distance travel and communications. It is surprising, then, that commuter couples nevertheless frequently reproduce traditional gender roles. It is typically the husband who is the breadwinner commuting to work and the wife who has ongoing responsibility for the household and any children. Even though couples report that both husbands and wives contribute to everyday tasks such as ironing, cooking and home maintenance, the heavier burden of responsibility for maintaining the family and household remains that of wives, with a few exceptions. When it is the woman who is the commuting partner, friends and family make it clear through their comments that she is deviating from the norm. As one commuting partner explained, 'They'll say "I bet Ted is so lonely"... they have more sympathy for the man in the relationship. I think that is a given, always' (Bergen, Kirby & McBride 2007: 288).

A big part of the problem for commuter marriages, according to Gerstel and Gross (1984), is the fact that non-cohabiting marriages are perceived as deviant, often by the couples themselves but particularly by their families, friends and social networks (Forsyth & Gramling 1998). As Karla Bergen (2010) demonstrates in the case of commuter partnerships in the USA, the master narrative of marriage continues to assume a couple living in a shared household (Bergen 2010). Commuting is seen primarily as a less-than-ideal strategy for managing diverging work, family and other commitments, rather than as a preferred way of living. New communication technologies mean couples can now engage in what is known as 'incidental intimacy', and stay in almost continuous contact, being able to send text messages as well as talk on the phone and see each other through Skype or other visual media. Long-distance travel, too, is cheaper and faster. Yet these tools tend to be used to maintain the ideal of the co-resident nuclear family, rather than create new ideals or models. The separation remains anomalous, rather than becoming normalized as part of the partnership (van der Klis 2008; van der Klis & Mulder 2008; van der Klis & Karsten 2009a, 2009b). There is a sense of having to justify their non-normative relationship to others and sometimes even to themselves. Karla Bergen (2010; see also McBride & Bergen 2014) points out that these justifications can take a number of forms, including emphasizing that it was a mutual decision or encouraged by the spouse in order to support two careers, or suggesting that one or both partners in the couple prefer the arrangement, either because they like time on their own or their work is too demanding for them to notice the time apart. In other cases, the quality of the time spent together is emphasized, or the quantity of time spent apart is dismissed as minimal.

Although commuter partnerships are sometimes used as a strategy to enable both partners to maintain a career, many commuter partnerships tend to reproduce more traditional divisions of labour in their relationship (Anderson & Spruill 1993). Evidence from the Netherlands suggests that they are often seen as a strategy for temporarily minimizing disruption of everyday life, but also tend to limit opportunities for greater gender equality (van der Klis & Karsten 2009b). In most cases, commuting is a strategy for delaying or avoiding family migration and a trailing spouse, rather than a means to create greater gender equality. Most of the time, the commuting partner eventually returns to live full time in the family home, with only a small number of couples deciding to relocate permanently to the place of work or opting to sustain the commuting strategy indefinitely.

LAT relationships

Since the 1990s, many scholars have turned to the 'living apart together', or LAT, relationship as a much clearer indication of the willingness and desire to create more equal couple partnerships. These relationships appear to be a clear alternative to the assumption that long-term committed relationships require co-residence. Instead, LAT couples are distinctive in their choice to maintain separate households, which they may or may not share with other people such as their children or parents (Levin & Trost 1999). Unlike commuter couples, LAT couples do not have one person living in the 'main' household while the other person lives elsewhere for periods of time for work or study reasons. LAT couples maintain separate households in which they sometimes spend time together. They perceive themselves as long-term, committed couples and are perceived by their close social networks as a couple, but this perception is not based on their co-residence.

Levin and Trost (1999) consider LAT relationships to be a new stage in the shift away from the dominance of a narrow definition of marriage towards a broader range of social institutions through which people organize their long-term couple relationships. These shifts include the increasing possibility of having a sexual relationship, bearing and raising children and sharing a residence without getting married. Not only have the social stigmas associated with these choices been disappearing, but as options they have been supported by new legislation that recognizes de facto relationships and parenthood outside of marriage, giving partners rights and obligations that were previously only instituted through marriage. These social, legal and cultural changes have produced new opportunities for people to reimagine their relationships, including being able to choose to live apart as a couple.

A study conducted by Levin and Trost (1999; Levin 2004) in the Netherlands identifies a range of reasons that might encourage people to consider a LAT relationship. For example, a couple with children from previous marriages might choose to live in separate households so as not to disrupt the lives of their children with their new relationship, choosing to visit each other's homes on the days when their children are with another parent. In some cases, a person might choose to live separately from their partner in order to be able to live with and care for an ageing parent. In other cases, a couple might choose a LAT relationship as an alternative to divorce, particularly if they want to maintain a loving marital relationship and raise their children together but find it too difficult to share their everyday life in the same home. As Mary Holmes (2006) argues, LAT relationships provide a means for negotiating the demands of emotion work and managing the clash between romantic narratives and the everyday demands of work and care responsibilities.

Another important reason identified for pursuing LAT relationships is that women are able to use this household form in order to engage in the reflexive and strategic undoing of gendered norms (Upton-Davis 2012, 2013). For women who wish to avoid becoming a 'housewife', LAT relationships can provide a strategy for ensuring that they don't create expectations in themselves or in their partner that they will take care of all of the couple's domestic tasks. Instead, their partner is required to manage their own domestic sphere. Separate households also create an opportunity for people to maintain their own, individual, lifestyle, including having autonomy in the furnishing and decoration of their home as well as greater freedom to use their time in the way that best suits them. Thus, LAT relationships are one of the strategies that men and particularly women might adopt in order to manage the demands and opportunities of modern life, which require a balance of work, friendships, family and a long-term relationship while also maintaining a sense of independence and individual control in everyday life (Duncan & Phillips 2011; Hughes 2013).

However, there is limited evidence of this liberating novelty in LAT relationships (e.g. Duncan & Phillips 2010; Duncan 2015). Recent evidence suggests that, rather than providing a vanguard of new relationship possibilities, LAT relationships might be better interpreted as reflecting new constraints on how people organize their lives, while maintaining fairly conventional gender and family norms. This is particularly the case for young people, who seem to participate in LAT relationships as a stage in the progression towards marriage and/or cohabitation (Duncan & Phillips 2011; Reimondos, Evans & Gray 2011). That is, while some LAT couples may *choose* to live apart, others might be *unable* to live together. In some cases, this is because their work opportunities are located in different places, so that relocating the couple to a place that benefits one person's career would limit the employment opportunities for the other person, turning them into a trailing spouse with all of the disadvantages that such a status would entail. Others, who might prefer to live together, may not have the economic resources to do so while they complete their studies or training. Some may only be offered insecure or short-term employment in the new location, so that it is not feasible for their partner to leave a home and job in order to relocate with them. Sometimes there is simply no option of living together, as is the case with employees in resource extraction industries such as mining and oil which do not necessarily provide an option of living close to the employment site. Instead, they offer FIFO employment that requires workers to live on site for a period of time and return home for a period of time on a regular roster.

FIFO relationships

Fly-in-fly-out (FIFO) employment, whether it involves planes, buses (BIBO) or driving (DIDO), is a rapidly growing arrangement, particularly in resource-rich nations such as Australia and Canada. It has been defined by Keith Storey (2001: 135) as

> work in relatively remote locations where food and lodging is provided for workers at the work site, but not for their families. Schedules are established whereby employees spend a fixed number of days working at the site, followed by a fixed number of days at home.

By definition, FIFO employment is conditional on the employee agreeing to split their time between their home and their workplace. The rosters vary depending on the nature and location of the work, including diverse options ranging from one week on/one week off to six or more weeks on followed by one or two weeks off. This reflects the combined impact of more affordable air travel and tax concessions for companies that use FIFO, which contribute to an increased reliance on temporary, transient workforces rather than the development of large settlements. It is cheaper to fly people to the worksite and house them in temporary accommodation facilities for intensive shifts than it is to build a more permanent settlement (Storey & Shrimpton 1989).

There is significant and growing concern that the comparatively low financial costs of FIFO operations have been accompanied by increased social costs (e.g. Watts 2004, Gallegos 2006). Some consider the impact on existing nearby regional communities to be devastating, with the Mayor of Kalgoorlie calling FIFO the 'cancer of the bush' (Commonwealth of Australia 2013: vii). Concerns have also been raised about the role of FIFO in negative social outcomes that range from greater levels of drug and alcohol abuse to family violence and parenting problems (Storey 2001).

FIFO employment, like commuter employment, has been described as a rational response to 'a relatively inflexible occupational system' that requires workers to 'sacrifice an aspect of their family lives' (Gerstel & Gross 1982: 88). Keith Storey and Mark Shrimpton (1989), for example, argue that FIFO work schedules incur considerable personal and family costs (see also Torkington, Larkins & Gupta 2011). Yet surveys also suggest that the workers and their families tend to believe that the benefits outweigh the costs and that their relationships generally function effectively (e.g. Taylor & Simmonds 2009). Indeed, many couples and their families state that they have adapted well to the demands of FIFO work (e.g. Parkes, Carnell & Farmer 2005; Kaczmarek & Sibbel 2008; Mclean 2012). Those who are involved in FIFO work seem willing to sacrifice what is perceived as a more 'normal' family life, involving daily contact around local work schedules, in return for higher incomes and other benefits that FIFO employment is perceived to offer.

The impacts of FIFO employment are experienced differently by the workers and the family members left behind, and these differences are gendered.

Most FIFO work is in the male-dominated resource industries, meaning that most of the partners left behind are female. Like Australian mining town wives of the past, FIFO wives consider themselves 'a pretty independent and resourceful bunch' who are expected to be stoic and self-reliant (Pini & Mayes 2012: 77). They must deal with extended periods of loneliness during which, if they have children, they are effectively single parents. They must also deal with the repeated transition into intense periods of intimacy and togetherness, during which their partner typically expects them to be fully available (Gerstel & Gross 1982: 89). In order to manage this transition, the female partners of FIFO workers counsel each other and themselves not to become 'too independent', as this could lead their male partners to feeling they are not wanted or needed, which could lead to relationship problems (Pini & Mayes 2012: 79).

In effect, the female partners of male FIFO workers are required to organize not only their time but also their emotional self around the demands of their partner's work. The women in these arrangements bear the heavier burden of what Arlie Hochschild (1983) calls 'emotion work' in the relationships. They are responsible for ensuring that they manage their own emotions when their husbands are absent or present, the emotions of their children, and also their own emotions, to ensure a family unit that remains functional and supportive for all of its members.

There are a number of strategies the women use to manage this responsibility. Those who work tend to have casual employment, where they are more able to increase their hours during the 'on' weeks and decrease their hours during the 'off' weeks to accommodate the family's needs. Other activities and interests, such as volunteer work, must also be organized around the FIFO work schedule. Those who have children must develop mechanisms to manage the periods of absence and presence so as to protect the children from the potentially damaging effects of disruption (Kaczmarek & Sibbel 2008). Any sense of independence and egalitarianism that is developed as a result of periods of time spent alone must be managed, so that they do not become a problem during periods of time spent together.

In contrast, the men seem to be largely protected from the negative effects of FIFO work by their partners, with one man even suggesting that there was significant pleasure to be had from the lifestyle, saying: 'when you come out here [to work] it's almost like you're in this little fantasy world where all of those stressors at home – bills, marital difficulties, neighbour's dog barking, bloody councils and all those little things, you're away from all that' (Torkington, Larkins & Gupta 2011: 138). Because he is unable to actually do anything about the management of everyday life stressors, being so far away, he finds it easier to ignore them and relinquish responsibility. This is not the case for all men. Indeed, some men find the separation difficult, particularly when they have young children, and there is widespread recognition of the return-to-work 'blues' that tends to settle on men in the final day or two of their 'off' week when they are at home, but anticipating returning to work (Pini & Mayes 2012).

In each of the examples above, it is the intimate social relationship that is prioritized in the analysis. This means that the role of place is downplayed, becoming significant only to the extent that it signifies a particular geographic distance between 'home' and 'away'. Yet terms such as 'home' and 'away' also have the potential to evoke a sense of connection (or lack of connection) to particular places that are important in and of themselves in the wellbeing and relationship satisfaction of couples who live apart. Home is defined to be the desired place, meaning that the partner at 'home' is assumed to have a better situation. This underpins the sense of empathy that is often expressed towards the commuter or FIFO spouse who must travel away in order to work. It is this assumption about the desirability of home that also reproduces the gender inequalities that accompany home as a feminine domestic space. LAT relationships appear to address this problem by defining both of the places in which the couple live as a 'home', meaning that neither is advantaged nor disadvantaged by access to a particular geographic site of the relationship. To date, little attention has been paid to the role of a place itself in shaping the experience or practice of a relationship. Interestingly, it is through studies of mobilities that greater attention is now being paid to the role of place as a key factor in social relationships (see In Focus 3.2).

Transnational marriages

It is clear from the descriptions of both commuter and FIFO marriages that, in spite of some clear benefits, many people struggle with the strains placed on their relationship by extended periods of time spent apart. However, in both of these cases, the periods of time spent apart are rarely longer than a few weeks, and are more commonly only one or two weeks at a time. In contrast, some married couples involved in transnational labour markets spend years apart from each other. The experiences of these couples vary depending on whether the migrant is male or female, and whether the spouse 'stays behind' in the home country or also migrates for work but to another place. Another important factor is the extent to which the migration of one or both spouses challenges local expectations regarding couple relationships and gendered roles within that relationship.

Left-behind wives

The transnational marriage arrangement that fits most closely with the nuclear family model is one in which the husband migrates overseas, while the wife remains at home caring for the household and children. This is the arrangement of the families researched by Deborah Boehm (2008a, 2008b, 2011, 2012), exploring the experiences of wives who remain in Mexico while their husbands risk an illegal crossing into the USA in order to earn the family's income. Both men and women expect and encourage men to migrate as a means of fulfilling the role of a good husband who is able to provide for

In Focus 3.2 Marriage as commitment to place and culture

The examples of marriage in this chapter reflect the dominant Western model of marriage as a companionate relationship, in which the primary commitment within the marriage is expected to be to the spouse. However, marriage can take many different forms and have a range of functions and meanings. Iain Walker (2012) describes one of these varieties as it is practised on the Comorian island of Ngazidja in the western Indian Ocean by the Wangazidja (the people of Ngazidja).

The island of Ngazidja has long been a site of migration and population flows, including between Zanzibar, Madagascar, France and the UK. The local population would be unable to survive without persistent emigration, due to the lack of economic opportunities on the island. Ngazidja provides an important base for escaping occasional violence in the host country, and is also an object of communal identity and personal status. In spite of a long history of migration, the community remains insular and able to resist incorporation into other dominant cultures they encounter.

Among other ritual affirmations of belonging, one of the key strategies for maintaining cultural connection is the customary *aada* marriage. Participating in an *aada* marriage is an essential prerequisite for the groom to receive adult status in the community, including his rights to wear high-status clothing, occupy a special place in the mosque, participate in village politics and benefit when others host their *aada*. The bride, too, acquires a higher status as a result of her *aada* marriage. The centrality of the ritual to social status means that many people choose to migrate specifically in order to acquire sufficient wealth to host their own *aada*. The event is expensive, requiring a groom to provide and a bride's family to prepare ritual meals for all of the men in the village. A home must also be provided for the bride.

The *aada* marriage acts as an investment in ultimate return to the island, usually upon retirement. This has the simultaneous effect of limiting a person's interest or capacity in establishing a home or business outside of the island in spite of living most of their lives earning an income away from Ngazidja. That is, the *aada* marriage is a form of spatial anchoring that acts as an expression of commitment that migrants make to their home village. An *aada* needs to only be performed once to achieve the requisite status. Indeed, the bonds to place represented by this ritual are stronger than the bonds to their marriage partners, as divorce is common and multiple marriages acceptable, yet the commitment to the village represented by the ritual remains long after the marriage has dissolved.

his family. The extended periods of separation are rationalized as the price that must be paid in order for a man to be perceived as a good husband, fulfil his responsibilities and thus maintain a good marriage. This fulfilment of a masculine identity is, at the same time, characterized by a loss of autonomy, as men give up the control over the labour they enjoy on their own farms, and instead submit themselves to the long hours, low pay, low status and low autonomy of wage labour in the US economy.

Even as this transnational marriage arrangement reproduces some gendered norms, it is also disrupting others. Back in the *rancho*, the wife is expected to maintain the household and children, and care for any extended kin in her husband's family. However, the women left behind often find that their roles are also expanded and they are required to perform the sorts of household and farming tasks that men usually undertake. As Rosa, a participant in Deborah Boehm's (2008b: 16) research, explained

> I take care of the fields, our animals. ... I'm currently painting our house. I have to do all the work my husband used to do. And I'm still responsible for everything I did before – cooking, cleaning, caring for the children ... Now I am a man *and* a woman.

Rosa's comments are echoed by women in Bangladesh whose husbands migrate overseas for work. As Abdullahel Hadi (2001) explains, the non-migrant wives are required to take on additional roles around the household, but they also have increased control over the household's resources, greater decision-making powers and greater independence from their in-laws. They also tend to invest more in the education of their daughters than do non-migrant families (see also Gardner 1995). Thus, women find that their sphere of influence and their level of autonomy can be expanded, even as their husband might experience the reduction of status associated with menial, low-paid work in the destination country.

This is not to suggest that migration of husbands is always experienced as liberatory by their wives. As Boehm (2008b) argues, the Mexican women she works with are simultaneously constrained and liberated. Their capacity to migrate with their partner to the USA is severely restricted, requiring permission and support from either their husband or another family member, even as their experience at home is of increased autonomy. Their experience of independence and autonomy is also typically limited to the periods of time when their husbands are absent, stripped away during the periods of time the husband returns to the *rancho*.

The expectations of fidelity that are the foundation of most cultural models of marriage can also be difficult for transnational couples to fulfil. As Sarah Mahler (2001) explains, when the circumstances of separation lead to long periods of time apart, husbands and wives tend to 'fill in the gaps with their imaginations'. Non-migrant wives, in particular, imagine the sexual infidelity of their migrant husbands, while their own fidelity is closely supervised by neighbouring kin. This is also the case for the couples in Mexico and the USA described by Boehm (2008b), where it is the women who feel particularly at risk of being abandoned by their absent partner, and who must often turn a blind eye to his infidelity in order to maintain the marriage.

Concerns about infidelity are not the domain of women alone. Dinah Hannaford (2015) describes the ways in which new technologies are employed by migrant husbands to closely monitor their wives from a distance. It is customary in Senegal for women to be confined to the home and ask permission to leave in order to visit family or perform daily tasks. In practice, this is typically an act of courtesy, with women relatively free to move. However, some jealous and suspicious migrant husbands, who lack the reassurance of being able to see their wives on a daily basis, are using communication technologies to impose this custom more rigorously on their wives. One young woman had her outfit approved by her husband during a daily Skype session. Another was required to be at home to answer the landline telephone whenever her husband called at random times of day and night.

The experiences of transnational couples have been transformed by the emergence of new communication technologies, which have produced both new opportunities for contact and new capacities of surveillance. In the 1990s, wives living in El Salvador would hear from their husbands infrequently. Mahler (2001) describes the effort required for Maria to communicate with her husband in the USA in the 1990s, entailing a long journey to collect a letter and another long journey to receive a phone call. By 2000, she was able to have more regular contact, up to a few times a week, with her husband on a mobile phone, enabling them to once again function somewhat effectively as a family unit, albeit across distance. Yet the example of Senegal demonstrates that these same technologies can become tools of surveillance that increase inequalities between men and women.

Left-behind husbands

Since the 1990s, there has been a growing awareness of the feminization of migration – of the fact that more women are migrating independently of men, to more destinations, and under more diverse migration categories (Piper 2013). In particular, women from nations such as the Philippines and Vietnam have been migrating to work as domestic servants in nations such as Italy, Hong Kong and Singapore. Migrating husbands are able to fit the gendered norms of the heterosexual nuclear family with relative ease, because their absence is an extension of the existing norm that he should be absent at work while the wife remains in the home. In contrast, migrating wives present a direct transgression of these norms. It is widely expected that women should remain in the family residence, as the 'light of the home' (Asis, Huang & Yeoh 2004), the recipient of the benefits of her husband's labour. However, with masculine overseas employment declining, and feminine overseas employment increasing, migrating wives and left-behind husbands have become an increasingly common experience.

One of the most widely discussed examples of female labour migration is that of women from the Philippines, who are supported by their government to undertake overseas labour migration or 'overseas foreign worker' programmes. Cecilia Tacoli (1999) points out that an economic analysis alone is not sufficient to understand these migration decisions. The capacity to earn a higher income is important, but it must be recognized that most of the women who leave the Philippines to work overseas are among the more highly educated and those who already earn higher, professional incomes. It is this status that provides them with the resources necessary to take an employment opportunity overseas, which requires significant payments to migration agents as well as knowledge about the process. Thus, they do not migrate overseas to simply earn an income and avoid impoverishment (Tacoli 1999). Rather, their labour migration is part of a strategy for upward mobility, usually directed at achieving a private education for their children, the purchase of property, or accumulating the capital necessary for establishing a small business. In addition, women might use the opportunity offered by labour migration to pursue a culturally legitimate pathway to adventure and seeing a bit more of the world. In some cases, it also provides a handy escape from local marriage problems, important given that there is limited capacity for divorce.

One of the clearest consequences of female migration is that men tend to suffer. Their masculine role is undermined by their loss of breadwinner status, and this is expressed in depression, drinking, gambling and domestic violence. On the other hand, it rarely translates into increased contributions to housework or childcare (Gamburd 2000; Kabeer 2007). Those men who do thrive when their wives migrate overseas usually benefit from strategies and circumstances that protect their sense of masculinity (Gamburd 2000; Pingol 2001; Kabeer 2007). This can include their own good employment prospects in the home, their previous earnings having already secured a family home, or their local status as community leaders. For some, it might also be secured by spending the remittances sent by their wives in order to maintain a role in the local masculine drinking culture.

One of the strategies through which men and women maintain good gender relations is by ensuring that the husband maintains authority over the family even though the wife is earning the primary income (Hoang & Yeoh 2011). In Vietnam, for example, couples agree that men are the authoritative head of the family and make all decisions regarding members of the family. They also draw on a strong cultural expectation, supported by the government, that women will make an economic contribution to the household and that men will contribute to household work and childcare. Women and men are considered equals when it comes to maintaining the household and raising the family. This means that when women migrate, men in Vietnam are highly likely to take on full-time care of their children, rather than relinquish this to female members of the extended family (Hoang & Yeoh 2011). In some cases, they return from their own overseas migration to take on this role, in acknowledgement that migrant women are able to earn a higher income overseas than migrant men.

This is in contrast to other contexts, such as left-behind husbands in the Philippines and Sri Lanka, where gender norms make it more difficult for men to take on the caregiving roles left by their migrant wives (e.g. Gamburd 2000; Parreñas 2005). In spite of being perceived as deviating from the norm, some nevertheless do adjust to the situation. As Andy explained, he was confused when his wife first migrated from the Philippines to Singapore:

> I was taken aback. Who would take care of the children when they went to school, things [like that]? [I realized that] I would be the one to take care of them…Yes, when nobody could wash clothes, I would wash clothes. Suddenly [Edna] was not here … the children, all the chores in the house, such things…I am the one who [had to] perform all those. (Asis, Huang & Yeoh 2004: 207)

After an initial period of adjustment, some men – both husbands and sons – come to accept their new roles in caring for children and the household. This is not to say that women are excluded from this role. Rather, their role is reimagined as being performed across a distance and during visits. Yet many men simply refuse to take on those chores and responsibilities, preferring to leave them to other women in the family, such as grandparents, siblings or eldest daughters, rather than risk damage to their masculine identities. Furthermore, even when men do take on these roles while their wives are absent, the inversion of gendered roles is recognized as temporary and is rarely sustained. Once the women return home after having worked overseas, the gendered division of labour is typically resumed.

Conclusion

The examples in this chapter point to an interesting contradiction. On the one hand, there is a wide variety of ways in which men and women are able to maintain marriage and marriage-like relationships across distance, ranging from the decision to migrate together to the decision to spend extended periods of time apart. Yet there is also an equally surprising lack of variety in the central issues that they negotiate and how these are managed. Who will earn the income? Who will care for the children? Who will do the housework? Who will make the decisions, about migration, investment and large purchases? And can this partner be trusted, or can their sexual infidelity be accepted?

Underlying the answers to these questions are gendered norms and expectations that are maintained and reproduced through gendered subjectivities. In many cases, the answers to these questions are provided in advance, by gendered norms that are experienced as appropriate ways of being masculine or feminine. When circumstances do not allow for a response that fits with gendered norms, then couples must invent new ways of making the circumstances acceptable. Thus, for example, women who take on the masculine role of income earning work hard to ensure that their partner is respected as the male authority of the household. Men, meanwhile, who perform the feminine work of childcare or domestic labour work hard to maintain their income-earning status and family authority. It is in the fulfilment, rather than the challenging, of these gendered norms that people find satisfaction and self-worth.

This likely contributes to the lack of progress in the transformation of intimacy in heterosexual couples. Even in those societies where democratic intimacy is presumably ascendant, it is not always far progressed nor necessarily capable of progressing much further. Even as women seek greater autonomy, they are not necessarily willing to give up the value they place on caring for others, especially those in their family and those they love (Duncan et al. 2003). Care is an important aspect of feminine subjectivity, and of marital subjectivities, which is not easily set aside in favour of autonomy and economic opportunities. Similarly, income earning is an important aspect of masculine subjectivity and of being a husband. Even for those men who accept a caregiving role within the family, this needs to be interpreted as a temporary or part-time role, one that should also be accompanied by more conventional masculine roles of authority and income earning.

The evidence points to the capacity for people to create and sustain intimate, caring, supportive relationships in spite of long periods of time spent physically separated. The extent to which they are satisfied in these relationships seems to depend on the construction of cultural models that support their willingness to accept these as successful relationships. The most significant problems emerge when couples find it difficult to explain their relationship to others in their social circle, and have to constantly defend themselves against suspicion or sympathy. The demands of employment provide both a motivator and a rationale for the diverse couple arrangements that people create. In some cases, careers and financial constraints make migration or a distance relationship seem inevitable. These also offer ready-made acceptable justifications for individuals who seek adventure, opportunity or a relationship that combines both greater autonomy and romantic intimacy that is intensified by absence.

The transformation of intimacy, with its emphasis on the capacity for individuals to choose, has no doubt contributed to the sense of satisfaction that people are able to derive from their diverse relationship strategies. Yet it does assume a certain level of equality in the relationship. Women are expected to and often want to perform more of the emotional labour and care work in a relationship, relative to men (Duncombe & Marsden 1993; Holmes 2004). This lack of attention to inequalities has long been a critique of Giddens' (1992) claims regarding the transformation of intimacy, with not only women but also children identified as less equal than men in claiming the rewards of democratic intimacy (Jamieson 1998). It is to the experiences of these children and their parents that we now turn, in the next chapter.

Transnational Parents and Global Care Chains

What it means to be a good parent varies widely across social and cultural contexts, and changes over time. By the start of the twenty-first century, a middle-class model of parenting has spread across the world that emphasizes the need for children to receive the nurturing attention of their parents, a high standard of material wellbeing and a high-quality education. However, these aspirations of good parenting are also very expensive, usually requiring both parents to participate in a labour market that is increasingly competitive and highly demanding. Both parenting and employment require intense time commitments, producing a clash between the ideology of middle-class parenting and the ideology of middle-class work. In this chapter, I explore the ways in which global mobility is being used by many parents to achieve some parenting goals, while simultaneously undermining other parenting aspirations. I begin by exploring the contradictions of contemporary parenting and their origins in recent social change, before turning to an examination of some of the creative solutions people adopt in response to those contradictions. These include the emergence of global care chains, global nannies, distant mothering and distant fathering.

The contradictory conditions of parenting

Leo and Ellen have a loving relationship in a companionate marriage; they enjoy spending time together and their intimacy is based on equality, mutual desire and a close emotional bond. They live in a large New York apartment, where they are raising their daughter, Sophie. Their relationship with her is also a loving relationship, in which affection is freely expressed. The three enjoy playing together, laughing, teasing, and taking pleasure in each other's company. Both Leo and Ellen are ambitious and successful. Leo is an executive in a global corporation who travels first class to locations around the world. Ellen is a surgeon in a busy hospital emergency department, responding to urgent health crises. Their skills earn them high incomes that support their expensive lifestyle, but both of their occupations are also highly time intensive. Ellen works long hours that are unpredictable, depending on the emergencies she is required to respond to. Leo is often required to travel overseas at short notice and for unknown periods of time. He can spend weeks waiting in hotel rooms with no clear end date, unable to return home until the project reaches the point at which his particular skills are required. While he waits, he relies on a range of technologies to keep in touch with his wife and daughter back home.

Leo and Ellen rely on Gloria, their live-in nanny, to care for Sophie and look after their home. It is Gloria who takes Sophie on outings in the city, who sings her to sleep, helps her with her homework and holds her hand when they walk down the street. They also have a loving, caring relationship. Gloria prepares meals and sits down to eat with Sophie; she is able to anticipate Sophie's needs and knows how to fulfil them. Meanwhile, her own children remain in her own home in the Philippines. Their mother has only recently accepted the work in New York, and they are struggling to adjust to her absence. They live with their grandmother and are surrounded by other extended kin. However, they miss their mother and wonder about her life. They call her on the phone to beg her to come home, and worry that they will not see her again until they are adults. At the same time, they also understand that they are the reason she is living and working in New York, so that she can earn enough money to build them a new house and pay for their education.

Leo, Ellen Sophie and Gloria are the central characters in the 2009 film, *Mammoth*, written and directed by Lukas Moodysson. It is one of the few films that try to capture the contradictions of late-modern family life, in which women from nations such as the Philippines are employed to care for the children of wealthy families on the other side of the world. Economically, it seems that everyone benefits. Leo and Ellen are able to devote themselves to their employment without sacrificing the care of their daughter. Gloria is able to earn money to direct towards her own children attaining a more prosperous lifestyle. However, as the film suggests, the emotional costs are also high. Leo struggles with the extended periods of boredom and loneliness while on overseas assignments, Ellen is left alone to manage the stresses induced by her work, and Gloria must balance the need to be constantly available to Sophie while not displacing Ellen as Sophie's focus of affection. While the emotional toll on everyone is evident, it is Gloria's children who are depicted as the clear losers in this situation, longing for the attention of their mother yet facing the prospect of being unable to spend their childhoods in her proximity. They must instead accept the telephone calls and gift boxes she is able to provide them from a distance.

Transforming parenting

The contradictions of late-modern family life produced by the demands of employment are central to the individualization thesis (see Chapters 1 and 2). On the one hand, there is an expectation that women will increasingly participate in education and the paid workforce. Indeed, the economic independence that comes from paid work is relied upon to improve gender equality in development programmes around the world. Yet it is becoming clear that economic participation alone is not particularly effective at creating gender equality. This is because expectations of greater employment participation come into direct conflict with another very powerful expectation: that mothers are naturally the best choice when it comes to caring for children. The clash between these two sets of expectations is often used to explain low and declining levels of fertility in many nations around the world (see Figure 4.1). On the one hand, women's participation in education and employment in combination with access to effective contraception is enabling many women to postpone childbearing until a later date. On the other hand, it is also thought that many women are postponing or even avoiding having children because of the difficulties in balancing their roles as paid employees as well as parents.

Since at least the nineteenth century, ideologies of the nuclear family and the 'myth of motherhood' have positioned women at the heart of the home and as the natural caregivers for children in nations such as the UK, Australia and the USA (Oakley 1974). Interestingly, this 'natural' role was also one that required expert knowledge and education, with women subject to increasing surveillance and instruction on how to perform their tasks correctly (Reiger 1985). While women from wealthier middle-class backgrounds might be able to allocate their housework to paid domestic servants, it was more difficult to pass on their childrearing tasks. This is because women's moral value became tied in complex ways to their capacity to nurture their children's talents and education and prepare them for the

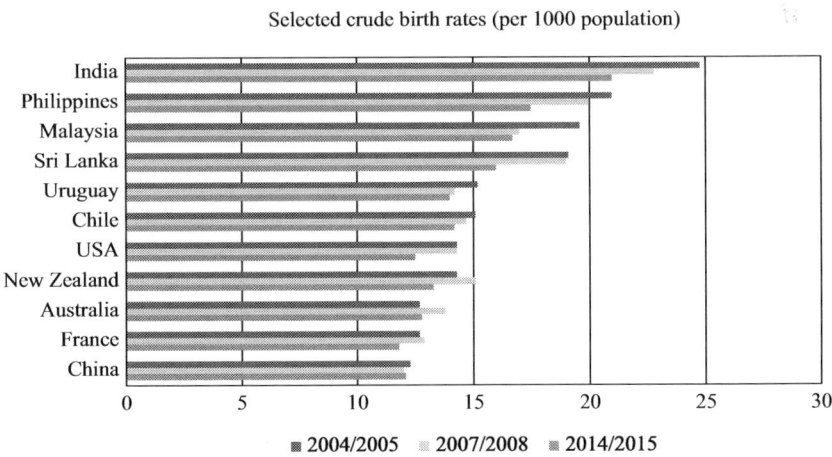

Figure 4.1 Declining fertility in select nations around the world

Data from UN Demographic Yearbooks, available at: https://unstats.un.org/unsd/demographic/products/vitstats/serATab3.pdf.

adult world of work, while also protecting them from the harsh realities of the public world. Mothers became the 'light of the home' (Asis, Huang & Yeoh 2004), and the good mother is always available to her children, always patient with them and attentive to their needs, and places their needs before her own (Pocock 2005). Hays (1996) called this set of moral expectations 'intensive mothering', referring to the requirement for women to constantly monitor and enhance their child's development and wellbeing. In some cultural contexts, this has resulted in new images and stereotypes, such as the Asian 'tiger mother' who invests heavily in her children's educational success (Guo 2013; Fu & Markus 2014).

Intensive parenting requires significant resources. Parents are expected to invest financially in the education and activities of their children, as well as spend 'quality time' with them in order to help them develop into successful individuals. In the traditional nuclear family, these two roles are split along gendered lines. The father earns the income that provides the financial resources, while the mother invests her personal time and attention in the children and the household. However, in recent decades this has begun to shift. Mothers are increasingly participating in paid work, contributing financially to their children's development, while fathers are increasingly expected to be emotionally involved with their children. This creates a set of contradictions for men and women who are employed and have children. On the one hand, competition in the labour force requires a full commitment to their career and employer. On the other hand, ideologies of parenting require full devotion of themselves to their children.

This contradiction has been described as a 'crisis' for women (Summers 2003), because they are made to feel guilty about failing to fulfil requirements in both their career and their maternal role. Others have suggested that maintaining a career and paid employment is one way in which women can manage what is termed 'maternal ambivalence'. This is the suggestion that not all women derive full satisfaction from their mothering role or wish to dedicate themselves so completely to parenting their children, yet they are morally compelled to display these feelings. The ideologies of intensive mothering make it difficult for women to acknowledge dislike for their children that goes alongside love and care, or to recognize that being a mother involves grieving the loss of some of the freedoms and pleasures of being childless, even as caring for children brings its own joys (Hollway & Featherstone 1997). Participation in paid employment and the development of a career can provide an alternative source of identity and value, which might help to alleviate the emotional pressures of mothering.

Fathers, too, are increasingly facing this set of contradictory trends. On the one hand, they continue to maintain responsibility as the primary income earner in the nuclear family household. On the other hand, the recent 'transformation of intimacy' has introduced new expectations for fathers (Giddens 1992). Conventional models of fatherhood, in which men were acknowledged as too caught up in the world of work to participate in the emotional world of the family, are in the process of being replaced by more emotionally available and open models of fatherhood. This is in part because children are no longer being raised to obey adult figures of authority in their lives. Rather, parents recognize that they must raise children who can thrive in an individualized, detraditionalized society in which negotiation and reflexivity are more valuable qualities. Fathers who perform the role of authoritative disciplinarians are becoming less common. Instead, fathering (and mothering) require more child-centred approaches, in which children are helped to think about their choices and predict the consequences of their actions.

Researchers have identified that multiple, contingent models of fatherhood arise from this transformation (Williams 2008). The most common outcome, interestingly, is a variation on the conventional breadwinner father – a man who remains relatively absent from the home because of work commitments, but is nevertheless aware of and tries to fulfil some of the expectations of emotional support and socialization of his children. A study by Tina Miller (2011) helps us to understand the dynamics that continue to produce these traditional models of fatherhood. She interviewed men and women who were waiting for their first child to be born, and then spoke to them again at intervals after the birth. What she found was that most men intended to be very involved fathers, providing physical and personal care to their babies and building close relationships with them. However, within a year of the children being born, they reported that work commitments had prevented them from being as involved as they would have liked, and that their female partner seemed to have more expert knowledge of the child's needs. As a result, their own participation was relatively minimal, even if it was somewhat greater than the participation of their own fathers in their lives.

Less common, but nevertheless significant, are the alternative models of absent fathers and fathers as primary caregivers (Gerson 1994). Absent fathers are usually produced by a combination of failure to maintain a relationship with the child's mother and a failure to earn sufficient income to financially support them. In the case of divorce and separation, there is still a strong conventional pattern of children being placed with the mother, reflecting the ongoing naturalization of maternal care as the most natural form of childcare. Fathers who are not co-resident with their children are less likely to be involved in their lives. However, this is further exacerbated if the father is unable to earn sufficient income to provide material support. In these cases, fathers typically remove themselves completely from their children's lives, unable to fulfil any of the role expectations that accompany fatherhood.

In contrast, some men are becoming primary caregivers of their children. In some cases, this is because they are awarded caregiving responsibilities for children following divorce or separation. However, more commonly it is because their female partner has greater income-earning potential and comparatively heavy work commitments. In these cases, a couple may make the joint decision to allocate the primary caring role to the father, and the primary income-earning role to the mother, either long term or temporarily. These fathers are often held up as the vanguards of a future in which parenting is no longer gendered. However, it should be noted that their numbers remain small, and they continue to face difficulties in being socially accepted. Dominant ideals of parenting continue to place women at the centre of a child's life, and fathers and extended kin as secondary care options, but not in all cultural contexts. Recent research in African nations, for example, point to different models of parenting and childcare, in which extended kin play a much more accepted and active role, particularly when parents have the opportunity to migrate in order to earn an income (see In Focus 4.1).

In Focus 4.1 Perspectives on parenting from Ghana

Cati Coe (2014) documents how migrants from Ghana living in the USA commonly place their children in the care of grandparents or other kin in Ghana for years at a time while they are working to earn an income. Sometimes this is because of obstacles to gaining a visa for children to follow their parents to the USA. On other occasions, it is because the time-intensive labour, low income and lack of kin support in the USA means that leaving children in Ghana is perceived as a more caring, supportive and cost-effective way of raising their children.

Coe (2014) argues that parents and children use the existing beliefs, practices and resources of family life, what she calls their 'family repertoire', to negotiate the separations that are part of their family practices and economic strategies. She argues that a family repertoire that normalizes parental absence for periods of time results in children who are less likely to suffer when their parents live at a distance (see also Olwig 1999). Parents, too, are less likely to suffer from the effects of leaving children behind when they migrate for work. Indeed, children are not considered to have been 'left behind', but instead are being cared for by family.

The Ghanaian model of parenting has a number of cultural assumptions and practices that enable this family repertoire to succeed. First, Ghanaians subscribe to a 'distributed' notion of parenting. This is the idea that not just the mother and father, but a wide range of kin are responsible for and involved in the care of children, including grandparents, aunts and uncles. Indeed, co-presence in a single household is not part of Ghanaian traditional family life, and up to 25 per cent of children in Ghana were routinely living outside of their parents' home even as recently as the late twentieth century (Coe 2011b). Children traditionally circulate between households, ensuring that they are raised within extensive networks of kin.

Second, Ghanaians recognize the materiality of care. Kin relations are 'maintained by exchanges of resources over the lifetime of the relationship' (Coe 2011b: 150). This is in striking contrast to most Western cultural norms, in which the monetary value of care is disguised or hidden behind the cloak of emotions (Coe 2011a). For Ghanaians, material contributions in the form of money and goods are interpreted as a direct and necessary expression of care and love. As a result, 'reliability of remittances, rather than presence, can characterize a good parent' (Coe 2014: 28) and parental neglect is more commonly perceived when there is a lack of financial support than when there is a lack of physical co-presence (Coe 2011a).

Repertoires of fostering and child shifting can serve transnational migrants and their children well, but are not always readily accepted by the growing middle classes in Ghana, who are increasingly subscribing to ideals of family households in which the children remain with their parents (Coe 2014). Migration and class mobility are thus creating complex family contexts that people are responding to with constantly changing family repertoires.

While there is some evidence of change in gender roles and parenting, there is also a surprising level of resistance to such transformations. It might be expected that women's participation in paid employment would disrupt the traditional nuclear family. Instead, the more common solution seems to be a reconfiguration of that conventional model. Men's rates of participation in unpaid care work remain low even as women's contributions are declining, producing what has been called a 'care gap'. This gap has been associated with declining fertility rates around the world, as women seem to be choosing not to have children rather than bear the burden of increased workloads in both paid employment and unpaid care. It is also associated with the emergence of what has been labelled the 'global care chain' – the shifting of responsibility for childcare from one woman to another along a chain of global inequality.

Global care chains and displaced mothering

Airlie Hochschild (2000) was one of the first to name the phenomenon of the global care chain. She used it to describe what she saw as the displacement of care responsibilities along a chain of inequality, demonstrated in the ethnographic work of Rhacel Parreñas (2000). At the top of this chain are men in wealthy nations, who devolve their care responsibilities to the women with whom they construct a family and have children. When women in wealthy nations entered the workforce in greater numbers, men did not enter the domain of childcare and housework to the same extent, leaving women to rely upon other women to fill the gap. In some cases, their own mothers were relied upon to provide childcare. In many cases, domestic servants and nannies were employed to become substitute wives and mothers.

This care chain became a global care chain when the women being hired to perform caring and household work were women imported from less wealthy countries. Meanwhile, the women migrating to work as substitute wives and mothers in wealthy nations would themselves rely on female kin in their home country to care for their own homes and children, or would employ poorer women from rural areas who would migrate to perform these services in return for wages. These migrant women, too, would rely on female kin in their rural villages to care for their own left-behind homes and children. It is this devolving of caring work along a chain of female inequality that is captured by the metaphor of the care chain.

Hochschild (2000; Isaksen, Devi & Hochschild 2008; see also Yeates 2005, 2009, 2012) critiques this global chain of care on a number of grounds. First, she argues that it prevents the necessary transformation of working conditions and improved gender equality in the wealthier nations (see In Focus 4.2). Rather than women's greater employment participation producing new social structures in which men and women also contribute equally to care, the care chains solution instead entrenches gender inequality and gendered norms of caregiving by relying on less wealthy women to fill the gaps left by their wealthier counterparts. This contributes to what Hochschild (1989) has called the 'stalled revolution'. Second, this global care

In Focus 4.2 The national production of global care chains

The decision to employ a nanny from another country, or to be employed as a nanny in another country, seems at first to be a personal response to personal circumstances. However, researchers have documented a range of policies in both sending and hosting nations that make this personal response both possible and logical, if not required (Yeates 2009).

In host countries the persistent devaluing of care work has created a 'care deficit', a gap between local supply and demand of care workers (Palenga-Möllenbeck 2013). There is strong resistance to paying for the care services that women have historically provided as unpaid work, including the care of children and the elderly. As women have been entering the paid workforce in growing numbers in the second half of the twentieth century, there has been a lack of any accompanying transformation in relation to care work. There are still strong expectations that women will provide this work, and this is accompanied by assumptions that such work will be rewarded with very low wages. Nevertheless, at the same time, 'labor market participation is seen as an adult citizen's duty, while states are no longer prepared to deliver the necessary support for the balance of waged and care work' (Lutz & Palenga-Möllenbeck 2012: 19). The solution to this set of contradictions has not been a reconceptualization of the role of the state in relation to employment conditions or care provision, but rather a new source of care workers.

There is a long history of nations actively importing care from other nations in order to meet local needs without improving the wages or working conditions associated with the caring professions. For example, the UK was very active in recruiting nurses from Ireland to meet demand following World War II (Yeates 2004). However, the increasingly rigid migration regimes of recent years have transformed such experiences of care work migration. Whereas Irish nurse migration to the UK was a pathway to permanent settlement and citizenship and protected by a range of rights, care workers are now typically employed on contracts that limit their own rights while protecting the rights of the citizens in the nations that employ them.

In response to the growing demand for care work in host nations, a number of sending nations have adopted a very explicit labour export model that encourages their citizens to migrate for work. Their objectives include alleviating local unemployment and providing a stream of remittances to support national development. For example, the Philippines codified its labour export policy in 1972, leading to the establishment soon after of the Philippine Overseas Employment Agency. Other nations have since developed similar initiatives, including Indonesia, Sri Lanka and Thailand. These nations actively support training, education and support services for migrant workers and the development of international agreements that facilitate migrant worker flows, including streamlined accreditation processes for care professionals such as nurses (Yeates 2009). This also requires state investment in educational programmes that meet the host nation's expectations for the training of care professionals.

Care professionals are employed as care workers, not as people who might have their own family care obligations and aspirations. It is rare for host nations to provide working conditions that allow the families of workers to join them, and even when visas make this possible the low wages of care workers usually make it economically impossible for family reunion to occur while they are employed overseas. The result is an ongoing transformation of the family care dynamics in the sending countries, even as migrant care workers are changing the context of care expectations and practices within the host countries in an ongoing process of transformative globalization (Vaittinen 2014).

chain displaces the costs of the unequal social structure onto those who are most vulnerable, further reinforcing existing inequalities.

Hochschild argues that the primary losers in the global care chain arrangement are the children of the poorest women living in the poorest country. These costs are not necessarily economic costs, but rather emotional and care costs. As Nicola Yeates (2012: 137–8) explains, 'care resources are extracted from poorer countries and transferred to richer ones', with costs borne primarily by 'mothers and their children who experience intense loss and deprivation at long-term separation'. Hochschild (2013: 121) refers to this as a 'global emotional inequality', in which 'the American child enjoys one more caring adult while [the children at the bottom of the chain] grow up with one less'. Hochschild's critique aims to highlight the persistence of global inequality by emphasizing that its effects are not only at the economic level, but also at the level of human emotions and relationships. Mothers are being pulled away from their children, and children are being raised without access to an essential human bond – the bond they share with their mother.

The global inequalities embedded and reproduced by the global care chain are worthy of critique. However, there is a need to be sensitive to the assumptions that underpin these claims. Otherwise, the critique itself is at risk of erasing cultural differences and reproducing the foundations of gender inequality. Some scholars suggest that the arguments identifying and critiquing the global care chain tend to reinforce the assumption that the mother is the best possible carer for a child (Brown 2016), and in the process 'foregrounds the pathos of dislocated biological motherhood' (Manalansan 2008). This assumption might be culturally valid for some people in some parts of the world, but by no means all of them. Parenting practices and experiences are highly variable around the world, and so are affected in different ways by migration of mothers and fathers away from their biological children. Mothering and fathering are social and cultural constructs. These are roles that are performed in different ways, and with different expectations and rewards. This can be difficult to recognize, because of the powerful assumptions that any given cultural group's model of mothering is 'natural' and 'right'. The 'myth of motherhood' is not experienced as a myth, but rather as a set of emotions, obligations and expectations that shape the options available to parents and their children. An investigation of the experiences of men, women and children positioned along the global care chain helps us to explore these issues, by pointing to the ways in which local and global cultural models of parenting intersect with caregiving and parenting practices.

The global nanny

There are a number of established pathways that women and men follow when they travel from poorer countries to wealthier countries in order to work in health, care and domestic service (Kofman & Raghuram 2012; Castles, de Haas & Miller 2013). One of the most well-known of these is the ongoing departure of women from the Philippines to work in Europe and North America as domestic servants, nannies and aged-care workers (Parreñas 2001; Madianou & Miller 2012). Remittances from overseas foreign workers have long been an established and substantial part of gross domestic product (GDP) in the Philippines. At first, this was the result of men leaving the Philippines to work as labourers in the Middle East or as seafarers around the world. More recently, in response to the decline in demand for male labourers and the increase in demand for domestic servants, the migration of women for work has been supported by the government. There are now a range of government services and private providers who match women with employment opportunities and provide necessary training and support. In the destination countries, the large numbers of women from the Philippines who share common challenges and concerns has resulted in the creation of numerous support groups and organizations. In Italy, for example, the Filipino Women's Council was established in 1991 (Basa, Harcourt & Zarro 2011), at first as a women's shelter but later also providing workshops and research as well as medical, legal and economic support for women from the Philippines.

Occasionally, the murder or abuse of a migrant nanny or maid becomes a public story. Migrant domestic servants are identified as vulnerable to the physical, sexual and financial abuse of their employers. Media outrage is expressed at the strict controls that employers are able to exert over their nannies, which can include deciding what they can wear, whether they can leave the house, and whether and how often they can have time off from work. It is undeniable that domestic servants are vulnerable to abuse and exploitation. But what is not discussed so readily in the media is the extent to which women employed in the household might also exert some agency and even share a family-like relationship with their employees. This is particularly the case when a woman is employed to look after a family's children, as was described in research by Michele Gamburd (2000).

Lakshmi was a Sri Lankan woman employed by British expatriates to work in their family home in the Middle East. Her employer travelled to England to give birth to a new baby, and on returning to Bahrain handed the baby to Lakshmi, saying 'This isn't my baby but yours' (Gamburd 2000: 197). Lakshmi describes a very intimate relationship with the infant, in which he began to identify her as his 'Mommy'. Women like Lakshmi are often the most significant presence in the lives of the children in the households where they work. They are the ones who know what food the children will or will not eat, how they express their hunger, when they are unhappy, and how to cheer them up. It is the nanny who cares for them when they are ill, bathes them and teaches them self-care, and makes sure they attend school. It is perhaps little wonder, then, that the children often cry when the nanny returns home for a holiday for a few weeks, sometimes once a year, sometimes less.

In many cases, the global nanny has her own children waiting for those occasional visits back to the home country, receiving the benefits of the financial support that she is able to send back on a regular basis but unable to receive her everyday attention. As Rosemarie, a nanny working in the USA while her children were in the Philippines, explained:

> I feel the gap caused by our physical separation especially in the morning, when I pack (her) lunch, because that's what I used to do for my children ... I begin thinking that I should be taking care of my very own children and not someone else's ... Sometimes you feel the separation and you start to cry. (Parreñas 2001: 119)

Sometimes, this emotional pain translates into women lavishing love and affection on the children they are paid to care for. As one woman, Maricel, explained: 'I missed my kids. So taking care of Clare was like taking care of my own child' (Hochschild 2012: 151). However, many women also noted the risks of this transference of affection – both for the child and for the nanny. While domestic servants and nannies have formal employment arrangements, it is the capacity of nanny and employer to negotiate the unspoken rules of intimacy and economics that contributes most to satisfaction or dissatisfaction with the arrangement. When a nanny becomes too attached to the children she cares for, or allows them to become too attached to her, it can upset this balance. Women who would like to improve their employment situation, perhaps by considering working for another family, find that their options are more limited if they feel sad or guilty at the prospect of leaving the child they have been caring for.

Care work, as reproductive labour, is not the same as productive labour. Care work necessarily involves the paid employee in intimate relations with their care receivers. In the case of domestic work, this also means that the paid employee becomes intimately involved with their employer. Families and their live-in domestic servants perform a delicate dance of interdependence that is framed by a search for balance between the intimate and the economic. Indrani's story helps to show how this can work to the benefit of both employer and employee (Gamburd 2000). Indrani had been working for the same employers for over 12 years, having been employed a month after their first child was born. She now cared for three children in the family, and felt that she knew them much better than their biological mother did. She was also confident that the children loved her, which was made clear by their tears and distress when she left for occasional visits back to her home country to see her own children. While the children did not speak Sinhala, they understood it when she spoke to them. She also felt she had a sister-like relationship with her employer, which helped to make the work more pleasurable. However, underpinning the success of this relationship was not just the affection she felt for the family, but also her sense that the family looked after her financially. Her rate of pay was generous compared with many similar employees and it had increased during her years of employment with them. She also received regular gifts both for herself (such as gold jewellery) and for her family (such as household goods).

The giving of gifts to domestic servants is perceived by the employees as a symbol of respect and appreciation. In contrast with Indrani, one of her neighbours in Sri Lanka, Hema, was very dissatisfied with her long-term employers. They paid her much less than Indrani was paid, rarely provided her with gifts, and required her to work longer hours and perform more household tasks for a larger family than Indrani. Yet it was the lack of gifts that she particularly noted when talking about her dissatisfaction with her employment. This, more than anything else, was an indicator that the family did not care about her or appreciate the care she provided to them. It made it difficult to feel loyalty towards the family, and fostered a sense of resentment.

While women consider it a matter of pride and self-respect to provide good quality care to the families who employ them, an important part of their work is also to perform the emotional work of deference and distance that retains them as part of the family while also ensuring they are considered separate to the family. If they become too much a part of the family, they risk losing their ability to negotiate for better work conditions. If too little, they risk not being valued sufficiently to receive the gifts and considerations that make the work bearable and worthwhile. Too much distance, and they risk having their sense of humanity within the household devalued. Too little distance, and they risk being exploited (Gamburd 2000; Parreñas 2001).

Central to this dance of distance and closeness is the expectation that the nanny will substitute for and shadow but also protect the maternal role and identity of the biological mother in raising the children (Macdonald 1998). On the one hand, it is the nanny who must be present to feed, clothe, bathe and entertain the children. That is, nannies perform all of the daily care activities that constitute mothering, and are expected to do so with affection and concern for the children. A nanny who is not emotionally invested in her care responsibilities is not a good nanny. However, at the same time, the nanny does not have freedom to raise the children as she might wish, or to fully replace the mother. Indeed, part of her role is to ensure that the children recognize their 'real' mother and treat her with more affection than they direct towards their substitute mother, who must always remain identified as the nanny. This is what Macdonald (1998: 27) calls 'shadow mothering', referring to the fact that nannies are 'not only performing mother-work, but masking the fact that they are doing so'. A good nanny will perform all of the necessary work of mothering, but also work at creating the boundary between the mother work they perform and the role of mother, which remains the domain of the biological parent. It is notable that this is not discussed in relation to fathers, who more easily retain their parental role regardless of whether the biological mother or a substitute mother is caring for their children.

Mothering from a distance

Many nannies in the global care chain also have their own children, who remain in the home country. Usually this is because the countries in which they work do not allow the migration of dependents. In other cases, it is because raising children where they work is too expensive, or because the children themselves are unwilling to leave their home country (Barber 2000; Basa, Harcourt & Zarro 2011). It is common for the children to live with their grandmothers, who are increasingly being called upon to care for grandchildren as part of the family's broader economic strategy. Women separated from their children for extended periods of time face significant difficulties in maintaining their sense of motherhood, even though their migration is usually motivated by a desire to earn the financial resources necessary for intensive mothering. Professional women in the Philippines, for example, often migrate to become maids not in order to avoid poverty, but rather so that they can fulfil expectations that their children will have access to a private school education and material comfort.

In their study of migrant mothers from the Philippines living in London, Mirca Madianou and Daniel Miller (2012) describe the transformation of long-distance mothering that has occurred in recent decades. In the 1990s and earlier, mothers who migrated sacrificed their capacity to spend time and build intimate relationships with their children. This resulted in heartbreaking stories of the loss of their status as mothers. Women would leave their babies in the care of female kin and, when they returned one or more years later, were horrified that their children treated them like strangers. The maternal identities they had taken for granted and had been working to fulfil were snatched away from them.

More recently, women have been making use of a range of new media to not only communicate with their children but also participate in their lives on a daily basis. Mothers who leave behind young babies are able to sing songs and play games with them on Skype. Mothers of schoolchildren can share a meal with them by webcam or help them with their homework. Some will share a meal with their family in the Philippines on a daily basis, or participate in family celebrations and parties from the webcam on a computer. Although living many thousands of miles away, the women are able to give their children a telephone that can be used to send text messages to update their mother on important news, ask for advice, or ask for money. Women are now able to take on the responsibility for their children's emotional wellbeing, even when they have left their children in the care of a father or other family member. They are more able to focus on the expression of care as well as the provision of material goods (Dreby 2006; Madianou & Miller 2012). The transformation of communication technologies has enabled women to be both income earners and active mothers. They have expanded their role, to encompass both the conventional fathering role of providing materially for their family and the conventional mothering role of providing emotional support.

In a context of intensive mothering that is supported by access to communication technologies, there may even be an advantage for women who are mothering from a distance. Madianou (2012) explains that migration overseas for work may be one strategy women in the Philippines use to negotiate their maternal ambivalence. By working at a distance from her children, a woman is more able to assert a sense of self that is distinct from the maternal identity that is imposed not just by her children, but also by the cultural context (such as exists in the Philippines) that associates her so closely and completely with her children. Moreover, the legitimation of overseas migration as essential to the Philippines national economy and to the family household economy provides a useful counternarrative to the one that otherwise confines women to the home and to caregiving roles. This is not to say that women are free to be absent from their children's lives. Rather, it provides a means for women to remain engaged with their children while also fulfilling their personal goals as independent working women.

Fathering from a distance

The majority of the evidence on transnational fathers suggests that men are not particularly involved in the care of their children, emotional or otherwise. In strong contrast to transnational mothers, the responsibilities of transnational fathers generally end at the point of providing remittances, sometimes extending to participating in communication (Dreby 2006; Parreñas 2008; but see McKay 2010; Kilkey 2014). The departure of a father rarely results in a significant reorganization of a household or care arrangements for the children (Ryan et al. 2009; Carling, Menjivar & Schmalzbauer 2012). This is likely because the migration of fathers tends to reinforce rather than disrupt conventional gendered norms of marriage and parenting. As Parreñas (2008: 1058) explains, 'transnational fathers tend to perform a heightened version of conventional fathering'. The conventional fathering norm in the Philippines that she reflects on is a version of the male breadwinner nuclear family model, in which the father would typically depart for work each day to earn the family's income. In the transnational version of this model of fatherhood, the absence is heightened – it becomes a period of months at a time rather than hours at a time spent apart from the family. Yet the core features of fatherhood remain the same, based on the performance of masculinity through projecting authority and discipline, providing a home and material security for the family through his income, and avoiding feminine expressions of care and communication (see also Dreby 2006).

Some of these aspects of fatherhood are readily available to migrant men. For example, their higher incomes mean that they are able to build a larger home and provide greater financial security for their families. As Parreñas (2008: 1063) argues, for migrant fathers with families in the Philippines, 'the ongoing project of building the home allows fathers to be symbolically present in the daily activities of transnational household maintenance' and serves to reinforce their breadwinner status. For Mexican men working in the USA, the capacity to send money to the family is the most important aspect of fatherhood: 'when they send money home, their symbolic position as father remains intact' (Dreby 2006: 51). The sending back of money becomes a symbol of love for the children who remain in the home country (Menjivar & Abrego 2009). This is evident in arguments suggesting that fathers tend to feel most distanced from their families when they are unable to send back money. If they face a period of unemployment or insufficient income, they are less likely to remain in touch with their children in the home country, prefer-ring to cease contact rather than experience the shame of failing to provide for them. When they are in contact, they continue to assert authority over the family, by determining how the money they provide is spent and making decisions such as where a family will live and where they will be educated.

However, what is lacking in the transnational nuclear family is an opportunity for fathers to develop intimate relationships with their children. A co-present father is often able to achieve this sort of relationship with his children through the mere fact of being present in the household. A few small words of approval, a gentle chiding for poor behaviour, and incidental intima-cies such as a pat on the back or sitting together at a table are often sufficient to express and reinforce a relationship in ways that are also considered suf-ficiently masculine. Instead, the maintenance of a transnational relationship requires participation in active communication or 'kinwork', such as sending cards and letters and making contact through telephone calls (di Leonardo 1987). These activities are typically performed by women, and most often by mothers, although new technologies do expand the range of people who become involved in communication (Mahler 2001; Wilding 2006).

Transnational relationships also require the explicit articulation and expression of emotions through words, in the absence of opportunities to show emotions through being present and sharing space. As Parreñas (2008: 1058) points out in relation to the Philippines, communication and emo-tional expression are often perceived as distinctly 'maternal acts', associated with femininity and seen as a potential threat to masculinity. The femininity of emotion work is also clear in accounts of intimacy in Western societies, where is it claimed that men tend to have lower levels of skill and experi-ence in expressing emotions, placing them at a disadvantage in fulfilling new expectations in intimate relationships (Giddens 1992; Jamieson 1998). When transnational fathers do communicate with their families, it tends to be limited to letters and telephone calls they exchange with their wives, rather than directly with their children (Parreñas 2008). When they contact their children, it is usually to reprimand them for poor behaviour or school performance. That is, they use communications to enact their gendered role in providing authority and discipline, rather than to discuss their emotions. This is not to suggest that fathers do not love their children. However, the means they use to express that love is gendered – and is typically associated with exerting authority, disciplining their children's behaviour, and providing financial support.

There is some recent evidence that the skills and expectations of fathers are undergoing a broader transformation. Majella Kilkey (2014), for exam-ple, argues that recent transformations in ideologies and practices of father-ing mean that it is now necessary for researchers to pay attention to men as 'embodied migrants'. That is, men as well as women need to be under-stood as both labour migrants and as participants in intimate networks of care exchange and commitments. Kilkey's research with Polish men work-ing in the United Kingdom demonstrated that the men expected to have a loving, intimate relationship with their children in addition to fulfilling their breadwinner role. Steve McKay's (2010) research with Filipino seamen reinforces this argument. He points to the ways in which men create opportunities to participate in hands-on care of their children in order to nurture and strengthen emotional bonds and expand their role beyond that of the breadwinner to a more involved mode of fathering.

The organization of childcare

While separation is typically described as difficult, many transnational parents nevertheless report that they are satisfied with their choices and confident that their children are happy. The relationships between the migrant and the left-behind caregiver are central to this satisfaction. A man who leaves his children in the care of his wife back home is reliant on her to ensure he remains a part of their lives. She, meanwhile, must trust that he will continue to support his children. This can become difficult when a marriage breaks down, requiring the family to reorganize their resources and care arrangements. Deborah Boehm's (2012) detailed study of Mexican families living their lives across the border of the USA and Mexico provides a useful example. Migration has been part of Mexican family life for centuries. In the twenty-first century, many – though not all – make the crossing illegally, taking their chances in what has become a common but very dangerous journey, when death and imprisonment are real possibilities. The journey is so common that there are experts who can be hired to facilitate the journey – *coyotes* and *coyotas*.

Typically, migrants are young men who enter the USA in order to make a living to support their families. Women also sometimes make the crossing, particularly if they have children to support and no male partner to earn an income. For example, Boehm (2012: 40) describes the situation of Reina, whose husband went to California to earn an income to support her and their three children. After a while, it became clear that he had met another woman and would no longer be sending money back. Reina then made the journey herself, with the support of her brother. She met and married another migrant who had citizenship, acquired permanent residency, and then called for her parents to send her children to join her.

The dangers of the illegal crossing do not stop people migrating, but they do reduce the frequency with which they make the crossing. Although most people would prefer to be able to freely travel between their Mexican and US homes, the dangers and the potential for deportation at any moment make it difficult to return on a regular basis. Couples regularly sustain long-distance relationships for many years, reuniting perhaps once every three or four years for only a short time, before the husband returns to earn more money. As sons reach adolescence, they commonly follow their fathers in order to contribute to the household income, perhaps also demonstrating their marriageability to young local women. Ultimately, the goal is for the family to reunite, but this is not always easy or possible. Husbands living in the USA must earn enough money to support themselves and their families and save to pay a *coyote* or *coyota* to bring their wives and children across the border. Some marriages, like that of Reina, fall apart before this becomes possible.

There is a strong element of trust required in these transnational relationships, and an ability to rely on extended kin to fill gaps that emerge. When Reina was required to migrate to support her children, her own parents became an essential resource. These family members have to be accepting of the decision to migrate, willing to care for the children for an indefinite period of time, and then willing to help the children travel to reunite with their mother when she indicates that the time is right. Throughout the period of separation, these caregivers are also responsible for negotiating the relationship between parent and child, something that requires the caregiver to manage communications and accept instructions from the migrant about how money should be spent (Madianou & Miller 2012).

Migrant parents are heavily reliant on left-behind kin to manage their success both as earners and as parents. Their sense of satisfaction in their employment strategy is very dependent on the care arrangements that they have been able to secure in the home country. This is much easier to manage and monitor now than in the past (Madianou & Miller 2012). New communication technologies mean that parents can see for themselves when a gift package has arrived and how it is distributed. They can also see for themselves when money has been spent on their children, and have more direct contact with their children through which they can reassure themselves that care is being taken of their physical and emotional wellbeing. This is probably why many migrants express a lack of concern about their children while overseas. Indeed, parents often expressed that it was they who suffered the most, because they felt the pain of being away from home and of watching their children grow up. Their children, on the other hand, were often described as well cared for back home. Often children are left with grandparents or aunts (Moran-Taylor 2008), in which case it is usually feared that the children will be too spoiled rather than feel unloved (Dreby 2006; Moran-Taylor 2008). Ofelia, who had left her son in Mexico when he was 2 in order to work in the USA, said:

> I know my son is missing the love of a mother, but I also know my son doesn't suffer terribly without me, he has food, material things, and love from my own mother. It is more that I am the one who suffers without him. (Dreby 2006: 49)

Indeed, just as money is an important symbol of parents' appreciation of the efforts of their nannies, migrant parents also use money and gifts as a symbol of their love for their children and their role as parents. Some parents go to great lengths to ensure that they are able to send as much money as possible back to their children. Esperanze, a live-in nanny in Los Angeles with children in El Salvador, was one such example (Menjívar & Abrego 2009). She earned $100 a week and sent $300 a month to her children, plus paying for the $10 transfer fee. This left her with little money each month to cover her own expenses. Once a week she would have a day off, when her food costs were not covered by her employer. Rather than spend her remaining money on eating out, she bought ramen noodle soup packets, eating them three times a day. Saying, 'I don't even want to see anymore' of these soups, she nevertheless continued: 'I was the happiest woman in the world because my daughter had something to eat!' (Menjivar & Abrego 2009: 173) Parents feel that because they are able to send back such strong expressions of their love their children are less likely to suffer. They are presumed to be protected by the constant reminders they receive of their parents' care.

Not all parents are equally able to provide these expressions of love through remittances, communications and visits. Some parents are able to visit less frequently because of their illegal status in the country where they are working. This is the case for the migrants from Mexico and El Salvador who enter the USA illegally. Their lack of a valid visa also places them at more risk in the labour market, due to their having to accept lower-paid jobs and enter into more risky employment. For migrants from the Philippines who participate in regulated labour migrant flows, visits are still infrequent (about once a year at most), but earnings tend to be more regular and trips can be planned in advance. Some even develop strategies for family reunion in the destination country, making use of programmes in nations such as Canada or Italy where dependent children can be sponsored to join their parents. In contrast, the children of migrants in America rarely travel across the border until they are old enough to make the risky illegal crossing themselves in order to work. Migrants from the Philippines are also likely to see more material benefit for their children from their migration, given that they are starting from a middle-class foundation and their parents are regulated migrants. Transnational parenting, then, is not just gendered. It is also informed by class and visa status, and the specific geographic pathways that migrants follow.

Conclusion

There is an ongoing struggle in parents, who must balance the demands of labour force participation with the desire to fulfil the expectations of intensive parenting. The nuclear family model and the roles within it have undergone some significant changes. Mothers are now expected to maintain a career as well as care for their children, and fathers are increasingly expected to supplement their income-earning role with emotional involvement with their children. Parents are expected to use not only their economic resources, but also their social and cultural capital, to produce children who become adults able to succeed in an uncertain, risky world through being adaptable, flexible and mobile, and not simply reproducing what their parents did before them. Parenting has become an active set of constructive practices, rather than a set of roles – mother and father – indicating conception and a gendered division of care of the child.

Around the world, the family is shaped by culturally specific models of parenting that typically associate women with caregiving roles and men with income-earning roles, but both men and women are now also required to expand those roles to incorporate elements of the alternative. As Tacoli (1999: 675) argues, we need to pay attention to 'the importance of gender-ascriptive roles (husband/wife, mother/father, son/daughter) in shaping individuals' constraints and opportunities'. Yet, importantly, the 'stalled revolution' has done more to push women into the world of paid employment than it has to pull men into unpaid caregiving activities (Asis, Huang & Yeoh 2004). This leaves a significant care deficit that is contributing to global care chains that leave some children feeling a lack of care, while providing others with a surplus of carers. These dynamics must not be assumed to occur within a cultural vacuum. Rather, local expectations of good mothers, good fathers, good parenting and good childhoods contribute to the family repertoires that are used to make sense of the circumstances that people are navigating.

The result is that, while both men and women experience separation from their children, their experiences of this separation, and their strategies for negotiating that separation, are culturally specific, gender specific and role specific. While men are sometimes more easily able to fulfil their fathering role through providing regular remittances, such men can struggle to find easy strategies to reproduce intimate relationships with their children, even with the emergence of new communication technologies and options. Many women, meanwhile, struggle to maintain their role as central to their children's emotional worlds, even as they successfully expand their maternal role to include providing for the material wellbeing of their children. At the same time, men and women both engage in creative adaptations to their opportunities and circumstances, producing new models of the family, motherhood and fatherhood that are more or less satisfying. Of course, how the children perceive the strategies adopted by their parents is another question; this is considered in more detail in Chapter 5.

Transnational Childhoods

Despite widespread assumptions that children are raised within a family household in a bounded locale, there is growing research evidence that many children's lives are stretched across time and place. In this chapter, I explore some of the ways in which children respond to the migration of their parents and even engage in migration themselves. Throughout this account, it is my intention to emphasize the capacity for children to be active agents in their own lives, in spite of clear constraints on their autonomy and capacity to make choices or influence their significant caregivers. This chapter explores these complex intersections of freedom and constraint by examining the experiences of left-behind children in global care chains, the astronaut and parachute families of middle-class families from Asian nations, forced child migration and international adoption.

Growing up in a non-traditional family

Menaka is a 13-year-old girl who lives with her mother, father and younger sister in Mount Gambier, a regional Australian city of nearly 30,000 people near the border of South Australia and Victoria (Insight 2010). Nearly 90 per cent of the town's population is Australian-born, tracing their ancestry back to England and New Zealand (ABS Census). This makes Menaka an exception. While her mother and father are Australian-born and have pale pink skin, she and her sister were born in India, to Indian mothers who gave them up for adoption. They have dark brown skin and dark hair, which identifies them as different from their parents and most of the city's population. They are related to each other by country of birth and adoption rather than biological parentage.

Menaka loves her parents. She feels particularly close to her mother, and enjoys sharing secrets with her. She also enjoys spending time with her extended family of cousins, aunts and uncles. 'If you hang out with them, it just feels normal really', she explains, but at the same time, 'we are the only brown kids in our whole family', so 'it feels a bit weird sometimes, like if you're taking photos for example'. She is sometimes made aware of her difference in public, too. For example, when she walks down the street she is aware that other children look like their parents, whereas she does not. Other children and parents at her local school often ask her where she comes from. It is clear to them that she does not come from 'here', even though she has lived here almost all of her life. She sometimes wonders what life would be like if she had remained with her birth family. She receives an update about them twice a year. What would it be like if she not only looked like her family, but also shared the same language, home, way of dressing and way of life? She plans to visit her birth family in India when she is older, something that her adoptive mother supports. She knows little about them, but is aware that she has two sisters in India, including an older sister who is about to get married. Apart from that, the occasional photographs are her only insight into what her life might have been like if she had remained in India.

Transforming childhood

One of the few human universals that we all share is our dependency on others to care for us when we are infants and young children. This is presumed to be the basis of 'childhood', a period of dependence in the early stages of all human life. However, like all other stages in the life course, childhood is a social and cultural construction that is subject to variation across time and place. How children are defined or perceived and how their care is organized is highly variable. For example, in most societies, babies are breastfed, but they are not always breastfed by their biological mother. In some societies, class status prevents some women from breastfeeding their children, so they hire a wet nurse instead (Roberts 1976; Fildes 1988; Golden 1996). Similarly, while in modern Western societies there is a strong assumption that children will be cared for primarily by their biological mother, this is not the case in all societies. The Sambia in Papua New Guinea, for example, keep their children in their mother's household. However, when boys are initiated at 7 to 10 years old they begin to live in male-only clubhouses nearby (Herdt 1993). The British have a history of sending school-aged children to boarding schools (Bamford 1967; Wakeford 1969). In other cultures, familial care remains common, but is not necessarily confined to maternal care. As is discussed in Chapter 4, it is sometimes not only possible but also preferable for children to be circulated through the kin network and raised by aunts, uncles, grandparents or fictive kin who are wealthier, have no children, or require assistance with household or other labour (Gittins 1985; Coe 2008, 2011a).

Modern Western childhood is distinguished from other models of childhood by a number of key characteristics. One of these is the assumption that children should live in a nuclear family household, with only their biological parents and siblings, their mother providing primary care and their father earning the family's income. This is constructed as an ideal context for socialization of children into their responsibilities as moral citizens of the nation. The state is heavily involved in surveillance of parenting and the regulation of childhood, contributing to the creation of particular forms of national subject (Rose 1999). This includes requiring extended periods of education, ensuring that children remain dependent on their parents for longer periods of time. Child labour laws now prevent children from earning an income until they are almost adults, creating the conditions in which children have become emotionally priceless, even as their economic contributions to the family have been reduced (Zelizer 1994).

State regulation of childhood coincides with a cultural perception of children as pure, innocent and vulnerable, rather than active agents in their own lives. Children are presumed to require their parents' care and guidance, and also to need significant protections and regulation of their lives by the state. Any children displaying delinquent or antisocial behaviours are presumed to be the product of poor parenting. In extreme cases, the state will replace the faulty parents with state-provided foster or institutional care. This assumption of dependence is simultaneously accompanied by an expectation that parents will raise children who are expert at making choices and negotiating uncertainty, and will be effective reflexive participants in modern individualized society. This is usually achieved by giving children increased power over their choices in consumption of media and material goods, rather than increased power over their broader life contexts.

It is within childhood that parents are expected to reproduce their society and culture, by raising children who share the same values and have the same goals of success. In modern Western societies, this is presumed to mean creating reflexive individuals capable of highly skilled employment. In practice, what this means is highly variable, depending on factors such as class, ethnicity and religion. For example, working-class parents have been found to place greater emphasis on their children obeying authority. Middle-class parents, on the other hand, expect their children to build cultural capital by participating in a range of activities (Lareau 2002, 2003; Griffith & Smith 2005; Vincent & Ball 2006). Working-class children are required to enter the workforce at a younger age in order to meet their own and their family's economic needs, while middle- and upper-class children have longer periods of supported dependency (Nelson 2010). Individualization, too, is a problematic assumption for some ethnic and religious groups, which have cultural models that place a much greater emphasis on collective participation in a larger family and community network.

Children are now members of increasingly diverse family forms. In modern Western nations, the two-parent nuclear family household is accompanied by a range of diverse models, including single-parent, extended, split and blended family households. New family models have also been generated by migration, either of children, as in the case of Maneka's international adoption, or the temporary or permanent migration of one or both of their parents. The experiences of children in the resultant transnational families have only recently been receiving the attention they deserve (Coe et al. 2011). What is emerging is a picture of great complexity. Some children, such as Maneka, have no opportunity to choose whether they leave their place of birth. They become migrants as infants, with consequences for the rest of their life. Yet they do have options as they grow up. Like Maneka, some choose to visit or even return permanently to their country of birth. Others do not. Some whose parents have migrated are accepting of those movements, others are resentful. Because they are reliant on the care of others, the agency of children in these transnational and international family dynamics is easy to overlook.

Recent research is beginning to document the range of ways in which young people are both enacting their own migration and responding to the migration of others in their own ways. What their stories help to highlight is a particular set of assumptions that underpin the nuclear family ideal: that a family is heterosexual, that its children are biological descendants of their primary caregivers, and that the nation in which they live corresponds with their physical appearance. The children discussed in this chapter do not fulfil these strong expectations that place, identity, physical appearance and family relations will converge.

Children's experiences in the global care chain

The global care chains critique discussed in Chapter 4 presents a very grim picture of young people who are 'left behind' by their parents. Vulnerable and abandoned, they are the ones who are argued to be bearing the costs of the ideal nuclear family model that is patched together by wealthy men and women at the top of the chain with care resources extracted from those at the bottom. It is commonly argued that the result is a range of negative outcomes for the children left behind (Grimes 1998; Smith 2006). As one research account explains,

> Many children are not able to cope with the situation. They can become overwhelmed by all the expensive gifts their parents shower on them to make up for their absence. They often do not do well at school, risk drug abuse and early pregnancy, and marry early. There is often a confusion of roles and responsibilities occurring between men and women left back home, and some report abuse of older daughters by fathers. (Basa, Harcourt & Zarro 2011: 16)

It is true that some 'left-behind' children have poorer educational outcomes and report negative experiences as a result of their parents working overseas. However, given the economic circumstances that prompt migration, it is possible that these children would have had poor educational outcomes and engaged in risky behaviour even if their parents had remained at home. Indeed, their opportunities for success might have been even further reduced if the family lacked the material advantages associated with the overseas income. Thus, it is important to recognize that negative perceptions of children's experiences in the global care chain are partly produced by a set of underlying assumptions about the necessity of a co-resident nuclear family to protect the innocence of childhood. Although some children struggle when their parents migrate, it seems that a majority are able to thrive (Paz Cruz 1987). This indicates that migration alone does not help to explain their experiences. Other factors, too, play a significant role.

In a cultural model that emphasizes maternal affection as central to child wellbeing, the most significant factor affecting a child's experience of migration is the combined influence of the gender of the parent who departs and the responses of the person who remains to provide care. When it is the father who migrates, the children tend to experience increased attention from their mothers (Parreñas 2005). This is likely to be because a father's migration is a relatively simple expansion of the assumptions of the nuclear family model. His increased earnings enable the left-behind mothers to participate more fully in intensive mothering practices, which are also supported by cultural expectations of her maternal role (see also Chapter 4). Children in these families tend to do well, and the absent father, as long as he sends back remittances, is also able to fulfil his role as a parent effectively (Battistella & Conaco 1998).

In contrast, there is often concern expressed that the migration of a mother is less likely to result in positive experiences for left-behind children. The problem here is not necessarily the absence of the mother so much as the responses of the people who remain to care for the children and the cultural context within which those care arrangements are interpreted. In some cases, it is the father who remains to care for the children. This arrangement can work well when fathers feel secure in their masculinity, either because they have already bought the family's home or because they continue in paid work (Parreñas 2005). Their secure sense of masculinity translates into more active contributions to the household through domestic labour and caring for the children. More commonly, fathers tend to devolve maternal tasks to the eldest daughter. One of the participants in Parreñas's research, Barbara, described the dramatic transformation of her home life after her mother left the Philippines to work overseas when she was still only 13 years old:

> Before my mother left, I did not have to do anything when I got home from school. All the work at home could be done [and my mother] … would help me with my homework. Well that stopped … now my grades are not so good anymore. It is because sometimes I cannot study because of all of the housework I have to do. See, my father does not do anything at home. (Parreñas 2005: 110)

Some daughters whose fathers fail to help them are supported by other women in the family or by a domestic servant, allowing them to maintain good grades. Parreñas (2005) found that some daughters even felt empowered by the new responsibilities they had taken on after their mother's departure. Ellen, a daughter whose mother had left when she was 10 years old and whose family had employed a domestic worker to manage the household, had not only maintained good grades at school but had also taken on new roles. She explained that her mother's absence had provided her with the training to help her become a good leader, by being disciplined in looking after herself and her siblings on behalf of her hard-working mother. At the time of the interview, she was completing medical school and preparing to follow her mother to work in the USA (Parreñas 2005: 111).

Aside from success at school, one of the common concerns about left-behind children is that they experience psychological distress or trauma as a result of their mother's absence. However, even in the Philippines, within a cultural context that emphasizes intensive mothering, this is not always supported by evidence. A survey by Parreñas (2005) that included 94 children of migrant mothers found that, of this 94, 61 indicated that they 'never' felt unloved or neglected, only two 'always' felt unloved, and three 'always' felt neglected. Most were in regular contact with their mothers, through at least weekly telephone calls or sometimes less regular letters or gift boxes. At the same time, the potential for increased intimacy through communication does not always translate into how children experience the relationship. Some children feel that their mother's constant monitoring of social media, persistent text messages and frequent telephone calls are an annoying burden. They suggest that, in spite of the regular and frequent contact they had with their mother, they do not feel particularly close (Madianou & Miller 2012). Intimate relationships with fathers are also reported as suffering as a result of migration. For example, in the Philippines, the children of migrant fathers talk about a 'gap' between themselves and their fathers (Parreñas 2005, 2008). They report that their fathers contact them only occasionally, and that when their fathers return for a visit, they feel uncomfortable around them. They particularly complain about fathers who primarily play a disciplinary, authoritarian role on their return, with little opportunity for building a bond.

An important part of the experience of distant parenting is how children perceive the migration of their parents. Many children express gratitude for the sacrifice their parents have made, especially if they experience significant improvement in their material wellbeing as a result of their parents' migration (Parreñas 2005). Marisa, a 16 year old whose mother migrated from El Salvador to the USA when she was 12, explains:

> Yes, you could say that we are living better now. I stopped going to public school because there were always fights there and my parents told my sister [the caregiver] to sign me up for this private school. And although I still have a hole in my heart because I miss my mother, because nothing can replace a mother, I remember how much she worked here, selling drinks at the outdoor market, and I am grateful that things are better. (Menjivar & Abrego 2009: 169)

It is typically older children who are able to express this sort of gratitude. They seem to be more able to interpret the parents' remittances as evidence of their love for their children, and also the absence of remittances as a loss of the parent. It is in these cases that they may begin to feel abandoned and direct their attention and affection elsewhere, usually to the available extended kin who have been supporting them (Menjivar & Abrego 2009), but potentially also to youth groups, including gangs. In contrast, younger children are more often described as demanding the physical presence and personal attention of their mothers, asking when they will see them next and sometimes crying when on the telephone (Dreby 2006; Menjivar & Abrego 2009). For them, material support is perceived as less satisfying than personal attention and physical co-presence in demonstrating parental love. However, the experience of separation must always be interpreted in the context of local social and cultural norms. Suffering is not necessarily the norm, even for young children, as a result of parental separation (see In Focus 5.1; see also Chapter 4).

In Focus 5.1 Satellite babies

In recent years, growing research attention has been drawn to the phenomenon of 'satellite babies'. These are babies who are sent to live in China with grandparents by their migrant parents. While some parents are working on temporary visas and earning low incomes, many are permanent residents or citizens of the host nations in which they are settled and working as middle-class professionals. For these parents, it is not the lack of legal options to raise their children in the country where they work that poses a problem. Rather, it is the demands of their employment, the lack of affordable childcare and a cultural preference to have their own parents raise their children that contribute to their decision to send their babies away. Parents complain that it is simply not possible to have the grandparents stay in the host country to perform this role, because of time restrictions on visitor visas and the lack of possibilities for their ageing parents to acquire a visa of their own. In some cases, the grandparents would also prefer to maintain their own lives in China while raising their grandchildren. It is common for the children to be returned to live with their parents when they reach school age so that they can enter the local education system, having received an early childhood informed by cultural traditions and knowledge of the home country.

The phenomenon of satellite babies has primarily been researched in terms of its potential to produce public health problems. Bohr and Tse (2009), for example, have asked the question of whether the repeated disrupted attachments of satellite babies might produce mental health problems later in life as well as depression and behavioural problems during childhood. However, they point out that most studies of disrupted attachment in Western contexts entail children being placed in institutional settings when separated from their parents. Moreover, there is little acknowledgement of the role of cultural norms in framing the experiences of infants who are relocated between households and carers. Satellite babies, for example, are remaining within the same kinship network even when they shift primary caregiver and household location. Their grandparents and parents are consistent throughout their childhood, although they play different roles in everyday care.

In their research with Chinese immigrants in Spain, González-Pascual and colleagues (2017) point to another public health issue raised by satellite babies: the loss of breastfeeding opportunities. Research has established the multiple and diverse health benefits for both mothers and babies of breastfeeding for the first six months after birth. However, only 48.3 per cent of Chinese mothers living in Spain are breastfeeding for this long. Their research demonstrates that the low rates of breastfeeding are not due to cultural rejection of breastfeeding. Indeed, in China the breastfeeding rate is estimated at 86 per cent. Rather, breastfeeding is not compatible with the structural positions in which women find themselves. They must return to work soon after giving birth, and when the baby is sent to China it is simply not possible to continue breastfeeding.

Importantly, children are not passive recipients of their parents' migration decisions. They are able to exert limited forms of agency within the family, which reflect their low positioning in the family hierarchy, using 'tactics' rather than strategies (de Certeau 1984). Emotions are particularly powerful tools in the repertoires of children, who are capable of making use of their capacity to instil guilt and sadness in their parents in order to achieve some of their own goals. This is something that Jason Pribilsky (2001) has explored in Ecuador, where he has investigated the increasing incidence of *nervios* among children with migrant fathers. *Nervios* is best described as a state of severe and profound unhappiness. If left unchecked, it can transform into expressions of anger or violence and, ultimately, can lead to attempts at self-harm and suicide. It is a condition most commonly associated with adult women. On the rare occasions it appears in children, it is usually believed to be an indicator of child abuse or maltreatment. However, it has become increasingly common among children in transnational families. This perplexes local people, who see only the benefits of father migration for the children left behind – children have fewer responsibilities in the household, more educational opportunities, and greater material support. What could possibly be causing *nervios* in these circumstances?

Pribilsky (2001) argues that *nervios* is not simply a psychological illness. Rather, he agrees with medical anthropologists who interpret it as a culturally acceptable expression of emotions, suffering and stress. In this case, *nervios* seems to be produced by the absence of the father who migrates. But it is also partly a response to a transformation in the role of the child in transnational families. There are a number of practical changes and cultural contradictions that children must manage and negotiate. Whereas, in the past, children were able to make important contributions to reciprocal relations in their families, their father's migration instead places them in a position of indebtedness that comes into conflict with local expectations of reciprocity. The increased time they spend in education and in travelling to and from the better schools that are further away means that they are not only exhausted but also spending less time contributing to community activities. Children are aware that this creates despair and anger among non-migrant families and local leaders, who expect to be able to draw on childhood labour to achieve community goals. Children of migrant fathers are also expected to be more individualistic than their local culture generally expects. They are given a bedroom of their own rather than required to co-sleep with other family members, creating feelings of isolation and loneliness in some. *Nervios* may well be a logical response to the contradictions that children experience as a result of their parents' migration, and their most readily available strategy for communicating their resultant trauma. In some cases, it even results in their father returning home prematurely or more frequently, if not permanently.

Children also exert agency when presented with the opportunity to reunite with their migrant parents across borders. The chance to return to a co-resident nuclear household with their biological parents is assumed to be the happiest possible outcome of long-term separation. The parents are able to continue working in a wealthier nation, but are able to spend more time with their children outside of working hours. The children themselves, meanwhile, are able to benefit from the educational opportunities in the wealthier nation and also the potential for employment themselves once they are old enough. However, not all children welcome this possibility. For example, Maria, a woman employed in Canada with a son staying with her parents in the Philippines, worked hard for many years to acquire the economic and visa status necessary to finally bring her son to live with her. He remained in Canada for only three months before returning to live with his grandparents. He rejected his mother's lifestyle, the cultural context of Canada and the educational opportunities she was offering, stating clearly that he preferred his life back home with his grandparents. She felt she had no choice but to accept his decision and continue caring from a distance, having to reconfigure her imagining of an ideal family to accommodate the desires of her son (Barber 2000; see also Menjivar & Abrego 2009).

Migrating 'for the children'

When migrants leave their children behind, it is common for them to tell researchers that they are migrating for their children, to provide them with a better life. Yet some family migrations place children more directly at the centre of decisions to leave than do others. The astronaut family was first identified in the 1990s as a strategy used by middle-class Hong Kong fathers concerned about the looming return of the colony to China in 1997. They exported their wives and children to 'safe havens' overseas while they remained employed in Hong Kong, waiting to see the outcome (Huang & Yeoh 2005). It is now a family arrangement that is practised by relatively wealthy middle-class families from countries such as China, Taiwan, Hong Kong and Malaysia, who fit the model of cosmopolitan citizenship described by anthropologist Aihwa Ong (1999). These are families who see opportunities in global, rather than local, terms, who celebrate flexibility and mobility, and instil these values in their children. They are also practising a form of intensive parenting based in the beliefs that 'the achievement of a mother lies in her children's education' (Chiang 2008: 516) and that the goal of parents is to ensure their children have the best possible chance of success in the future.

Families who choose to take their children overseas for migration explain that they have a number of motivations (Huang & Yeoh 2005; Waters 2010; Finch & Kim 2012; Nukaga 2013). Partly, they want to avoid some of the intense competition and narrow learning styles in their home countries. For example, in Korea the saying 'four in, five out' refers to the fact that a child who gets four hours of sleep a night is more likely to enter into a good university than a child who chooses to have five hours of sleep each night (Finch & Kim 2012). Some families also emphasize that they prefer the more relaxed lifestyle that is available overseas, in which mothers can also spend more time with their children (Chiang 2008). They also hope to improve the English-language skills and cross-cultural knowledge of their children, which might improve their prospects later in life. As one mother explained:

> China has opened up ... and foreign investors have stepped up on their investments [in China]. First, the English needs to be good, of a higher standard ... for one, it [migration and overseas education] is to develop the child's English. And then there are many people in China, and the competition is extremely strong. (Huang & Yeoh 2005: 389)

This model of family migration is not without its costs. Often, the father is required to remain in the home country to maintain his employment or the family business, meaning that the family only reunite during visits (Pe Pua et al. 1996). The parent who travels with the student, usually the mother, also sacrifices their own career prospects (Ip 2002; Chee 2003; Huang & Yeoh 2005). In a smaller number of cases, it is the father who sacrifices his career in order to remain with the children, while his wife returns to the home country to maintain a business or career (Chiang 2008; Waters 2010). Sometimes, children live overseas without either parent. These children, known as 'parachute children', are sent abroad to study, where they sometimes stay with other kin, but often live outside of a family context in boarding schools or paid homestay arrangements (Pe Pua et al. 1996; Ho 2002; Waters 2003; Chiang 2004, 2008). Sometimes, parents take it in turns to live with their overseas children, balancing both of their careers in the home country with their desire to support their children.

Education is not the only motivator for these strategic migrations of children. Some parents refer to the health benefits of living in a particular climate, while others use migration as a means of ensuring their children are not required to perform military service when they become adults. Changing political and economic contexts, as well as movement through the life course and into retirement, also influence when a family decides to migrate, which members migrate, and where they migrate to (Ley & Kobayashi 2005). At different points in the family's history, this could involve the entire family settling in the host country, or the entire family reuniting in the home country. In many cases, families become stretched across multiple countries, always ready to move and reorganize their households in response to the needs of the moment (Ho 2002).

While the future of the children is the motivator of the migration, this does not necessarily mean that the children themselves always feel that they benefit from their relocation. Some children struggle with adjusting to the new educational environment, particularly when they are required to rely on their limited English-language skills. Students who are accustomed to performing at a high level in their schools in the home country are reduced to tears by the stresses of adapting to a new school system. One mother described her son's experiences, who told her:

> I cannot understand a word of what's going on. I could not understand what the teacher was saying. I don't know what I should do. I don't

know what my classmates are going to do. I don't know what time the class ends. I don't know where to go and eat. I don't even know where to go if I need to go to the toilet. (Huang & Yeoh 2005: 390)

For other children, it is a shock to become part of an ethnic minority within a diverse social context after having lived in a relatively homogeneous society (Finch & Kim 2012). They also struggle with the clash between the freedoms they see their classmates enjoying and the strict monitoring of their own behaviour and study habits by their parents. Some also feel the absence of their parent keenly. As one boy explained, 'it's really hard to talk to my mom because I might hurt her feelings and because she's kind of emotional compared to my dad'. Children who live without either parent can also feel abandoned. One young woman said that her homestay family allowed her freedom to do what she wanted, but at the same time this left her sometimes wondering, 'how come no one cares about me?' (Waters 2003: 168).

For others, it is the lack of an ability to plan for a particular future that presents a challenge. Children will be reminded by their parents that they are staying in the country only for their education, after which they will likely return to the home country. Their parents remind them that they must retain their cultural background rather than adapt fully to the context in which they are being educated. For example, one young woman was told by her mother, 'we're not going to settle here. We don't know what's going to happen next, so you can't [behave like the other children]' (Finch & Kim 2012: 501). Instead, she had to remain Korean while living in America, in order to keep her options open for returning to Korea in the future (see also Jagganath 2015).

Some children miss their homeland and their overseas family, and count down the days until they return. But for others, the experience is much more positive, and they are willing to assert their own personal goals to stay. As one boy explained, 'If my Mum told me to go [back] to Hong Kong to study I would say no.' (Waters 2003: 174) He was enjoying his friends and the culture in Vancouver, and believed that he would not have the same opportunities to study drama and music if he were to return to Hong Kong. This capacity to make choices for their own future was particularly prevalent among children who had been sent overseas without either parent (see also In Focus 5.2). They had become accustomed to looking after themselves, and were no longer willing to accept the authority of their parents.

Forced return migration

Astronaut families use their global social and class positioning in order to choose from a diverse range of education opportunities and lifestyle possibilities. Yet not everyone has access to these resources. Towards the other end of the socio-economic spectrum are migrants who live in wealthy countries but earn low incomes. Their children are known as the 'second generation', a group whose experiences are different to their

In Focus 5.2 Unaccompanied refugee minors

For some children, the decision to migrate is made without the assistance or company of parents. Unaccompanied refugee minors are defined as young people under the age of 18 who request asylum as a result of a well-founded fear of persecution in their own country and who do not have a parent or culturally relevant parental authority responsible for their care (Kohli 2011). In 2014, 26 per cent of all asylum applications in the EU were from children over 14 and under 18 years of age. While 86 per cent of these young people travelled with family, tens of thousands arrived without a parent (Hebebrand et al. 2015). About two-thirds of unaccompanied minors are boys (Derluyn & Vervliet 2012).

Some unaccompanied minors are separated from their parents permanently. For example, a large number of Sudanese youths were separated from their parents during the civil war between 1983 and 2005. Children who lost their parents walked for long periods of time in peer groups in search of safety, relying on each other for protection. Many watched their friends die beside them, from starvation, violence and poor health. By the time they were provided with resettlement opportunities in a foster family, almost all were displaying symptoms of significant trauma (Luster et al. 2010).

In other cases, unaccompanied minors occupy a more complex position in the spectrum of forced migration. While they are defined by their practice of travelling alone, the migration of some unaccompanied minors is nevertheless prompted and sometimes forced by their parents or other community members (Vervliet et al. 2015). Sometimes this is in order to seek protection when they are in danger, particularly when young men are at risk of being forced into military service during war. Sometimes, migration is prompted in order to reunite children with family members who have already made the perilous journey to seek asylum but are unable to apply for family reunion. Others are motivated to seek employment in another nation that will enable remittances to be returned to the family, or are sometimes required by their families to establish the beginning of a family's chain migration pattern (Vervliet et al. 2015). For these children, the risks are also significant as they undertake their journey to seek asylum. They are at the mercy of people smugglers.

Unaccompanied minors are required to be provided with special protection in accordance with the Child Rights Convention. Care of these children is undertaken by the state and its agents, sometimes placing significant pressure on existing child and youth services in the countries of arrival. Research indicates that the children settle best if they have access to a safe and supportive place to live, a capacity to maintain a relationship with past social networks and cultural practices, access to meaningful education and opportunities to build new routines of everyday life activities (Wade, Mitchell & Baylis 2005). There is evidence that many unaccompanied minors succeed in establishing new social networks of friends in their host country and establishing their own family in addition to undertaking educational opportunities and finding employment (e.g. Wallin & Ahlstrom 2006). In explaining their own successful settlement, some young people emphasized the role of the families and communities they had left behind. They explained that they were compelled to succeed so that they could return and help the country they had left behind (Luster et al. 2010).

parents (because they were born in the country to which their parents migrated) but also different to their peers. They are distinguished from 'local' students by their physical appearance, their socialization into some of their parents' ways of speaking, dressing and behaving, and the ways in which their futures are shaped by their parents' non-local aspirations and expectations.

The success or failure of the second generation is often interpreted as an indicator of the extent to which a migrant community has successfully integrated into a host society (Portes & Rumbaut 2001). Some are celebrated. For example, the children of Australia's post-war Italian and Greek migrants have helped their communities become upwardly mobile, performing well in secondary and tertiary education and entering a wide range of professions (e.g. Baldassar 2001). They have benefited from the economic wellbeing and upwardly mobile aspirations of their parents. In contrast, the children of migrants from Lebanon, Turkey and Vietnam, who arrived in Australia later than the Europeans, tend to live in families with lower socio-economic status (Khoo et al. 2002). Their successes in employment and education are more variable, with many encountering discrimination and under- or unemployment. Their parents live in less wealthy areas of Australia's cities, and the children are more likely to be perceived as gang members with the potential to engage in criminal activity.

When faced with the problems of raising children in a different national context to their own childhood, some immigrant parents turn to tradition as a solution. Some reduce childcare costs by sending children to live with kin in the home country, which also ensures that children are being raised in accordance with their own social and cultural norms (Levitt 2001; Lee 2003). For many migrants, this is considered the best way of avoiding the negative influences of American or European society (Whitehouse 2009; Boehm 2012). Others, however, keep their children with them when they are young and instead send their adolescents back to the home country. Sometimes this is in order to manage problems of risky behaviours or non-attendance at school, or in other cases to try and prevent their children becoming involved in youth gangs or delinquency (Menjivar 2002; Moran-Taylor 2008).

Helen Lee (2009) describes one such case among children of Tongan families in Australia. Tongan labour migration to New Zealand, the USA and Australia has produced a significant diaspora, whose members remain closely connected to the home country. Tonga's economy relies on the remittances that are sent back, and regular visits are made between the diaspora and Tonga for weddings or funerals, as part of a church group, or simply to reunite with family and reconnect with place. Many take their children with them on return visits, ensuring they have some connection to family in Tonga and to the place itself. Connections to the homeland are much weaker among the second generation than in the migrant generation (Lee 2006). In part, this is because Tongan parents rarely teach their children how to speak Tongan, being too busy earning an income to pass on cultural and language knowledge. It can therefore be a shock for young people when their parents decide it is necessary to send them there to live for an extended period of time.

When Tongan migrants in Australia send their teenagers to Tonga, it is usually because they are concerned about their behaviour, but sometimes also because they want to help them build their Tongan language and cultural skills. Occasionally, young people decide for themselves that they want to live in Tonga for a period of time, so that they can 'help' Tonga and its people. However, many are sent to Tonga against their will. Sometimes they are not even aware of their parents' plan until the rest of the family return to Australia, leaving them behind in a boarding school or to live with extended kin. For the parents, this is likely to seem a logical solution. The young people, too, can often see the rationale. They recognize that they have been sent to Tonga because their school performance is poor, or their behaviour bad. However, all struggle with the experience of being 'returned' to a foreign country to live with family who are relative strangers.

One of the common problems reported among the second generation is the challenge to their identity that comes from 'return' to their parents' home country. The second generation in Australia, for example, are constantly identified with their parents' home country. Rather than being undeniably Australian, they are perceived as and constantly reminded by their parents that they are 'Italian', 'Vietnamese', 'Tongan' and so on (Thomas 1999; Baldassar 2001; Lee 2003). However, when they travel to their parents' birth country, they discover that this identity is rejected not only by the local community, but also by their own family. Tongan youth who are 'returned' to Tonga report encountering 'ambivalence or even outright hostility from other Tongans, who view them as outsiders and may call them *pālangi* ("white") or *pālangi loi* (someone trying to act "white"), which is regarded as insulting' (Lee 2009: 47). They unknowingly breach codes of conduct by dressing inappropriately or behaving in ways that are considered shameful and undesirable in the local context, and must adapt to local practices of disciplining young people and expressing affection and care.

For the young people from the second generation who are 'returned' to their parents' homeland, the disjunctures between self, family and nation are made clear to them on a daily basis. They receive painful reminders that both their parents and themselves are 'out of place', both in their own country of birth and in their parents' country of birth. They are required to learn two languages, two cultures, two ways of being part of a family, and two sets of expectations about being good sons or daughters and good potential partners who are capable of creating and supporting a family of their own. It is in the contradictions of their experiences that the assumptions about the convergence of self, family and nation become clear. All of the connections are there, but are somewhat mismatched. A Tongan self in an Australian nation is notable for its difference, in just the same way that an Australian-born child of Tongan parents is notable when in Tonga. Part of the challenge is that the biological connections are only partially supported by the social and cultural connections.

International adoption

One of the problems faced by the children of migrants is the persistent challenge they experience to their sense of identity. In their country of birth, they are identified by the ethnicity of their parents' country of birth. In their parents' country of birth, they are identified as belonging to their own country of birth. Katie Gardner (1995, 2002) explains that children born in Britain who are taken 'home' to Bangladesh to meet their family and come to understand their origins often come away feeling more rather than less alienated from their parents' background. They are sensitive to being identified in Bangladesh as 'British', a hard thing to hear after having been told so clearly in Britain that they are Bangladeshi. While some children of migrants develop a sense of belonging in both places, others start to wonder if they can ever fully belong anywhere. They begin to feel that they might belong nowhere, that their claims for identity are rightfully rejected in both the country where they are born and the parental home that their bodies signify to others as the place where they belong.

These questions about identity are even more acute for the children of international adoption, who share neither country of birth nor physical appearance with the parents who raise them. In many respects, international adoption has the potential to challenge the conventions of the nuclear family model of parenting, by directly contradicting assumptions that a man and woman will raise their own biological children. However, adoption is commonly hidden, often kept secret even from the child who was adopted, in order to protect that ideal. This is not possible in the case of international adoptions. As Menaka identified at the start of this chapter, it is immediately evident to anyone passing in the street that parent and child are not biologically related. International adoptions challenge the assumption that self, family and nation converge 'naturally' in the body and automatically reproduce the next generation in the model of its predecessor.

Anthropologists have demonstrated that both formal and informal adoption practices are a relatively common means for societies around the world to organize the care of children (Seligman 2013). There are also relatively long histories of adoptions occurring across ethnic and racial boundaries, particularly in colonial eras (Haebich 2000). However, the practice of international adoption is relatively recent, emerging after major military conflicts in the second half of the twentieth century, when Korean and Vietnamese babies were removed from their home countries to be distributed among adoptive parents in the USA (Volkman 2005; Yngvesson 2010). By the 1990s, the number and range of sending countries of adoptive children had increased, as had the number and range of receiving countries. However, the direction remained the same. Children from poorer parts of the world, such as India, China, Guatemala, Ethiopia and Kazakhstan, were relocated to live with families in richer parts of the world, including Europe, North America and Australia. Adoptive parents were attracted by the opportunity to not only create a family of their own, but to do so in a way that helped 'children in need'.

The increasing popularity of international adoption raised serious questions about the commoditization of children and the potential to provoke child abductions in response to demand for babies. The Hague Convention on Protection of Children and Co-Operation in Respect of Intercountry Adoption (1993) aimed to address these problems. It established the principles that, first, a child should 'grow up in a family environment, in an atmosphere of happiness, love and understanding'; second, that each signatory state should make every effort to 'enable the child to remain in the care of his or her family of origin'; and third, that an intercountry adoption should only be pursued when it 'may offer the advantage of a permanent family to a child for whom a suitable family cannot be found in his or her State of origin' (HCCH 1993). That is, intercountry adoption was represented in the convention as an option of last resort, to be implemented only when all other options were unavailable. Nevertheless, websites around the world continue to present images of children available for adoption, giving prospective parents an opportunity to imagine the sort of family they might create from a global smorgasbord of difference (Cartwright 2003; De Graeve & Bex 2015).

There is a difficult set of contradictions at play in international adoptions, which point to two opposing tendencies. The first is a set of ongoing assumptions that a child's best interests lie in their being placed firmly at the convergent intersection of body, family and nation. That is, a child's wellbeing is assumed to rely on them being supported to stay with their biological parents, in their parents' country of birth. This is the principle embedded in the Hague Convention. The second tendency, in contrast, lies in the perception that international adoption helps to challenge the conventions of a normative family model in which the body, the family and the nation are assumed to converge and intersect in the production of a unitary identity. This tendency underlines the rights of the individual to create a 'family of choice' that is not bound by biology or nation, but simply by the desire to exchange love, care and kinship through the practice of 'kinning' (Howell 2003, 2006).

Importantly, this process of kinning implicitly relies on an image of the adopted child as a blank slate, and as fitting the idealized image held by the adoptive parent. Indeed, a child who does not meet these expectations is readily rejected in favour of one who does (Blasco 2012). For the child who does fit expectations, a range of bureaucratic practices are implemented by both the sending state and the receiving state, and intense emotion work is undertaken by the adoptive family and the child, in order to achieve the erasure of the child's past relationships and the production of a new family identity (Yngvesson 2010). This is most easily achieved when children are very young, so that the language, family and nation that they were born into can be more effectively erased in order for the adoptive parents to create their imagined family.

Babies are considered most malleable to this vision of the family of choice. In contrast, many adopted children are old enough to recall their pre-adoption history. What they describe is a significant disruption to their self-narrative, caused by a transformation not only in their family and housing circumstances, but also in their language and culture. Everything, from their sleeping arrangements to expectations about their expressions of emotion, is transformed in a brief period of time. It is perhaps no wonder, then, that many feel that their pre-adoption and post-adoption selves are different people. For example, Jaclyn Aronson explains that Hyo Jin will never become 9 years old. When she was 8 and a half, she was adopted from the Angel Babies Home by an American family and became Jaclyn Aronson. Jaclyn describes looking back at her younger self, Hyo Jin, saying:

> I don't know if her growth was stunted when I became Jaclyn Campbell Aronson or when she stopped being Kim Mi Young's child. Or in the orphanage when she was no one's child. But my memories of life in Korea are vivid. (Yngvesson 2013: 356)

Hyo Jin's memories are a vivid part of Jaclyn Aronson's memory-scape, but she is also perceived as someone separate to and distinct from the person who now holds those memories.

It is through contradictions such as these that the children who have been adopted into families overseas experience the tension between biological models of identity and fluid constructions of family as part of their everyday lives. This is not a comfortable experience. As Eun Mi, a Korean-born adoptee, explained,

> Native Koreans often feel 'sorry' for us, pity us, but still don't want us marrying their son/daughter. I have ambivalent feelings towards them. Wanna be with them, feel left out and resentful of them. Blame them for having the attitude, yet want to be like them. That's why fellow KADs [Korean adoptees] have my love, respect, and my word that I will always defend and fight for them. They are more real to me than Koreans and every other group. They are my nation, and through them I have a country of my own. (Volkman 2005: 12)

One of the responses to this set of contradictions is for adoptive parents to encourage their children to engage with and celebrate their 'birth culture'. Children and their families are now able to participate in 'roots trips' and 'culture camps' (Yngvesson 2013: 359; Quiroz 2012). In South Korea, international adoptees can participate in government-sponsored 'cultural training' camps (Kim 2005). In other cases, adoptive parents seek to connect their children with migrant communities from the same country of origin, which is believed to help children discuss issues such as racism and discrimination.

Similarly, the experiences of international adoptees challenge romantic notions of the birth mother as somehow special and irreplaceable. As one adoptee explained, 'My mother was "replaced". Two times. I have my third mother now. At the same time, of course she is the only mother' (Trotzig 1996, in Yngvesson 2013: 361). Adoptees who are able to meet their birth mother can find the experience confronting, particularly if their mother continues to live in difficult or impoverished conditions. Yet others find the experience of reunion a positive one. Indeed, for a small number, the adoption experience effectively disappears once they reach adult independence, when they are able to become attached to and maintain relationships with both mothers (Yngvesson 2013).

Conclusion

Transnational adoption presents a powerful opportunity to acknowledge the social and cultural construction of kinship. The naturalized imagery of the nuclear family, in which dependent children are linked automatically and biologically to their parents, is challenged by the realities of children who look physically different to their parents. This disjuncture of appearance and familial identity is also present in the cases of second-generation immigrants, whose country of birth and presumed country of origin are placed in tension when their physical appearance positions them in one place, while their childhood experiences locate them in another.

In an age of individualization, these points of difference should not be significant enough to warrant attention. Identities are proposed to now be fluid, and traditions no longer relevant in determining a person's life choices or life paths. Yet childhoods shaped by migration point to the many ways in which this is simply not the case. Children embedded in so-called global care chains have limited choices regarding their co-presence with their parents, restricted by the national borders and economic inequalities that serve to keep low-paid labourers and service sector workers in one place and their dependants in another. For the children of migrants and international adoptees, the fiction of fluidity and choice is made clear in every expression of surprise at their identity, every rejection of their claims to be either one thing or another, and every time they are asked 'but where do you *really* come from?'.

It is the case that there are now many ways in which people can construct families and relationships, including through international adoption, through choosing to live in one country while raising children in another, and by sending children back to the home country while continuing to work in another country. Yet it is also true that there are strict limits on these fluidities and freedoms. Children are particularly limited in the extent to which they can claim freedom to choose where to live and who to be. Babies taken from one country to be raised in another have no capacity to choose, any more than children left behind while their parents migrate elsewhere can do more than appeal to their parents' guilt when they seek reunion. It may be the case that gender and class no longer constrain the options available for men and women in wealthy countries in constructing their own life path. However, at the other end of global economic inequality, children from less wealthy nations continue to have their identities and their fates determined by others. Their identities continue to be strongly linked to both family and nation through the evidence of biological inheritance that their bodies are presumed to signify. Stepping outside of these links is harder than individualization theory seems to suggest, binding children into larger networks of relationality and kinship that are produced both through discursive possibilities and through everyday practices.

Stage in the family life course is another significant factor framing and constraining the options and possible outcomes of migration that are available to not only children but also adults and those who are ageing (Wall & Bolzman 2014). The capacities for children to exert agency over their own and their parents' migration are linked to their lack of legal autonomy and positioning as dependants. For adults, the requirements to provide care for older and younger generations in their families constrain the possibilities that they consider desirable and feasible. For the elderly, other factors – including physical immobility and cognitive decline – also constrain options and possibilities. It is the role of this other end of the life course, old age and the care requirements it invokes, that is the consideration of Chapter 6.

Aged Care and Intergenerational Relations

There are two distinct models of aged care around the world. The first is a model of intergenerational care that relies upon the co-presence of family and friends to provide support for elder kin as they become frail and less capable of contributing to the daily reproduction of the household. It is assumed that older people will reap the rewards of the long-term intimate relationships of care, support and companionship they have shared with their kin over the course of their lives. The second, more closely associated with an individualized society, assumes that older people will rely on formal care services to keep them safe and well in their old age, paid for either through private wealth or public welfare programmes. Global population ageing has disrupted both of these models of aged care. Informal family care has typically been provided by women and children, who have now been pulled away from the family home and into paid work and education, increasing the reliance on formal care. Meanwhile, formal care is becoming less affordable for governments, who are increasingly turning to families and communities to accept a larger role in caring for their ageing kin. In this chapter, I explore some of the diverse ways in which intergenerational relations of care are organized by adult children and their ageing parents, including some of the important roles that ageing parents can play in caring for their grandchildren as well as the challenges faced by working adults who find themselves in the so-called 'sandwich generation'.

A transnational care crisis

Keira was born to the north of Dublin, where she also met her engineer husband. They left Ireland in the late 1980s when he was offered a job with good pay in Western Australia. They had been living there ever since, where they had been raising their two children in the suburbs of Perth. Their eldest daughter was now 13, and their son was 11. Keira was an only child, born to older parents. At the time of our interview, she was struggling with her transnational family life. Her father had been ill for a few years, requiring increasing levels of daily care from her mother. This had been working relatively well until recently. Keira had been able to speak to her mother on the phone a few times a week to check in and make sure everything was going well. She also sometimes sent a bit of money or a gift, such as a hamper, as a way of helping her parents and brightening her mother's days. Each year she travelled to Ireland for a few weeks to give her mother a short break from looking after her father. During these visits, her mother would take a holiday to visit a sister in the south of Ireland for one of the weeks, and then spend time with Keira in her home.

Recently, circumstances had changed dramatically. First, Keira's mother was hospitalized after a fall. Keira used telephone calls to liaise with the health services in Ireland to make sure that a nurse and other care were able to be delivered to her father while her mother was in hospital. She travelled to Ireland soon after, when she was able to check that the arrangements had worked and so that she could also spend some time comforting her father. He was frustrated that he was not able to visit his wife in hospital or provide her with any support. Things became worse when, soon after, Keira's mother was diagnosed with dementia. At the time of our interview, Keira was preparing to travel back to Ireland, so that she could organize appropriate long-term care for both her mother and her father. She cried frequently as we talked, clearly stressed by the demands being placed on her. The journey would take more than 24 hours each way, and she was not sure how long she would need to stay there in order to organize her parents' care needs. She was aware that she would have to start the process of selling their house and moving out their belongings.

The list of responsibilities was long, and growing, and so she resigned from her work as a nurse in order to have more time and flexibility to care for her parents. Meanwhile, she also had to patch together arrangements for her own children, as her husband was often required to travel for days at a time for his work. Keira had found herself in an unforgiving situation. Like many women in the so-called 'sandwich generation' (see In Focus 6.1), she wanted to provide care for both her own children and her ageing parents. This situation was made even more difficult by the fact that her parents were not living just down the road, but rather on the other side of the world.

Ageing populations and the care 'crisis'

Many parts of the world are experiencing rapid population ageing. There are a number of factors contributing to this transformation, including the ageing of the large baby boom cohort that was born immediately after World War II, declining fertility rates and increasing life expectancy as a result of improved health across the life course. There are now larger numbers of people surviving into old age (65 and over) and old-old age (75 and over) than at any other time (Kinsella 2000). The result is that older people now represent

In Focus 6.1 The 'sandwich' generation

Elaine Brodie (1981: 471) first pointed to the issues of the 'women in the middle', saying that 'such women are in middle age, in the middle from a generational stand-point, and in the middle in that the demands of their various roles compete for their time and energy'. Dorothy Miller (1981) named this group the 'sandwich generation'.

The challenges faced by the sandwich generation are the result of complex and simultaneous demographic changes. People are having fewer children, and having them at a later age. Children are also remaining dependent on their parents for longer periods of time while they participate in education and delay the formation of their own household. Meanwhile, more people are surviving into old and even old-old age, and are living for longer periods of time. This also means that many older people live for extended periods of time with health concerns that need to be managed. All of these factors combine to create a generation of adult children who are more likely to be caring for their ageing parents while still raising their own children, and to be doing so without the assistance of a large number of siblings or other extended kin available to help.

While most research on the sandwich generation discusses the role of women as primary caregivers, there are also examples of men finding themselves caught between responsibilities to care for children and parents while working. For example, Hong-kin Kwok (2006; see also Lam 2006) explains that men in Hong Kong are just as involved in the emotional and financial care of their ageing parents as are women. It is also important to recognize that not only the children of elderly parents but also the spouses and partners of those children make significant con-tributions to elder care.

The sandwich generation is typically described as facing a heavy burden, and this is certainly the case for those who are required to provide substantial care to both older and younger kin. However, some argue that the metaphor is better under-stood as a modern myth that characterizes a very rare experience, rather than an experience that is common to an entire generation (Künemund 2006). First, while it is clear that many people in their middle age have both ageing parents and chil-dren while they are also employed, it is not clear that many of this generation are actually required to provide significant care to either their children or their ageing parents. This is linked to the second point, which is that it is important to recognize that older people themselves are not only living longer lives, but also longer and healthier lives. As a result, many ageing parents continue to contribute to the care of their children and grandchildren as they age, providing a particularly valuable source of childcare when their grandchildren are younger. Similarly, it is impor-tant to recognize that the children of the sandwich generation can make significant contributions to the family as they enter adulthood, including providing care and companionship to their ageing grandparents.

much larger proportions of the population in many nations. In Japan, for example, people aged 60 or over accounted for 33 per cent of the population in 2015, a figure that is expected to climb to 42 per cent by 2050 (Bloom 2011; United Nations 2015). In Australia, people aged 65 and over were only 4 per cent of the population in 1901, but represented 14 per cent of the popu-lation in 2011 (ABS Census 2012a, 2012b). It is projected that worldwide by

2050 the proportion of the population aged 60 or over will reach at least 20 per cent (United Nations 2015).

These broader figures disguise significant variation both within and between nations, with some population groups ageing much more rapidly than others. Within Australia, for example, Indigenous Australians make up 3 per cent of Australia's population but only 0.7 per cent of its population aged 65 and over. In contrast, among the Italian-born population in Australia, 42 per cent were aged 65 years or over in 2001 (ABS 2005). International comparisons are also highly variable. The UN Population Division (2015) reports that, in addition to Japan, high-income countries such as Germany, Italy and Finland have populations in which over 27 per cent are aged 60 or above. In comparison, it is anticipated that with population ageing, by 2030 older people will account for 6 per cent of the population in Africa and 17 per cent in Asia, Latin America and the Caribbean (United Nations 2015).

One of the fears commonly associated with an ageing population is that there are fewer people of working age available to support those who are entering old age. This has two consequences. First, it is feared that welfare state arrangements are becoming less affordable for governments, which have a smaller working population contributing to the support of a large and growing retired population. Many governments have responded to this issue by raising the age at which people become eligible for retirement and an aged pension (Rechel et al. 2013). However, this creates its own problems, with older people facing significant employment discrimination that can leave them unemployed as well as ineligible for the pension for long periods of time in their later life (Posthuma, Wagstaff & Campion 2012; Krasovitsky et al. 2016).

Second, it is widely feared that the informal support that seemed to be freely available and was widely relied upon for elder care only a few decades ago is rapidly disappearing. Some scholars describe this as part of a larger social decline in modernity, in which people are becoming more selfish, less concerned with their families and communities, and more interested in living 'a life of one's own' rather than 'living for others' (Lasch 1979; Beck & Beck-Gernsheim 2002). Yet it is not necessary to assume that people are selfish in order to recognize or understand the transformation in patterns of aged care (Myers & Nathanson 1982). David de Vaus (1996), for example, has demonstrated that, while adults continue to accept *some* obligation to care for their ageing parents, they are likely to reject *significant* caregiving responsibilities, particularly if it could impact on their own quality of life or that of their children. Moreover, their ageing parents are also likely to reject such offers of support and care, perceiving it as undesirable or inappropriate. Their own internalized cultural models of independence and individualization make it difficult to accept increasing dependence on others.

One of the factors significant to contemporary aged-care practices is the shift of women into the paid workforce, without a simultaneous shift of men into the unpaid care sector. This has contributed to what some describe as a 'care gap' (Hochschild 1989; Beck & Beck-Gernsheim 2002; see also Chapter 4). This is further exacerbated by the tendency for women to have children at a later age, meaning that many are confronted by responsibilities in the paid workforce that coincide with responsibilities for the care of dependent children and ageing parents. This is usually described as more of a problem for women than it is for men, because women remain the preferred care providers for elderly parents in most contexts (Abel 1991; Dooghe 1992; Evans 1996; Shaibu & Wallhagen 2002). Moreover, when it is sons who are preferred providers of care, they tend to draw on the unpaid labour of their wives to help provide this care, as in the case of family care in Chinese families (Cong & Silverstein 2012). Rather than hands-on providers, they are often positioned as 'managers' or coordinators of care (Kwok 2006).

However, it is also clear that large numbers of both men and women actively reorganize their lives in order to sustain substantial caregiving responsibilities for family members. In spite of the evident clash between work, childcare and elder care faced by many people, women, in particular, remain actively involved in providing care and support for their family members, including those who are older (Bengston & Achenbaum 1993; Finch & Mason 1993; Arber & Attias-Donfut 2000; Phillipson et al. 2001; Wilding & Baldassar 2009). Men tend to make more contributions to care when it is required by someone they are co-resident with, such as their spouse. In contrast, women tend to provide more care than men both for people living in the same household and for people living in other households. Moreover, they are more likely to sacrifice paid work, leisure time and other activities in order to provide this care (Finch & Groves 1983; Horowitz 1985; Arber & Ginn 1995; Murphy et al. 1997; Bittman et al. 2004; Pyper 2006). For example, some women in professions such as nursing choose to participate in paid employment in part-time and casual roles, and avoid promotion to more responsible roles, in order to ensure that they are available to provide care to kin when necessary (e.g. Wilding & Baldassar 2009). This can have significant consequences for women in their own later life, as it potentially means they have fewer opportunities to save for their own retirement needs or earn a pension, even though they are likely to live longer than men (Evandrou & Glaser 2003).

At the same time, it is important to keep in mind that being older does not necessarily mean being infirm, incapacitated or a burden to others (Featherstone & Wernick 1995). It is now well established that 'most old people are neither ill nor disabled and do not need looking after' (Borowski, Encel & Ozanne 2007: 9). The vast majority of older people remain valuable contributors to their families, communities and nations, with most retaining independence until late in life. In fact, a growing body of research suggests that older people are net providers rather than recipients of care and support within family networks (Bengston et al. 2000; Dench & Ogg 2002; Baldassar, Baldock & Wilding 2007). This includes the care they provide for grandchildren while parents are at work, but also care for spouses, older relatives, neighbours and as volunteers in the community (Arber & Ginn 1995; Goodman & Silverstein 2001). This is also the case for families living in different countries. As Judith Treas (2008, 2009) demonstrates, older people negotiate significant obstacles in the form of visa restrictions and limited access to healthcare in order to care for their grandchildren living in other countries. In the process, they make important contributions to domestic work as well as raise their grandchildren as bilingual and instil in them the cultural norms of their home country (Treas & Mazumdar 2002, 2004).

Within families, it is important to recognize the reciprocal nature and ongoing circulation of care across the life course (Finch & Mason 1993; Finch 1995; Baldassar, Baldock & Wilding 2007; Baldassar & Merla 2014). Janet Finch and Jennifer Mason (1993) demonstrated this process in their account of how British families negotiate responsibilities to support each other. While it was clear that a person's gender and role in the family (such as daughter, mother or aunt) played a small role in determining who might be considered the logical person to provide support to someone in need, much more important than this was the family history or biography. Members of a family would make decisions about whom to receive support from, or whom to provide support to, based largely on their assessments of past support given and received within the family. This was calibrated by perceptions of who was most able to provide the specific type of support needed and who had the closest emotional relationship. What emerges is a picture of family life in which individuals do not necessarily feel obligated to provide care for an older parent simply because they are the parent, but rather acquire a sense of obligation through the development of a relationship over time, and in light of the present circumstances.

Significant to building up this sense of relationship is the exchange of support and care over a lifetime. Finch and Mason (1993) describe five key forms of such support: financial support; emotional support; accommodation support (providing housing when required); practical support, such as helping with the garden; and personal support, such as providing meals. In most cases, parents will have provided most, if not all, of these forms of support to their children, which helps to explain why most adult children in Britain recognize that they have some obligation to provide care to their ageing parent if needed. However, the extent of the care provided, the types of care provided, and the specific person who should provide that care (whether a daughter or son, oldest or youngest child) are negotiable. When there are multiple children in the family, they will generally share the burden of care. However, the form this sharing takes will vary, depending on the emotional closeness, past histories of support, current capacities to care and, importantly, geographic proximity.

This last point was explored by Eugene Litwak and Stephen Kulis (1987) in their study of what Litwak termed the 'modified extended family' (Litwak 1960b; see also Chapter 7). Litwak and Kulis (1987) argued that, due to advances in travel and communication technologies, proximity is no longer necessary in order for family members to care for one another, because many important forms of care and support can increasingly be provided across distance. They analysed the effect of distance on the types of support provided to older Americans by a 'main helper' such as a son or daughter, and found that some service provisions dropped dramatically, but others did not. For example, housekeeping help was one form of support that dropped significantly across distance, with 77 per cent of older people living in the same household as a main helper receiving light housekeeping help, compared with 25 per cent of those whose main helper lived a few blocks away, and only 8 per cent of those whose helpers lived further than 30 minutes away. In contrast, 87 per cent of people living in the same household received emotional support, which dropped to 83 per cent when helpers lived a few blocks away, and 73 per cent when they lived over 30 minutes away.

There are two interesting points to draw from this study. First, that some services decline only a small amount over distance. That is, distance is not necessarily an obstacle to caregiving, but may rather be one of a number of factors that shape the caregiving and support older people can access. Second, that the largest drops are often connected to very small distances, suggesting that the types of relationships with family members are more significant than where they live. This points to an important issue in Western societies, where older people are now more likely to be living at a distance from family. For example, in post-war Britain, older people usually had at least one relative living within one mile of their home. However, a survey in 2007 found that '44 per cent of respondents over the age of seventy had no close relative living nearby' (Chambers 2012: 98).

Cultural models of ageing and care also have a significant impact on practices and expectations of the support provided to older people (Zhan & Montgomery 2003; Baldassar, Baldock & Wilding 2007; Scharlach et al. 2008). In some cases, it is expected that older sons will be the main person responsible for parental care, and in others it is youngest sons. In some contexts, daughters are more likely to be the preferred carer, while in others there is an assumption that formal service providers will provide most forms of care. The forms this care takes vary significantly, too. In some cases, co-residence is preferred, while in others independent living or retirement housing is the ideal option. In some cases, families prefer to be able to provide personal care in close proximity, while in others it is more appropriate to provide financial contributions to pay others to provide personal care.

Migration, whether within the nation or across national borders, is also transforming expectations and practices regarding who cares, what form of care they provide and how this care should be provided. This is partly because of the movement of adult children away from their family homes and away from the residence of their ageing parents. It is also partly because of the ongoing circulation of alternative ideas about care and ageing in a global marketplace of cultural models. Migration is also significant because it is an important moment in the family's biography. When an adult child has been granted 'licence to leave' (Baldassar 2001), it is possible that they will be better able to sustain reciprocal caring relations with their ageing parents left behind. In other cases, migration represents a disruption in the emotional relationship between parent and child, which has negative effects on their reciprocal relations of support (Mason 1999; Baldassar, Baldock & Wilding 2007).

The examples that follow describe families in which adult children have moved across national borders and live in different countries than their parents. They help to highlight some of the complex issues faced by adult children and their parents as they negotiate transforming contexts of family support and care. What becomes clear is that families use a range of innovative strategies to care for and support their elderly kin and to receive care and support from their elderly kin. Yet these strategies incur a range of costs for the family members who adopt them.

The 'left-behind' elderly

In many countries, concerns have been raised about the impacts on older people of the three simultaneous processes of population ageing, mass rural–urban migration and large-scale international migration. These concerns point to the growing numbers of older people, who are increasingly being left without care as a result of younger adults leaving to work in cities or overseas. Rural-dwelling older people are considered to be particularly at risk of being abandoned and left without care or support (Kreager 2006; Knodel et al. 2010; Chambers 2012). Thus, for example, the United Nations (2002, paragraph 29) explicitly identifies older people in rural areas as vulnerable to the 'exodus of young adults' that leave them without either traditional family support or adequate financial resources, raising questions about how older people will manage as they age.

Without wanting to contribute to a sense of alarm, it is nevertheless apparent that migration is adding to the disruption of past modes of informal support of older people in at least three ways. First, in many cases potential caregivers no longer live locally with their own spouse and children, removing immediate sources of support. Second, local cultural expectations of who cares and how are undergoing transformation as a result of the global circulation of not only people but also ideas, media and cultural models. Third, migration creates a moment in each family's biography that affects how family members interact with each other. It changes the nature of a given relationship and affects the ways in which kin experience a sense of obligation to exchange care with specific family members. That is, not only the practical 'doing' and circumstances of care are transformed, but also how people 'think' about the care that they give and receive within their networks, including what they perceive as acceptable and appropriate. As Kreager (2006: 39) argues, 'the process by which people interpret past events shapes the meaning of current events and relationships with family members and others in the community; these, in turn, condition the kinds and levels of support that are available' (see also Finch & Mason 1993; Zechner 2004).

Researchers have provided important insights into the transformation of elder care across these three dimensions. Two examples help to highlight the issues at stake, chosen because of the different contexts of everyday life and migration they represent: one from India (Miltiades 2002), and the other from Albania (King & Vullnetari 2006). What they also demonstrate is the many experiences that are shared in common by families negotiating the ageing of key family members.

Parents in Calcutta with children in the USA

Helen Miltiades (2002) explains that care for elderly Hindu Bengali parents in Calcutta is framed by laws that historically prescribe obligations of sons to care for, and ideally live with, their parents; daughters are expected to marry and live in their husband's family's household, providing care to his elderly kin. Although there have been legislative changes to provide equal rights for women, norms of self-sacrifice to the family and obedience to the older, usually male, authority figures in the family tend to prevail. Yet some adjustments are also evident. For example, daughters who are economically independent often choose to provide care to their own ageing parents as well as their parents-in-law. In her research, Miltiades considers the impact of adult child emigration to the USA on the lives of their Hindu Bengali parents who remain in Calcutta, India.

When Miltiades interviewed the elderly parents in Calcutta, she found that they often emphasized the positive aspects of their lives. For example, they said that their children were happy in the USA where they were able to access better jobs, higher incomes and good education for their own children. As one man explained, he gave consent for his children to migrate to America because 'it is the best country in the world to live in, very affluent, and at that time I thought they were better off to stay there' (Miltiades 2002: 47). Furthermore, the parents all indicated that they were part of supportive informal networks and felt they had good access to care and support if or when they needed it. Indeed, relationships with locally living children were often described as intimate, with 'a special warmth and emotional closeness' (Miltiades 2002: 44), resulting from the everyday interactions they shared by visiting or phoning each other and small ongoing exchanges of mutual support. Those who had no children in India described the alternative family or neighbourhood support networks they were able to draw on, which were similarly described with warmth and affection. For example, one man described the help his wife's younger brother provided, and another woman explained she had developed a close relationship with the extended family of her son-in-law. For others, paid help in the form of maids and servants were an important source of support.

Despite these 'happy family' scenarios, Miltiades (2002: 47) is also sensitive to the undercurrent of pain and anguish that is simultaneously expressed by the parents, arguing that 'emigration places a heavy psychological burden on the parents'. Of the 27 parents in her study, 20 reported 'loneliness, depression and/or ill health due to excessive worry over their children' (Miltiades 2002: 48). The departure of children was described as 'unbearable' and, in contrast with the descriptions of social support provided above, parents also described feeling 'totally alone', with a 'lonely life' (Miltiades 2002: 49). They said they were worried about the future, when their health might deteriorate and make independent living more difficult. For those who were married, the thought of life after the death of their spouse was particularly worrying. As one man explained:

> One will remain and one will die. In our situation it is very painful, since my daughter is so far away. I don't know what she will do. I don't

think. I don't like to think. Because thinking will not give me any solution. (Miltiades 2002: 50)

Parents are forced to reconsider their own expectations for their ageing experience, which they recognize will be different to the one they observed in their own parents. Some suggested that the best they could hope for was to die soon. Furthermore, rather than a lingering demise, they hoped death would come as quickly as possible.

The movement of adult children away from the family home does not create an absolute loss of support for the parents in Miltiades' study. They continue to keep in touch with their children and feel supported by them. However, it does transform their experience of ageing. They are unable to assume the availability of their children overseas to support them if they become ill or frail, and so most are required to reimagine their support networks. Those with no children living locally or in India must extend their networks beyond the normal parent–child dyad to consider others as significant sources of informal support, including people who are kin only by marriage rather than by birth.

The movement of children also affects the types of support parents feel able to accept both from their children and others. Several, for example, rejected the norm of receiving financial support from their children, preferring instead to continue working in later life in order to remain financially independent. Although children remain willing to provide financial support, parents feel unable to accept this support because it is normally predicated on the child receiving in return the benefit of being housed under the parents' roof. When this norm is disrupted, both parent and child must negotiate a new arrangement for thinking about and practising the delicate balance of dependence and independence that is so important to their dignity and social status. If parents are prevented from providing the normal forms of support to their children, they may then feel unable to accept forms of support from their children that have traditionally been considered culturally normative.

Everyday moments of support and care may appear to be insignificant on a day-to-day basis, but over time they provide the foundations that enable an older parent to more readily accept care and support in later life when they become less capable of retaining independence. By moving away, the adult child is reducing the opportunities for parent and child to contribute the 'infrequent and quotidian exchanges of all kinds [that] manifest the solidarity and respective roles of the family members' (Kreager 2006: 50). It is in these everyday exchanges, which may not always be economically necessary, that family members reinforce their mutual ties and establish the conditions for drawing on support in the future in a system of generalized reciprocity. These exchanges are important ways of dealing with the anticipated or actual experience of periods of dependence in later life without losing self-respect, which are made more difficult to achieve when adult children have moved to live at a distance, or migrated to another country.

The capacity to sustain a social status to be proud of should not be underestimated as necessary to a positive or 'healthy' ageing experience or to family relationships following migration (Shaibu & Wallhagen 2002). For an older parent in a social context where emigration is prized, the resulting remittances are only one of the benefits of a child's emigration, with the improved social status also significant. In contrast, emigration in other contexts can be seen as a source of shame, and so parents are less likely to grant approval for the decision to migrate. The parents' satisfaction is also affected by whether their migrant children continue to remain in touch with them, when ongoing intergenerational support – even when provided at a distance – remains important to social status and perceived wellbeing (Guo, Aranda & Silverstein 2009).

Parents 'left behind' in Albania

In their account of the impact of migration on older people in Albania, Russell King and Julie Vullnetari (2006) describe the mass emigration of young adults from Albania that has accompanied the end of communist rule. It is estimated that a quarter of Albania's population (approximately a million people) emigrated in the 1990s and early 2000s, most to Greece and Italy, with large numbers also undertaking internal rural–urban migration. Emigration was perceived by many young people as 'a route to self-realisation and of escape from a still-paternalistic, convention-bound society' (King & Vullnetari 2006: 790), and was sometimes necessary to escape revenge killings. Many older people accepted emigration of the young people as a means of improving the situation of the whole family, particularly when associated with education. However, the dramatic loss of young people from rural areas has raised concerns about the wellbeing of the elderly left behind. One man described how his neighbourhood of 25 families had been reduced to only five, saying 'if you go there now you would be shocked, only abandoned land and houses, nobody there; I mean nobody, everyone has gone' (King & Vullnetari 2006: 791).

The older people in Albania recognize the economic necessity of migration, with remittances estimated to account for up to 20 per cent of Albania's GDP (King & Vullnetari 2006: 792). Money sent back by children living at a distance supplements inadequate pensions and helps older people survive day to day. However, this is at the cost of being able to access other forms of support from their children. Because emigration from Albania to work in other countries is typically illegal, adult children are not able to return easily. The older people left behind feel that they are effectively abandoned, unable to call on support from their children in the case of illness or other difficulties. They report feeling very insecure, not only about their own prospects and circumstances, but also about the future of their families.

One of the greatest heartaches reported by older people is the sense that the family has been ruptured by migration and cannot be restored. Older people in Albania talk about crying daily about their loss, often believing that they will never see their children again and may never meet the grandchildren they know only through phone calls and photographs. Their family structures and expectations of care have also been disrupted. The norms suggest that Albanian elderly should be cared for by their youngest son in the family home, but when youngest sons migrate overseas these expectations cannot be fulfilled. Even more painful, the elderly are not able to contribute to the care of their children and grandchildren, to provide them with the support and advice they believe should flow from older members of the family. There is a clear sense of the loss of 'normal' family life, with their children and grand-children living utterly foreign lives in foreign places.

At the same time, the laments of the older people are balanced by a simul-taneous recognition that they are lucky their children have migrated. Having them remain at home would have resulted in poverty and unemployment for the entire family. It is important to recognize, therefore, that migration is not in and of itself the source of their anguish. Rather, it is the dire economic circumstances in rural Albania that contribute to their pain and heartache.

Some of the elderly have children who have been able to legalize their migration through a Diversity Visa that enables settlement in the USA. This sometimes makes it possible for the elderly parents to also apply for visas to visit family for extended periods of time or even migrate to reunite with their children. However, it is unusual for them to accept an opportunity to migrate permanently. Indeed, those who are lucky enough to be able to visit their children overseas describe remaining in the house all day while their children are at work, unable to navigate the foreign streets, people and lan-guage outside. The lack of social contact and being in an unfamiliar place are often considered too high a price to pay in order to be with children and grandchildren permanently. Instead, they try to visit as often as their limited financial means will allow, spending most of their time at home with siblings, neighbours and friends. Their children, too, return home to visit when they can, and sustain the idea of a family reunion with (often unfulfilled) plans to return and establish small businesses.

The examples of elderly left behind in Albania and India point to the com-plexities of the impact of migration on older people who are impacted by migration even though they themselves never leave or cross borders. In con-trast to alarmist depictions of the impact of migration on older people, these examples suggest that older people have not been 'abandoned' (see also Guo, Chi & Silverstein 2009; Knodel et al. 2010). They continue to sustain rela-tionships with their children across distance, even when these are difficult. They are not perfect relationships that meet all of the preferences and desires of either the older people or their migrant children all of the time, but they are relationships that are maintained across time and space, and that enable families to pursue hopeful futures in spite of and in response to global eco-nomic inequalities and local unemployment.

Transnational aged care

Since Litwak and Kulis's (1987) study, there have been further significant advances in the affordability and availability of both travel and communica-tion technologies. What has been the impact of these advances on the lives of older people whose family members have migrated to other countries? This was the question driving a major research project on transnational aged care conducted in the early 2000s by Loretta Baldassar, Cora Baldock and Raelene Wilding (2007a). Rather than investigating older people 'left behind' by their migrant children, this research project sought to understand the exchange of support and care between ageing parents and their migrant adult children within the context of broader family networks, local communities and cultural norms, and nation-specific policies of aged care and migration.

Interviews were conducted both with migrants living in Perth, Australia and with their ageing parents in the home countries of Italy, Ireland, the Netherlands, Singapore and New Zealand, as well as with refugees accepted for resettlement in Australia and their ageing kin living in the transit country of Iran. The interviews explored the experiences of migration from the perspectives of both the migrants and their parents, and the ways in which they maintained their relationships after migration. This included specific questions about the quantity and quality of communication through letters, phone calls, emails and faxes as well as the frequency and quality of visits, both by migrants back to the home country and by parents to Australia. Aged care and informal family support were examined using Finch's model of five types of family exchange: financial, practical, emotional, personal and accommodation, with the goal of finding out which of these were able to be effectively exchanged across distance and national borders.

This research demonstrated that ageing parents and their migrant children sustain family relationships across time and space, by using regular visits and communication. Moreover, they are able to exchange all five forms of support in spite of living across national borders. Yet while the practice of care and support is common across all of the sample groups, the specifics of how people cared, what forms of support were considered desirable and appropriate, and how satisfied people were with transnational family life were highly variable both across and within the sample groups.

With the exception of the refugees, most of the elderly parents in this study were financially independent and, if not wealthy, able to meet their living expenses easily. The refugee families, in contrast, expressed a high sense of anxiety about meeting the demands for financial support from their kin in Iran. In addition to regular remittances, they were often asked to send money for specific purposes, including emergency healthcare. As a result, phone calls with kin could be highly fraught and stressful, with the migrant children negotiating the financial demands of their overseas kin with the limited incomes and high costs of living they were experiencing themselves in Australia.

The refugee participants were not the only ones to send money back to parents. For the Singaporean-Chinese migrants in Australia, sending small sums of money back to parents was not a financial necessity, but was an important symbolic representation of the adult child's cultural obligation to care for parents. In some cases, this obligation was met by paying for the parents' airfares or expenses during a visit to Australia, and in others by paying for a maid or servant within the parents' home. Some of the Italian migrants also chose to pay for in-home care for their parents, the financial contribution serving as the provision of personal care by proxy. One Irish woman decided to start sending her mother small gifts of money on a regular basis when she discovered that her mother did not have enough money to buy herself new clothing. The money was intended to improve her mother's material wellbeing. However, the daughter later discovered that in fact the additional income was spent on more and better gifts for the grandchildren. She laughed, reasoning that it was obviously more important to her mother to be able to give generously to her grandchildren than to buy herself a new coat. At least, she concluded, the money was helping to improve her mother's emotional wellbeing even if it was having very little impact on her material wellbeing.

Emotional and moral support was provided across all groups, reflecting the patterns of intergenerational support identified in more proximate families (Rossi & Rossi 1990; Bengston, Biblarz & Roberts 2002). Indeed, emotional support was particularly important at the time of migration, when many migrants and parents described feeling 'devastated' or 'very upset'. This was especially the case for the parents of Irish and Italian migrants, who often found it difficult to understand why their children would move so far away from their family. Italian and Irish migrants described feeling guilty and pressured to return, and so unable to talk with their parents about any emotional difficulties they might be having adjusting to their new home country. At other times, telephone calls and letters were used on a regular basis to provide an ongoing sense of care and emotional support. The telephone calls would increase in frequency and duration at times such as the birth of a new baby, a visit across the two countries or the death or illness of a family member. Indeed, sometimes the need for emotional support prompted an emergency return visit, particularly if a family member was hospitalized. Even if little could be done to help on arrival, simply being beside the hospital bed and holding a hand was seen as important and necessary.

For some, the telephone helped to make it seem like parents and their children were not far from each other at all. One woman said that she called her mother every day to just have a chat and maybe ask how to cook a particular family recipe or deal with a situation she was having with her young child. For others, the internet provided a means to keep in touch on a daily basis about more mundane features of everyday life, providing a means of ongoing social interaction and support. The weekly telephone call served the same purpose, despite being a little more ritualized and sometimes requiring preparation to make it effective. Such support and advice also extended beyond the relationship between ageing parent and adult child, with the children of migrants using the internet to communicate with their grandparents and cousins, for example. These were all described as the small, mundane routines of everyday life that helped to sustain a sense of the relationship in the absence of daily face-to-face contact.

Practical and personal care were less likely to be possible via communication technologies, and typically occurred during regular visits. For most of the migrants in this study, visits were made to the home country every two to three years, with parents visiting Australia less frequently but often for longer periods, sometimes for up to six months. During the visits, adult children and older parents would typically stay in each other's homes and provide a variety of forms of assistance. For example, older parents would look after grandchildren when visiting Australia and sometimes worked on the garden or renovations of their children's homes. Migrants, on the other hand, would assist with the renovations and gardens in their parents homes as well as use the visit to assess their parents' ongoing care needs. Migrants would sometimes be struck by the transformation of their parents' health or conditions in the time since their last visit, and would be able to perceive needs that local kin and even the parents themselves had not noticed in the incremental changes over time. On these occasions, a visit might prompt a new service or facility to be located for the older parent, helping them to manage their everyday life more comfortably. On other occasions, a visit would be timed so as to be able to offer support following a planned medical procedure, or to enable a local sibling caregiver to take a holiday knowing that their parent had the full-time support of the visiting migrant.

These support strategies are culturally specific and are negotiated in response to specific family relationship histories of support as well as relative capacities and resources (Finch & Mason 1993). They are also clearly gendered, with women remaining the most common caregivers and continuing to bear significantly larger burdens of informal care and support than men. In spite of claims that feminism is no longer needed and that equality has been achieved, there is an unequal burden carried by women in relation to elder care, which has negative effects on the life experiences and future prospects of women who care.

Most instances of care and support were thus routine, everyday sorts of care that were managed across national borders rather than in close proximity. This does not address the question of whether distance reduces the care available to older people who are frail, disabled or ill. Given that such circumstances require hands-on personal care, are transnational family members able to play a role in providing this sort of support? The study did not have many instances of such intense caregiving requirements, with most of the parents in relatively good health and requiring little ongoing care. One Dutch mother was institutionalized with dementia, meaning that her son in Australia was unable to phone her and resorted to regular postcards as a way of seeking to remind her of his love and care. In this case, the quantity of care he provided would have been very similar whether he had been living locally or at a distance, with the Dutch preference for aged care being the use of formal services (Baldassar, Wilding & Baldock 2007).

Another woman, from Ireland, played a particularly important role in her mother's care, even after her migration to Australia. Anne had been living in Australia for nearly 25 years when she was informed by telephone that her mother in Ireland had been diagnosed with a virulent cancer. She arranged to be on a plane to Ireland within 36 hours, leaving her own husband and children to manage without her for an indefinite period of time. The surgeon predicted that her mother would live no more than four months, and so Anne resolved to remain and use her professional nursing skills to contribute to her mother's care. Prior to her migration as a young woman, she had promised her mother that, as her eldest daughter, she would make sure that her mother would never be sent to a nursing home and that any care she needed would be provided in her own home. Anne had organized her life in Australia to ensure she would always be able to fulfil this promise, keeping a savings account that would pay for emergency travel to Ireland and working in part-time and casual positions that she could leave at short notice if she was required to return to Ireland. Her husband and children were also aware and supportive of her possible need to return for an emergency.

Anne used her professional knowledge to care for her mother in her own home for the last months of her life. As a result, her local sisters were able to continue with their own employment and care responsibilities while supporting Anne as the primary caregiver. Their relationships were not straightforward, and Anne had to be sensitive to the fact that with her sisters she 'had to be really rather careful, you know, breezing in from overseas, and sort of telling them what was best'. Spending time with her mother, she became aware of how much of her everyday life she had lost touch with. Following her mother's death, the rest of the family would reminisce about things their mother had said or done, or places she liked to visit, and Anne was forced to recognize that she no longer knew the woman she had been caring for.

Anne had the benefit of siblings in Ireland who were able to care for her mother prior to the need for more intensive nursing care. Keira, in the opening story of this chapter, had no such additional support. She also had younger children of her own, and a husband working in an industry requiring significant amounts of travel. Even if she had wanted to spend months caring for her parents, it was not possible for her to make the necessary arrangements. Instead she was forced to accept the stresses and emotional trauma of trying to care from a distance. It is in moments like this that the limitations of communication technologies become evident.

One important aspect of caregiving that is difficult to measure in terms of its costs to the carer is the sense of being 'on call' to respond to an emergency (Bittman et al. 2004). Anne was effectively 'on call' for most of her life in Australia, while Keira found herself 'on call' from the time of her father's diagnosis. The experience and practice of being 'on call' may be one of the key differences in the experiences of proximate and distant caregivers, with proximate carers in some senses more able to balance the demands of providing care and maintaining employment than distant carers. Providing care to family in Ireland while living in Australia cannot be managed through strategies such as finishing work earlier or reducing hours each week. Simply travelling from one country to the other takes at least a full day, and so carers need to be able to leave their employment for at least a week in order to travel and provide just a couple of days of care (Wilding & Baldassar 2009). This might explain why the women caregivers in this study provide such a clear contrast to Zechner's (2004: 651) study of proximate caregiving in Finland and Italy, which suggests that 'few participants changed their work arrangements for care reasons'. Some employers are better than others at recognizing the demands of long-distance care. Yet the migrant women in this study tended to manage the situation by either working in insecure casual employment that could be dropped quickly, or leaving a job at short notice if necessary to be able to return and provide care, itself contributing to job insecurity in the future.

Transnational grandparenting

While many research accounts address concerns about how to care for the growing elderly population, in fact it is important to recognize that only a small proportion of the elderly require ongoing care. Those who do require intensive care usually only require it for a relatively short period of time. For most older people, most of the time, independence remains the norm. Indeed, many older people are active contributors to their families and communities well into old age. They not only maintain their roles as parents, but also acquire new roles as grandparents and great-grandparents. These roles are an important source of identity, status and wellbeing. When children migrate, this requires the grandparent role to be reimagined in response to the new circumstances.

In China, it is common for mothers and fathers to migrate to large urban centres for work, leaving their children in the care of the paternal grandparents (e.g. Liu & Erwin 2015). This is a culturally acceptable solution to the simultaneous demands of earning an income and caring for a child. However, many of the grandparents express concern that it is a less than desirable situation. Some consider themselves too frail to have sole care of young active children or too lacking in authority to guide potentially delinquent adolescents (see also Pantea 2012). However, of at least equal concern is their sense of being unable to support the grandchildren through their education. Not having been educated themselves, they fear that they will be unable to help the children succeed at school and have the opportunities they deserve in the future. This is particularly problematic when one of the most significant motivations for migration is to earn sufficient money to improve the educational and employment opportunities of the next generation. They fear that they might be playing a role in the lost potential of their grandchildren, and some thus place pressure on parents to return to care for their children while they attend school.

In other cases, grandparents must travel in order to play a role in the lives of their grandchildren. This might include annual holidays spent in the country where their children and grandchildren might live, or sometimes living for extended periods of time in their children's homes. Some Chinese grandparents, for example, would travel to live with a new mother for several months following the birth of a new grandchild in order to fulfil their grandparenting duties (Baldassar, Baldock & Wilding 2007; Lie 2010). Grandparents in the USA whose daughters have migrated with their partners and children to live in Israel describe visiting their grandchildren on a regular basis, and encouraging the children to visit them at least once a year (Sigad & Eisikovits 2013).

Some pay for flights to facilitate this travel, thereby ensuring they are able to enact their grandparenting roles on a regular basis. This also has the added benefit of providing opportunities to enculturate grandchildren in the social and cultural norms of their ancestors (see also Urrieta & Martínez 2011). Nevertheless, some complain that they are unable to get to know their grandchildren well, feeling constrained in their relationship by the distance and lack of time spent together (see also Banks 2009). They also struggle with the cultural norms that they see their grandchildren adopting, particularly when these are contrary to the American norms they value and assume themselves. Intimacy becomes a more difficult achievement in grandparent-grandchild relationships under these conditions.

Many immigrants from China living in Canada find it necessary to call on their ageing parents to travel to Canada to provide childcare while they work long hours. As Neysmith and Zhou (2013) explain, the grandparents rarely reject such a request. Intergenerational love is a cultural norm, and they feel pride and satisfaction from being able to make a contribution to the lives of their grandchildren. However, making this contribution is not easy. The visa process is complicated, expensive and restrictive, sometimes requiring multiple attempts before entry to Canada is finally granted. The visas are also for a limited time, usually six months, requiring applicants to return to China before applying again. Grandparents face language difficulties and dramatic cultural adjustments, while also living without the support networks and companions they are accustomed to having when at home. Yet, by caring for their grandchildren, the grandparents are also expressing care for their children, reinforcing their roles as both grandparents and parents. As one grandmother explained, 'if I take good care of these two grandchildren, then my daughter will have peace of mind and can concentrate on her work' (Neysmith & Zhou 2013: 149).

In some cases, ageing parents are able to migrate on family reunion visas and join their children and grandchildren permanently. Some Albanian migrants, for example, made the decision to join their children and grandchildren in Italy (King et al. 2014). This enabled them to become a part of the everyday lives of their grandchildren, while simultaneously freeing the parents to work longer hours and earn a higher income for the family by providing childcare within the home. There was also an added benefit of being able to access higher quality healthcare as their own needs began to increase. However, these advantages came with a significant cost, in that many elderly people were then left isolated in a country where they knew few people and did not speak the language. They described missing the homes they had left behind.

Conclusion

In spite of fears that migration is resulting in the abandonment of older people, migrants clearly care for their ageing parents from a distance. Moreover, ageing parents actively contribute to the care of their migrant children and grandchildren. Those who can, use their access to travel and communication technologies to provide care on a regular basis, including providing support during illness, sending money and simply talking, sometimes as often as every day. For those in more precarious migration situations, phone calls and photographs must often suffice, although even then family members sometimes risk their lives in order to be together.

This is not to suggest that transnational family life is somehow more perfect than proximate family life, or that migrants care more for their ageing parents than do local children. It is clear that some elderly parents never fully accept the absence of their children and grandchildren. It is also true that some migrants find that the additional distance between them and their parents help to manage what can be difficult relationships. In spite of these challenges and problems, the prevalence of transnational aged care provides an important antidote to the arguments about individualization and decreased willingness to care for family members. Families persist in the exchange of support and care, in spite of distance and of encountering multiple diverse models of care and support. This attention to the persistence of practice despite the transformation of the geographic and ideational contexts of everyday life is also important in understanding the ongoing significance of broader networks of extended kin, whose experiences are considered in the next chapter.

The Global Extended Family: Identities and Relatedness

Anthropologists have long contributed to documenting the dizzyingly wide variety of models that humans have developed in order to make sense of our relatedness to each other. There are diverse strategies for understanding shared lineage and ancestry, as well as for imposing responsibilities and obligations of care towards the young and the elderly. In addition to the role of parents, children and grandchildren, some cultural groups emphasize the important connections between sisters or brothers, while others emphasize the significance of aunts or uncles. In all societies, cultural norms exist to help those who are not identified as kin by blood or marriage to be transformed into family through the labels, practices and rituals of fictive kinship. In this chapter, I begin by outlining a pathway beyond the concerns of the nuclear family and modified extended family to consider the broader array of extended kin relations that are significant for many people. In particular, I focus on the ways in which migration produces transnational social fields that both facilitate further migration and transform existing kinship networks into transnational families. I then explore three examples of transnational extended kin networks: those found among Caribbean, Tongan and Indian transnational families.

A dispersed refugee family

La Pree estimates that she was 8 years old when she arrived in Australia. She had been living in a refugee camp on the Thai-Burma border all of her life, and was both excited and nervous at the prospect of relocating. She arrived with her older sister and her mother's sister. Her father and older brother had been resettled in the USA several years earlier, when it had been decided that the two sisters should remain with their aunt and continue to apply for resettlement with her, as she was their primary caregiver. La Pree was too young when her brother left to remember much about him, but her older sister was still in touch with him on Facebook and spoke to him on the phone around once a week, meaning that she received regular updates about his life. Her mother had also had another sister, with two children, who had been relocated in Europe a few years earlier. One of these children was close in age to La Pree, and the two had a close relationship. She regularly communicated with her on Facebook, and was planning to visit her on a trip to Europe in the year or so that followed, for which she was saving. She had no plans to visit her father and brother in the USA. She had, however, returned to Thailand once every two years to spend time with some cousins and close friends who had decided not to resettle. Her family, she explained, were 'everywhere in the world'. But this did not make her sad. Rather, she saw it as a great motivator for her to travel and visit them. Also, she explained, it was so easy to talk to them on the phone and get updates on Facebook. Really, they didn't seem so far away at all.

Stories such as that of La Pree describe a picture of the family that is quite distinct from the nuclear family dyads that have been the primary focus of earlier chapters. For La Pree, a parent is not necessarily more significant than an aunt, and a cousin can be more significant than a brother. Sharing a household is not a necessary condition for feeling part of a family. Indeed, it is not even necessary to live in the same country in order to recognize particular members of the extended kinship network as significant to everyday life. Rather, a set of practices of communication and visits can be established across time and distance to maintain a sense of belonging to and feeling connected to particular members of the family network. In spite of the challenges members of this family face in communicating and visiting, the maintenance of ties is something they commit substantial resources to achieving. La Pree not only communicates daily with her extended kin – such as cousins, aunts and uncles – but also directs economic resources to spending time in their presence. She is part of a family network of support, in which money, goods, ideas, advice and care are circulated on a constant basis. She sends support and receives support. She feels a part of their life, and feels they are an important part of hers.

The nuclear and extended family

When Talcott Parsons (1943, 1955) argued that the nuclear family had emerged as the most logical and functional family form for American capitalism, he was asserting that the past model of the extended family household was coming to an end. Households were becoming smaller in order to more efficiently meet the economic and socialization needs of reproduction. This contraction of the family was arguably reaching its logical endpoint when, in the 1990s, it was asserted that individualization was attaining dominance (Giddens 1992; Beck & Beck-Gernsheim 1995). The nuclear family was being replaced by individuals who more easily and readily discarded social ties when they no longer fulfilled the individual's life plan. Instead, people participated in loose-knit networks in which learning to untie relationships was just as important as knowing how to tie them (Bauman 2003).

The image of an ever-declining family size, from the extended to the nuclear to the individual, is supported by statistics that show us the declining rate of nuclear households and increasing rates of people living alone. More important than this, though, is that the shift from extended family to individualization is a set of ideas, ideals and moral assertions that serve to normalize certain practices and beliefs. As David Cheal (2008: 1) argues, 'to be recognized as living in a family is to have one's lifestyle socially validated and socially supported'. The image of the traditional extended family is one that is hierarchical and collectivist. Patriarchal norms ensure that the father at the head of the household is legitimated in making decisions for and on behalf of the entire family group. Meanwhile, all of the members in the family household accept the authority of the patriarchal head because they are invested in the success of the family household and lineage; personal satisfactions are sacrificed and overlooked in the interests of the good of the collective. In contrast, the image of the nuclear family is strongly tied to a set of ideas that families should be based around a much smaller conjugal unit comprising a heterosexual couple and their children, their union framed by marriage laws and the social stigma attached to divorce and other family forms perceived as either deviant or irrelevant (Bernardes 1999).

These ideas, powerful as they might be in establishing what passes without comment, must always be recognized as ideas. In practice, families, households and perceptions of relatedness are much more complicated. The traditional extended family household may have provided a model for behaviour, but families and households in the past would necessarily have been required to respond to the dynamics, opportunities and challenges within which they actually existed. Thus, for example, while cultural norms may have required a father to pass on leadership of his household to his eldest son, this norm would require a renegotiation if the couple had no son. A son-in-law might suffice, married to the eldest daughter, or perhaps a fictive son adopted from another household, such as the younger child of a brother or sister. This degree of variability between the uniformity of ideals and the complexity of practice is important to keep in mind when considering social change and global cultural variation.

The norms of the nuclear family from the middle of the twentieth century began to lose their power by the end of the century. A greater diversity of family arrangements is now acknowledged, including families in which couples are not necessarily heterosexual, in which they cohabit rather than marry, and in which they potentially separate, divorce and repartner. Accompanying these norms of family diversity is a new cultural norm and expectation, characterized by a tendency to assume that individuals are 'free floating', as in the case of individualization theories, or that the only families that require attention by researchers and policy makers are those that feature co-resident parents and dependent children – the nuclear family. Other family ties, including the extended family and fictive kin, remain a background note to the main game, assumed to be of a much lower priority and providing a relatively unimportant backdrop to the individual, their love partner and their children.

Fortunately, this set of assumptions is now being contested by a growing body of research (Smart & Neale 1999; Mason 2004, 2008; Baldassar, Baldock & Wilding 2007). Indeed, even at the height of the nuclear family's dominance in the middle of the twentieth century, scholars such as Eugene Litwak (1960a, 1960b) were contesting Parsons' assumptions by pointing to the ongoing significance of extended kin in the everyday lives of people in modern societies. Litwak argued that the requirement for occupational mobility in modern capitalism did not result in the demise of the extended family, but rather in its modification. He coined the term 'modified extended family' to describe extended families that did not live in the same household, but nevertheless exchanged support with each other and perceived themselves as part of a valued and valuable family network. Unlike the traditional nuclear family, the modified extended family is associated with ideals of egalitarianism rather than hierarchy. The patriarchal norms associated with the traditional extended family are diluted. Like Parsons' model of the nuclear family, the modified extended family is also associated with capacities for mobility. There is no expectation of the extended family sharing a household, meaning that they are not required to live within close geographic proximity in order to maintain their sense of familyhood.

The ideal of the modified extended family is a set of ongoing close relationships that persist without the need to share a household. These can extend both across the generations, such as between grandparents and grandchildren, or aunts and nieces, as well as within the generations, including between siblings or cousins (Bengston, Biblarz & Roberts 2002; Charles, Davies & Harris 2008). In some cases, they are characterized by close emotional relationships. In others, they include substantial support being exchanged, including financial support, emotional support and accommodation support, as well as personal and practical care (Finch & Mason 1993). Under conditions of partnering, divorce and repartnering, they can include a complex range of kin connections and assertions of relatedness. The modified extended family has been identified as particularly important in combating the effects of poverty or social exclusion, by providing both a more secure economic basis and an alternative form of belonging, and includes extended family households in which multiple generations collaborate to meet needs such as childcare and aged care (Ruggles 1994; Hartley 1995; Shaw 2000).

The relationships and care exchanged within a modified extended family are not usually understood as the outcome of straightforward rules of obligation – in this respect, they differ from the ideal model of the extended family household, with its imposition of patriarchal authority. Rather, as Janet Finch and Jennifer Mason (1993) have argued, the provision and receipt of support within the family network is negotiated on the basis of long histories of relationship and biographies of exchange and support. Factors taken into account might include a sense of emotional closeness and a sense of having been supported by the person in need or potentially being supported by that person in the future, as well as a complex assessment of who in the family network is best positioned to provide the type of support that is required in that moment. Thus, a busy working mother on a low income might be expected to provide less support than a woman with adult children, part-time work and a substantial income.

This points to the growing awareness that definitions of the family – and of the extended family – are somewhat fluid and changeable. Members of a family network will engage in rituals and routines, in 'family practices' (Morgan 1996, 2011) and 'family displays' (Finch 2007), that help to constitute a particular family's membership and identity. Most serve to maintain the family, for example, through annual events at which members are reunited. Some are designed to encompass new members, such as a new baby, an adopted child, a marriage partner, domestic servant or family friend who becomes 'like family' through the support they provide or receive. Others serve to separate from the family individuals who were once considered core members, such as a divorced partner, a deceased aunt, or a family-like domestic servant who has left the family's employ.

As David Morgan (2011) points out, the family is something that we 'do', rather than just something that we 'have' (see In Focus 7.1). At the same time, we need to recognize that families are not simply created out of our own reflexive activities or desires. As Michael Gilding (2010) points out, families are also social structures and framed by normative conventions, some of which are enshrined in national law. This is made clear by inheritance laws and practices, which continue to prioritize the claims of some members of the family over others. It is important to recognize that these institutional features of the family ensure that some ideas and ideals of family connections and relatedness will be more readily accepted, validated and supported by larger social structures and practices. Thus, the creativity with which people engage in their relationships is limited by other factors, such as norms about gender, power, authority, intimacy, care and support. While in the past these norms may have been strengthened by local agreement, in the twenty-first century they have become complicated by the stretching of relationships across national and cultural borders. The institutional constraints are disrupted by the necessity of negotiating multiple social, political and legal fields, even as the capacity for negotiation is impeded by local institutional constraints.

Transnational families

The 'transnational family' was defined by Deborah Bryceson and Ulla Vuorela (2002: 3) as referring to 'families that live some or most of the time separated from each other, yet hold together and create something that can be seen as a feeling of collective welfare and unity, namely "familyhood", even across national borders'. When members of a family are co-resident in a household or live in close proximity, a sense of familyhood is produced relatively automatically and almost unintentionally by the simple sharing of space. However, when a family becomes separated by distance, this sense of co-presence must be actively produced (Baldassar 2008; Baldassar et al. 2016). The use of communication technologies to 'keep in touch' as

In Focus 7.1 Family displays

David Morgan (1996, 2011) introduced the concept of 'family practices' to emphasize the need to understand family as something that is 'done' rather than something that 'is' an established and unchanging institution. Adopting this approach helps us to better understand the fluidity of any given family across the life course of any given individual. Yet this also raises the question of how 'family' persists in the context of such fluidity and change.

Janet Finch (2007) offers one solution, by drawing attention to the practices by which families are 'displayed' and thus given materiality for both family members and broader public audiences. Finch (2007: 67) explains that 'Display is the process by which individuals, and groups of individuals, convey to each other and to relevant audiences that certain of their actions do constitute "doing family things" and thereby confirm that these relationships are "family" relationships'. She argues that family displays are used to communicate to others that this is a family and, moreover, that this assemblage of relationships works well as a family, even if it varies from the established norms of families in that time and place.

Display can take a number of forms. During periods of change within a family group, such as following divorce, or as a child becomes an adult, or as an elder becomes more dependent, the individuals making up that family group are required to rework their roles within the family. They display new versions of their role as parent or child, not only to each other through their interactions, but also to a broader audience of observers who might then affirm that yes, this is indeed a family and a family that works well.

Every time a reminiscence is shared or a gift is given within a family group, the family itself and the relationships and roles of the members within it are on display. Similarly, when gifts are arranged in a home the family is placed on display, made material in the spaces of everyday life. Families are also displayed in the photographs that are carried in phones, purses and wallets, arranged in albums and placed in frames on walls. These displays of stories, gifts and images can change over time, especially when previously happy memories become tainted by danger or the undesirable (e.g. Phu 2014).

Importantly, the display of family is not a matter of reproducing a generalized account of what families normally should be or do. Rather, displays are moments in which the specifics of this particular family and its complex, anomalous sets of relationships are placed in dialogue with the larger ideologies of kinship and family within which particular families are situated, and through which they are constantly interpreted and evaluated by themselves and others. It is through their displays that families assert their right to recognize themselves and be recognized as familial, and have their claims to being 'a family that works well' validated and legitimated.

well as regular visits are important and common tools used to produce a sense of ongoing familyhood, by providing moments of virtual or physical co-presence. Other strategies are also significant. For example, older people left behind by children and grandchildren in Lahu families in Thailand sometimes maintain the migrant's room in the home for extended periods of time. As one farmer explained, referring to the belongings left behind by a migrant son, 'we didn't touch [them] because it is his things. So when he comes back, he knows exactly where they are' (Tan & Yeoh 2011: 52). Maintaining the migrant's room helps to retain the migrant in the family home, and at the core of the family imaginary, even when they are physically distant. Zoe Robertson and colleagues (2016) describe how, for many people whose families have been disrupted by forced migration, physical reunion is an impossibility. However, young people are able to use digital photographs to stitch together a sense of family by placing images of their kin alongside each other in cyberspace. These digital images are then printed, circulated and discussed in social media in ways that give the images a new material form. They gradually and persistently produce a new family imaginary that takes a visible, tangible form, which becomes the foundation of a sense of familyhood and co-presence.

What these examples reinforce is the knowledge that a transnational family does not simply 'exist'; effort to sustain it over time and place is required. This work of creating the family has been given a range of terms, including 'kinning' and 'family practices' (Carsten 2004; Morgan 2011). Deborah Bryceson and Ulla Vuorela (2002: 14) use the term 'relativising', which they define as

> the variety of ways individuals establish, maintain or curtail relational ties with specific family members. It is intended to stress the sense of relativity, or being related, that occurs in transnational family relations that are created by active pursuit or passive negligence of familial blood ties and the possible inclusion of non-blood ties as family members.

Relativizing is a selective process through which individuals in a family network reinforce some ties with available others, while de-emphasizing other ties. Thus, for example, some family members may use migration as an opportunity to create distance from specific kin, while others might use it to further reinforce their relationships by positioning themselves to fulfil their economic role in the family.

Elaine Ho (2008) further argues that an equally important component of the transnational family is the set of strategies that nation-states use in order to bind their emigrant citizens to the nation by emphasizing the link between the family and the nation. Her example is Singapore, where government discourses emphasize the essential interdependency of family and nation in statements such as the following, from the Ministry of Community, Youth and Sports:

> Families serve as an important pillar of support for the nation. At the individual level, families are the primary source of emotional, social and financial support. At the national level, they contribute to social stability and national cohesiveness as they help develop socially responsible individuals and deepen the bond Singaporeans have with our country.

This statement underscores the centrality of the family to the maintenance of cultural values and Singaporean identities. It also emphasizes the role of the family and its members in securing the future success of the nation. Similar statements are made by governments around the world, such as that of the Philippines, which seeks to simultaneously encourage emigration (as beneficial to national economic development) and also encourage continued connection to the nation and commitment to those left behind.

The nation-state, then, is not simply a backdrop to the transnational family. It is an active participant in creating opportunities and obligations for families to become transnational. Migrants and their families are required to negotiate not just their relationships with each other, but also their relationships with the nation-states in which they reside, work and raise families. How this is accomplished depends on a range of factors, including national policies regarding citizenship, residence, travel and remittances, as well as histories of family relationships of support, neglect, affection and indifference. The other important factor that shapes the transnational family is the roles and identities available to individuals within specific national and cultural contexts and within particular families, at particular life stages. Any given individual makes decisions about their own migration and responds to the migration of their kin within the framework of a set of cultural expectations about how someone of their age and gender should or could behave, and the opportunities and challenges they encounter in both the country of emigration and the country of immigration. This is the case for members of all families around the world, as is demonstrated by examples throughout the chapters in this book. In the remainder of this chapter, these complex intersecting forces are explored in the context of specific families in specific social, cultural, economic and political contexts. Families from the Caribbean, Tonga and India have been selected for discussion, because they are associated with cultural models that emphasize the continuing role of the extended family in the lives of the individual. My intention is not to suggest that these are unique or exotic forms of familyhood. Rather, the cultural norms that are emphasized in these contexts help to illuminate the ongoing significance of relatedness in all families. What distinguishes these examples is the ways in which global householding practices (see In Focus 7.2) are made more explicit as a result of the cultural norms and values that members of these families emphasize and encounter in their transnational social fields.

A Caribbean transnational family

From at least the nineteenth century, the Caribbean family has been identified and imagined by colonial powers as deviant and dysfunctional. This is not necessarily an accurate reflection of the functionality of families in the Caribbean. Rather, it can be interpreted as reflecting the differences between families from Caribbean backgrounds and the nuclear family model that was upheld as the ideal by Christian missionaries and European colonial masters. As Mary Chamberlain (2006: 4) explains, the Caribbean family has commonly

In Focus 7.2 Global householding

For many population censuses around the world, the standard unit of analysis is not the 'family' or even the individual, but rather the 'household'. Households are distinct from families in that they might have a single person living within them, a nuclear family, a set of non-related adults, a multi-generational family or any of a wide range of other possibilities.

The household has been argued by some to be the basic unit of all societies. It is at the level of the household, rather than the family, where social reproduction is suggested to occur – that combination of activities that entails both economic production and material wellbeing as well as physical reproduction of the species and emotional wellbeing. Relying on this understanding of social reproduction as the most logical site of analysis of social change, Mike Douglass (2006, 2014) argues that recent migration patterns require the new concept of 'global householding' in order to best capture the impact of international migration on productive and reproductive lives.

Eleonore Kofman (2012) adds that a framework based on the household rather than the family enables the diverse activities of social reproduction in a global context to be more usefully connected. It demands that researchers pay attention to the role of migration in both the activities of economic production and those of physical reproduction, such as childbearing, childrearing and care of the elderly. A focus on global householding thus also helps to highlight the gendered division of labour that perpetuates inequalities not just within the household, but also beyond.

A focus on the household rather than the family can help to highlight the ways in which migration for care, family reunion or employment often overlap and intersect. For example, a woman might first migrate as a domestic servant to earn money, then become a migrant spouse who performs the same tasks without pay. She might at some point be mobile as an unpaid girlfriend, and at another point as a paid sex worker. She might be required to care for elderly parents overseas for money as a paid employee, or for free as part of her unpaid obligations to the overseas kin of her spouse. The slippage across different migration categories and different paid and unpaid roles points to the ways in which social reproduction is accomplished through both the labour market and the unpaid circulation of family care, and the ways in which diverse migration categories shape what is possible for individual households.

An important insight arising from the notion of global householding is a recognition that the social reproduction of the household is increasingly conducted across national borders, rather than just within the nation-state that records the household within its population census. Households within any single nation are increasingly having their strategies of marriage, fertility, economic productivity and exchange, caregiving and division of labour shaped by the policies, opportunities and constraints imposed by nations elsewhere and framed by geographically distant social and cultural contexts. Meanwhile, even as these nations are impacting on the practices and choices of individual households, the households within any given nation are also undergoing shifts that are not produced by local conditions, but rather by the contexts of other nations in which members of their households are participating through their engagement in the global labour market as well as through their relationships of care and intimacy.

been negatively compared with the western European nuclear family model, as follows:

> Varieties of conjugal unions, high illegitimacy rates, female-headed households, female employment, child fostering, and an inclusive embrace of all kin (and fictive kin) as family members stood in marked contrast to the (apparently) stable unions of Christian marriages, predicated on the autonomy and exclusiveness of family life, on the subservience of women and children to the authority of the male, and on the prominence given to the male line in inheritance and family identification.

In practice, the Caribbean family, like families in all nations, are actually very diverse. People's opportunities, expectations and family practices vary depending on which island in the Caribbean they were born or raised upon, their own and their family's socio-economic position, their position on a spectrum of racial identities, and their family's experiences of and opportunities for migration (Goulbourne 2002, 2003; Chamberlain 2006; Olwig 2007).

Karen Fog Olwig (2002, 2007) has conducted research with diverse family networks in the Caribbean, exploring their transnational family practices. One of the families she describes, the Smith family, is a set of siblings and their parents from a relatively impoverished background, on a relatively impoverished island in the Caribbean, Nevis. They fit many of the expectations about 'the' Caribbean family, and so help us understand how that model of the family might produce a particular form of transnationalism and transnational familyhood.

The story of the Smith family begins with Patrick and Miriam. When they married, they already had two children. As is relatively common in the Caribbean, their marriage was more a confirmation of the success of their union and Patrick's economic success than a celebration of the start of their relationship. Although marriage is a valued goal, it is something that is usually achieved in later life, particularly for those from poorer backgrounds. It was not until Patrick had accumulated enough money to buy land and build a house that Miriam married him, after which she and their two children left her parents' home to come and live with him. The couple went on to have ten children together, nine of whom survived.

Patrick and Miriam worked long hours to make a living from the land, and the children recalled looking after each other and their household, which they balanced with attending school. Their parents raised them to share and to care for each other, and Olwig (2007: 167) argues that it was through this 'relationship of sharing and caring that kinship was constituted'. This is not to deny the significance of biological ties, but rather to emphasize that biological ties were not sufficient (or even necessary) to produce a sense of familyhood.

In practice, not all members of the kinship network contributed equally, and not all biological relatives were able to be relied upon for support. The children describe fraught relationships with their maternal and paternal grandparents, who gave little or no support. Yet other members of the kin network in their village on Nevis could be regularly relied upon to help out. They had aunts who would often give food or clothing and godparents who displayed their relative wealth in the village by being generous with their godchildren. As they became older, the children left school at an early age in order to participate in paid work and contribute more to the family's material wellbeing. Unfortunately, they also quickly discovered that local employment was difficult to find and poorly paid. They soon realized they would need to migrate if they truly wanted to make a contribution to the family.

Patrick and Miriam's eldest son, Edwin, was the first to leave Nevis. He accompanied his girlfriend Syvilla to the UK, where she was being sent by her parents. They left their son with Syvilla's parents in Nevis until they established themselves. Edwin borrowed money from his father to pay the fare. He planned to earn money to support his parents' home in Nevis and also to save enough to establish a family household of his own back home with Syvilla and their children. This proved much more difficult than he expected, with work difficult to find, wages very low, and living costs high. Decades later, he still claimed he was living temporarily in the UK, even though the goal of returning remained out of reach. In the meantime, he bought a house in the UK where he raised and educated his children, and was an active participant in the local Nevisian community. As his retirement was approaching, he and Syvilla were exploring the options for retiring on Nevis, in a newly built home that displayed the product of their long absence.

Changes in visa regulations meant that none of Edwin's family joined him in the UK. His father, Patrick, migrated to the US Virgin Islands only a few months after Edwin had left, where he stayed with his brother and aunt while he established himself. His daughter Claudette later came to live with him and take up employment, and when she needed someone to care for her children, her sister Lisa migrated to look after the household. Other siblings also arrived, relying on the family network for support during periods of unemployment or relationship problems, and providing support to other family members during their times of difficulty. These were relatively frequent, as most of the siblings lacked the labour certification necessary to work legitimately and so were forced to accept work that was low paid and insecure. After 11 years, Patrick returned home to Nevis following an accident that left him unable to work, and the network of siblings continued to send back money and boxes of goods to sustain him and Miriam as well as others who remained in the household. Several of the siblings left their own children in the household with Miriam while they established themselves overseas, and some sent back children born overseas whom they were struggling to care for without local family support. Remittances and communications, then, were not simply between Miriam and her children, but encompassed a range of relationships between parents and children, grandparents and grandchildren, and co-resident cousins and their parents.

It is easy to see this as an ideal extended family network, in which all of the members contribute and receive support in a complex web of interdependence, rights and obligations. This is an important part of the picture, but it is not the full story. Olwig (2002) describes a wedding for one of the sons, in which the siblings converged on the family home, not long after the death of both of their parents. She argues that this wedding was a symbol of the family's success, not only materially as a result of their migration strategies, but also as a collective unit of care and support. The siblings were generally pleased with the outcome, happy that they were able to pool their resources in such a public display of the family's achievements.

However, they were also in the process of working out their parents' will and the distribution of the inheritance, and it was in this process that some of the tensions within the family became more obvious. For the first time, the siblings were required to evaluate each other's contributions to the household, in order to determine the fairest way of distributing the family's assets. This was a difficult process, not helped by the fact that some of them disagreed with the provisions in their parents' will. Some of the siblings had been sending back regular remittances, others sent regular and substantial gifts, and others remitted or gifted on a more occasional basis. Some had sent children back to live with their parents, explaining their larger remittance contributions, while others had returned to care for their parents when they were ill. What Olwig (2002) makes clear is that this was a turning point in the family's history, in which some siblings were able to reinforce their connection to the family and to the home in Nevis, while others began to direct their attention either to another home in Nevis or to the home they had created with their children in the country where they had been working (Olwig 2012). The second generation, the children born overseas and attending education overseas, made this picture even more complex as they were also beginning to make their own life plans, which may or may not involve return to the parental home (Reynolds 2011).

The fluidity and flexibility of this family provided a distinct advantage, enabling the siblings to relocate to other places for work, to relocate children to other places for care, and to invest in a collective identity that provided a sense of belonging. However, this same flexibility and fluidity also contributed to the potential demise of the transnational family network. Biological links had provided an initial foundation for their sense of familyhood, but were not sufficient on their own to sustain it into the future. Rather, the family is produced by the continuous exchange of goods, support and care throughout the network over time, and changes as these flows change (Olwig 2014). As the siblings raised their own children, with or without the help of each other, and encountered obstacles and opportunities in the countries where they were working, they were constantly renegotiating their contributions to and support from the family.

Many of the siblings were able to reflect with pride on the growing size of the family network, exhibited at family reunions. They emphasized that how their family was perceived in the local village was important to them. It contributed to how they perceived their own lives and measured their own successes. It also enabled them to withstand some of the challenges of migrating into low-paid work overseas where they experienced discrimination and exploitation. The extended family, for them, was a project of the self as well

as a collective endeavour. Yet for others the family was becoming less significant. They felt that their contributions were not sufficiently recognized by
their kin, and so began to contribute less. They began to orient their hopes
and ambitions away from the family, towards other contexts, either in Nevis
or overseas. In the process, they were contributing to the family's reconfiguration and decline, by contributing less, and receiving less, from the extended
network, and thereby making that network less meaningful and less effective.

A Tongan transnational social field

It has been suggested that transnational families have existed in the Caribbean
since the nineteenth century. Tongan transnational families, on the other
hand, have arguably existed for millennia. Tevita Ka'ili (2005) traces the
existence of Tongan transnational social fields back to ancestral origins when
he ponders the exploits of Maui, a cultural hero who captured the sun from
a mountain summit in Hawai'i to make it travel more slowly across the sky,
raised islands up from the sea with fishing hooks and smuggled fire into this
world from the underworld. He explains,

> In Tonga, people talk about the same sun-snaring Maui as the people
> in Hawai'i. As I pondered Maui's presence in all of the Moana islands,
> I wondered how he kept ties with all of them ... how Maui sustained
> relationships with many of his relatives who were dispersed yet con-
> nected across distant physical spaces. (Ka'ili 2005: 84)

Tongans have been travelling to other islands across the Pacific for centuries,
long before European contact, and this travel involved the maintenance of significant social ties across time and space (Small 1997). Since the 1960s, this
transnational orientation has been extended by the large numbers of Tongans
who migrated beyond the Pacific, to live and work in New Zealand, the USA
and Australia (Lee 2003, 2007; Ka'ili 2005). More Tongans now live overseas
than in Tonga, and their remittances are essential to the Tongan economy
(James 1997; Lee 2007). Tongan migrants are extremely active in maintaining their ties to Tonga and to Tongan communities living elsewhere around
the world. In part, these ties are maintained through family networks. But
they also extend beyond what might be perceived as the nuclear or extended
family, to include relations maintained through community organizations
and, in particular, church groups. The familyhood they are sustaining is not
just a matter of the present, but also of maintaining ancestral roots.

In order to understand the persistence of these strong relationships across
time and space, Tevita Ka'ili (2005: 89) argues that it is necessary to acknowledge the fundamental cultural value of *tauhi vā*, translated as 'caring for
sociospatial relations'. Tongans are able to trace their connections to each
other through their genealogical histories, linking themselves through shared
ancestors and shared connection to land. These links are manifested in the
social space between those points, which is not thought of as empty, but is

rather perceived as a sort of object that must be tended and maintained. Thus, identifying the connections between kin is not sufficient. Once these connections have been identified, they must also be tended to, cared for and maintained. This is achieved through acts of hospitality, in particular sharing food and accommodation, but also through giving gifts, sharing resources and providing support such as advice, education and employment opportunities.

The caring and tending to sociospatial relations can require substantial resources, which might limit individual upward mobility, but it is also a source of support that provides a sense of security and belonging in the world. Because *vā* is conceptualized as a social space, rather than a physical space, geographic distance is neither an impediment nor a facilitator of *tauhi vā*. It can be achieved regardless of geographic distance. Moreover, *tauhi vā* is reciprocal and exchanged across the generations, so that the grandchild of someone who tended to their *vā* with other kin will likely benefit from that in their own life, receiving the support of kin who were supported by others in the past. It is also something that is produced through connections to place. For this reason, Tongans living overseas will contribute both to their families in Tonga and also to village projects such as a new water pump or a church building (Small 1997).

The reciprocal nature of *tauhi vā* ensures that Tongans in Tonga do not only receive from their migrant kin, but also provide support to their migrant kin. This can take the form of sending kava root or traditional handicrafts for consumption or sale overseas (James 1997; Ka'ili 2005). From this perspective, migration overseas is not a simple matter of someone moving to a wealthier place in order to support those who remain in a less wealthy place. Rather, it is an opportunity for kin to engage in reciprocal exchanges of a wider range of resources. The migrant kin are able to draw on and contribute resources from modern capitalist societies, while those who remain in Tonga are able to contribute to the maintenance of tradition – both materially and in terms of cultural practices. This exchange of resources from different contexts is what reproduces the family as an entity. The maintenance of social space occurs over both time and space, both within and beyond the family network, and is the responsibility of all members of the network, who must commit all available resources to *tauhi vā*.

This helps to understand the sheer volume of exchanges that occur between Tongans in the diaspora and their kin and communities in Tonga. Helen Lee's substantial and longstanding work with Tongan migrants and their children demonstrates the extent of these connections (e.g. Lee 2003, 2004a, 2004b, 2007, 2011). Tongans in the diaspora regularly send money and goods to Tonga, either independently to kin or through their church or village networks. They use a range of communication technologies to keep in touch with a diverse range of kin and make regular return visits. In some cases, children are sent from the diaspora to Tonga to stay with family or attend boarding schools, where they receive childcare and an education in the *anga fakatonga*, the 'Tongan ways' (Lee 2003, 2009). The enculturation of children is an essential resource, matching or even exceeding the value of the financial resources being sent to Tonga from overseas.

Importantly, Tongan social relations are not maintained just between Tonga and the diaspora. Those who are living in the diaspora also maintain strong connections with each other, between Australia, North America and New Zealand (Lee 2011). They maintain websites and an active social media presence, enabling them to observe each other's lives from a distance and inform and update each other of their activities over time. Unlike the example of the Caribbean family discussed above, support in Tongan families and communities flows in multiple directions across multiple national borders, with some choosing to sustain stronger relationships across the diaspora than they do with Tonga. This is particularly clear within the second generation – children born to Tongan parents outside of Tonga. While they recognize their role in Tongan social fields, and participate in Tongan cultural activities, they often identify more strongly with each other than they do with their peers who have been born and raised in Tonga. There is some concern that this will ultimately result in the children of migrants failing to support Tonga economically in the future (Lee 2004a).

An important element of this diasporic consciousness is the emergence of communication technologies that enable people to produce and maintain relationships that do not rely on physical co-presence (Lee 2003). These technologies are also transforming the ways in which people maintain their relationships, as has been described by Makiko Nishitani (2014). The polymedia environment enabled by access to mobile phones, landline phones, social media and websites has produced a set of resources that Tongans can use to manage their cultural obligations and reputations while also achieving their individual goals. Thus, for example, young women are able to use social media to maintain close relations with some kin, while avoiding online contact with other kin. This does not reduce their obligations in the offline world, but does provide them with some control over their reputation and status within the family and the community. Similarly, young men who are keenly aware of their obligation to provide financial support when requested to do so by older kin are able to manage these expectations by simply not answering their phone when they have no resources to share. Thus, rather than having to face the shame of declining a request, they are able to avoid the request altogether, at least in the short term.

Importantly, the diverse uses of communication technologies point to a common theme throughout studies of Tongan transnational social ties. In spite of the transformations that are introduced by engagement with capitalist economies, migration to Western, English-speaking nations, and the adoption of a range of new communication technologies, Tongan social relations remain deeply embedded in cultural traditions of reciprocity and obligation (Small 1997; Evans 2001; Lee 2003). These shape gendered relations and enmesh people in social hierarchies that inform their contributions to the family and the community. As Nishitani (2014: 211) explains, 'While the daughters of Tongan migrants may work as independent women in Australian institutions outside the Tongan social field, they may act as submissive daughters or nieces within the kin-based Tongan social field, because each field has its own logic'.

It is the maintenance of this Tongan social field, alongside of participation in non-Tongan social fields, that ensures that money, goods, reputation and status continue to circulate and retain meaning throughout the Tongan extended family and community networks that spread across the globe. Furthermore, it is the circulation of these resources that sustains the social fields of Tongan identities and family networks. This not only ensures that a sense of familyhood and of Tongan identities is maintained, but also provides valuable resources for people from Tongan backgrounds. It is through their Tongan identities and social networks, argues Small (1997), that Tongans are able to better negotiate the harshness of life overseas, acquire social status, feel secure about ageing and their futures post-retirement, and provide their children with a supportive social network from which to plan their own futures. The Tongan social field provides an important alternative to the global capitalist economy, from which people might draw meaning, support and a sense of being valued members of a social group.

Indian transnational households

The Western model of the family would suggest that the nuclear family and the conjugal marriage bond are the most important focus of attention. However, studies of migration and transnational families have demonstrated consistently that the maintenance of cultural and family identities beyond the nuclear family remains essential. Supriya Singh (2006; Singh, Cabraal & Robertson 2010; Singh, Robertson & Cabraal 2012) demonstrates this effectively in her analysis of Indian transnational families. Her unique contribution is to draw particular attention to the meanings and functions of money as organizing and maintaining the Indian family.

India is a very diverse nation, consisting of numerous religious, ethnic and cultural groups. Nevertheless, the model of 'the' Indian family that is reproduced in popular culture and accepted as the cultural ideal and norm is the patrilineal joint family (Singh & Bhandari 2012). This cultural model assumes a shared household of three generations – a son, his parents, and his wife and children. It is the male head of the household who controls the money in this family household. The son will direct his earnings to his father, who will then distribute a small amount back to the son for his own needs. The women in the household typically have little involvement in the management of the household's income and expenditure. The mother might be responsible for managing the kitchen, but will not necessarily have a role to play in managing the household budget or paying any bills. She will make requests to her husband for any expenditure she wishes to make. If the son's wife wishes to make a purchase, she will pass her request to the son, her husband. He, in turn, makes requests to his father. Even if the son and his wife leave the household to establish a new household, it is nevertheless expected that he will continue to contribute to the family money, and will draw on their savings to contribute to large investments or purchases being made by the father. Thus, a son interviewed by Singh and Bhandari (2012: 53) explained that he contributed his and his wife's savings to pay for a house his father bought, saying: 'We bought the entire house together in Dad's name. He will give it back to me in a couple of years. It is all in the same family.'

In practice, the joint family ideal can result in a variety of arrangements, which change over time in response to changing circumstances and the life stage of the family members. For example, when there are no sons in a family, the daughters are more likely to contribute to their parents' household. When one son is earning more than other members of the family, he may support not only his father but also his siblings. In some families, all of the sons in a family will share responsibility for managing the family money with their father, while in other households the father maintains strict control over expenditure and rarely involves his sons in conversations about management of the family money, or might involve only some of his sons in these conversations. In some cases, the father will share management of the family money with his brothers, with his sons playing a junior role in the family money. Yet the basic principles remain the same: adult children routinely send money to their parents, as well as routinely receiving money from their parents when needed. Also, it is more important for men to contribute to the family money than it is for women. Indeed, contributing money to their father's household is an essential part of being a 'good son'.

People have been migrating from India to diverse countries around the world since at least the nineteenth century. Typically, this migration has been organized through kinship networks and sustained by chain migration (Voigt-Graf 2005). In recent decades, Indian migrants have been strongly associated with multiple migrations, with members of the family network dispersing across multiple locations. For example, Singh (2006) describes a series of migrations leading to a family being dispersed across India, Malaysia, Australia and the USA. Carmen Voigt-Graf (2005) notes that marriage strategies contribute to this dispersal of kin over time, by encouraging the continuous flow of people as well as money and goods between India and countries such as Australia and Fiji.

When Indian families are transformed by migration, the norms of family persist, including the norms of family money (Singh, Cabraal & Robertson 2010; Singh, Robertson & Cabraal 2012). After they have migrated overseas, sons continue contributing to the family by sending money to their fathers. This financial support ceases only when the parents die, or it will sometimes transform into a combination of in-kind and financial support if the parents relocate to live with the migrant child (Singh, Robertson & Cabraal 2012). Daughters will typically contribute to their husband's family rather than their own parents, although there are exceptions to this, particularly if there are no sons (Singh 2006).

It is important to recognize that this remittance activity continues regardless of whether the parents are in need of the money. As Voigt-Graf (2005: 380) argues, 'while there may be some material benefits resulting from participating in transnational kinship networks for migrants and non-migrants alike, these are not the main underlying reason for engaging in them'. Making a financial contribution to the family is sometimes less a matter of economic necessity, and more a symbol of the continuity of the family as a collective, which is an important goal in and of itself. Gifts are also important in this respect, particularly for women. Both men and women send gifts (of both money and goods) to their parents, siblings and other extended kin as a way of demonstrating their continued commitment to the family, and they receive gifts in the same spirit. In many cases, the transnational family can be dispersed across multiple nations (Voigt-Graf 2004), meaning that more gifts are sometimes sent to other countries in the world than are sent back to the original home in India.

While the sending of gifts and money is perceived by the migrants as important and valuable contributions to the family, they are not always received in this way by non-migrant kin. Indeed, migrants can begin to feel resentful about the imbalance in the relationship over time. Non-migrant kin rarely understand the sacrifices that their migrant kin make in order to be able to send contributions back to the family, and rarely notice that it is the migrant who takes primary responsibility for keeping in touch. The migrant can sometimes feel ignored and overlooked by the kin who remain at home, an issue that can become particularly acute with the death of parents, when inheritance issues are brought to the fore.

In the Indian joint family, it is the norm for sons to receive a family's inheritance and for daughters to be excluded, even though legislation provides for equal inheritance by men and women. In the transnational family, it is also likely that the migrant will be excluded from inheritance of the family home in favour of children who are living locally. In some cases, migrant men and women choose to waive their rights to inheritance of the family property, preferring to maintain good relations with their left-behind kin rather than benefit financially from their parents' death. Being excluded from discussions of the dispersal of the family property can also create tensions within the family and emotional pain for the migrant. As one woman, Hema, explained, 'it hurts emotionally in some ways when I am not taken into consideration, when things are happening there I am completely outside'.

In other cases, migration is a deliberate family strategy for upward social mobility. As Singh (2016) documents in her recent work on international student migration from India, it is often family decisions that result in the departure of children. In these circumstances, the flows of both money and communication have become more reciprocal than was the case for earlier waves of migration. Parents contribute to the initial expenses of travelling and studying overseas and continue to provide financial support if necessary. As soon as possible, students send money to their parents to help pay off loans and return on the investment in their education and migration. If the students settle in the new country, purchasing a home, establishing a business or marrying overseas are also family decisions, often prompting further economic support from the parents to the children. The joint family household might then be recreated if the parents follow their child to the new host country.

In many respects, the joint family relies on a sense of trust that the family will not only receive the contributions of the adult children but will also return financial support to those adult children. Transnational migration disrupts these assumptions of trust. On the one hand, those who remain behind might perceive that those living overseas have no need for the family property. They are living in wealthy nations where they are able to benefit from a better position in the global economy. Generous remittances might reinforce this impression that economic flows will generally flow in only one direction in the global economy, from family in the wealthier nation to family in the poorer nation. Maintaining the image of the successful migrant requires the migrant, too, to accept this interpretation. Asking for money or demanding a share of an inheritance might undermine their status as successful members of the family. At the same time, being included in the inheritance is an important symbol of their status as an equal member in the family, not just financially but also in terms of belonging. When a migrant is not included in these discussions, it can provoke questions about their position within the family. The distribution of money and property, and the decision to remain apart or reunite in the same household, are not simply economic activities. They are the ways in which a family displays who belongs, who is on the periphery, and how valued each member is within the family network. In the absence of everyday opportunities to share intimacy with kin, these symbols of family can become particularly important.

Conclusion

What this tells us is that the intersection of migration and family is a complex picture of opportunities and obligations. Importantly, sustaining transnational families and one's position within those transnational families requires the ongoing commitment and participation of both the migrants and the non-migrants in a kin network in order to be successful. This is something that was easily overlooked by analyses of migration that assumed economic factors as the primary motive for migration. In fact, there is a wide range of reasons prompting the movement of some people from one place to another. Underlying these reasons is a sense of the desire to 'improve' something, usually described as 'helping the family', or 'making a better future'. This is commonly interpreted as the desire to improve material wellbeing for the self and the family. Yet such an interpretation is too narrow to account for the experiences of the transnational families described in this chapter.

While diverse in their details, the accounts of transnational kinship from the Caribbean, Tonga and India do have a number of features in common. Central to this commonality is the role of reputation and status in prompting not only migration but also sustained transnational relationships. When various members of the Smith family left their home on Nevis, they did so not as individuals, but rather as sons, daughters, parents and siblings who hoped to fulfil these culturally prescribed roles to the best of their ability. This was also the case for men and women leaving India to live in Australia, and for examples discussed in earlier chapters, such as those of people leaving the Philippines to work in the UK. From their perspective, migration is a strategy that enables them to better fulfil the economic aspects of their role, by placing them in a better position to provide financial and material support to their parents, children and siblings as well as other extended kin.

The benefits of migration, then, are not only or even primarily economic. Rather, migration allows members of extended family networks to build their reputations as good people, as good members of a family, and as belonging to something larger than their individual ambitions. This requires the migrant to not only succeed economically, but to also succeed socially. Prior to the emergence of the telephone in the 1960s, this social success was likely an imagined one, based largely on memories of what the family and community of origin would have deemed a good person living a good life. Or, for those migrants living in the confines of an ethnic community, success would have been defined by others from the same cultural background who were living nearby. Nevertheless, in both cases, the reference points were in the imagined past, reconstructed from early memories of what a family and a community would have considered valuable and desirable.

Since the emergence of affordable and accessible international communication and transportation, the family of origin can be more readily maintained across time and distance and despite migration. This produces both obligations and opportunities, by both enabling and requiring the migrant to maintain ongoing connections to their family regardless of where they live. The migrant is able to more clearly remain a part of the family network they were raised in, and to fulfil the social expectations of their family of origin. Yet the transnational family is not a straightforward extension of the co-present family. There is a sort of schism that creates the potential for tensions and conflict within the family, which arises out of the perception that things continue as they always have, alongside the reality that the context in which the migrant now lives is actually significantly different to the context in which their left-behind kin remain. While geographic distance may no longer be an issue, cultural distance remains a problem.

Beyond Heteronormative Relationships

It is difficult to think about the family without falling into heteronormative assumptions. These are the assumptions that heterosexuality is not only common, but is the only natural and normal model for human relationships. However, human history and cultural variation is replete with not only diversity in family structures and forms, but also diversity in relationship types, sexuality and gendered norms and behaviours. In this chapter I explore the ways in which global migration and transnational social fields shape the opportunities and constraints of non-heterosexual intimate relationships. After a brief example illustrating the transnational complexities of non-normative relationships, I begin the chapter by considering the concept of 'families of choice'. This concept was introduced in the 1990s to highlight the ways in which non-heteronormative families are required to work within the bounds of heteronormative assumptions while carving out new models for their relationships. I then outline the research on 'queer migrations' and non-heteronormative transnational families. Finally, I discuss the practices associated with transnational friendships. This last section helps to demonstrate that transnational intimacies are not restricted to the heteronormative nuclear family. Indeed, it is through an examination of intimacy across a spectrum of relationships that the limits and insights of individualization theory become apparent, by highlighting the ways in which individuals and groups continually negotiate and renegotiate their roles and relationships, but always in the context of larger cultural norms and social structures.

The right to be a family

Fedora and Turandot had been living together for some years in a same-sex de facto relationship, which was formalized in Germany in 2005

(Hernandez-Losada 2016). They were Colombian citizens, but it was when they were living in Europe that the German government authorized their use of artificial insemination to have their first child (Nagle 2012). Fedora gave birth to their daughter in 2008. When they returned to Colombia soon after, they lodged a request to formalize Turandot's adoption of their daughter. The case became a media sensation in the country when the Instituto Colombiano de Bienestar Familiar (Colombian Institute of Family Welfare) rejected the application, on the grounds that the Colombian constitution did not permit same-sex adoption. The couple began a lengthy legal battle to have their relationship with each other and their joint guardianship of their child recognized as valid and legitimate. They demanded their rights to be seen as and treated as a family by the state.

The constitution in Colombia had been amended in a series of changes from 2007, enabling the formal recognition of the legal property, inheritance and other rights of same-sex couples for the first time (Nagle 2012; Hernandez-Losada 2016). However, it was unclear whether these rights extended to the right to have same-sex parents recognized as equal partners in parenting. The case went through the Superior Court, which found in favour of the couple; it was then successfully appealed, before being heard in the Constitutional Court. Finally, after many years of court attendances and public debates in the media, their claims were legitimated. Meanwhile, the broader set of Colombian laws and regulations concerned with gender, sexuality and families were also undergoing significant change, including a 2015 court decision to allow homosexual couples to adopt and the legalization of same-sex marriage in 2016. After decades of Colombians fleeing the country to seek asylum in the USA on grounds of being persecuted for their sexuality, Colombia was arguably leading the way in marriage equality (Nagle 2012; Brodzinsky 2016).

The story of Fedora and Turandot helps to highlight the complexities of non-heterosexual families and migration in an age of globalization. Couples who are recognized as having rights in one nation have those same rights challenged or ignored in another nation. They become aware of Western discourses of human rights and sexual equality through the global circulation of Western media, culture and ideas, and yet their capacity and desire to access those rights and equalities vary depending on where they are geographically located, what forms of citizenship and visas they are able to access, and their positioning in local social and cultural contexts. At the same time, national discourses, laws and policies are under pressure to transform in response to global shifts in social and cultural expectations regarding human rights and the circulation of their citizens through international spaces. For example, by conceiving and giving birth to a daughter in Germany, something that would have been virtually impossible in Colombia, Turnadot and Fedora effectively forced their own government and society to more fully debate the rights of non-heterosexual couples to have a family of their own.

Heterosexuality and the family

One of the central pillars of the nuclear family is the assumption of heterosexuality. Parsons' model of the functionality of the nuclear family was based on the idea that the only valid form of family was one consisting of a co-resident adult man and adult woman who produce their own biological children. This assumption provides the necessary support for the further assumption that men and women naturally have different, complementary roles within the nuclear family, the man earning an income in the public sphere and the woman providing unpaid care in the private sphere. It is a model of the family that relies on heteronormative assumptions about sexuality, gender identities, gender relations, intergenerational relations and social reproduction. It is also a set of assumptions and ideas that fails to withstand the growing evidence of diversity. This diversity takes multiple forms. Many people never live in households and families that are recognizably nuclear family households. Moreover, even people who do live in nuclear family households are not likely to live in them for their entire lives. They are likely to live in arrangements deviating from this norm at various points in the life course, including when they initially leave their parental home (when they might live in a shared house or live alone) and when their own children leave their home as adults (leaving them in a couple household, living alone or possibly in a shared house arrangement).

There is also considerable diversity in how the nuclear family household reproduces itself. The gendered division of labour, for example, is gradually undergoing a transformation. Men are increasingly participating in caregiving activities and responsibilities as well as paid work. More often, it is women who disrupt expectations that they remain at home as unpaid caregivers, by entering the public world of paid work (see Chapter 4, Chapter 6). These are often seen as a challenge to the nuclear family household model, sparking various complaints that the family is 'in decline' or 'under threat'. Yet the alternatives that tend to be perceived as a more fundamental challenge to the nuclear family household are drawn from a different set of alternatives. They are present in the growing awareness of the various families, households, relational and living arrangements of gender- and sexually diverse people.

Families of choice?

Gender and sexual diversity is not new. What is new is that throughout the second half of the twentieth century, gender- and sexually diverse people have been participating in social movements and organizations aimed at seeking equal rights (Altman 1993; 2013). Part of this has included lobbying for full recognition of the rights of same-sex couples to have their unions recognized and to have their parenting rights and their children respected and acknowledged (Weeks, Heaphy & Donovan 2001). That is, they have sought recognition of alternative models of living within families and family households that go beyond a male breadwinner, female carer and dependent children model of heterosexuality. This is not to suggest that all gender- and sexually diverse people expect or desire their household or living arrangements to be recognized as familial. Indeed, many seek to live completely outside of the practices and discourses of 'the family' (Weeks 1991). However, some do wish to have their social relationships and intimate practices recognized as a form of family, with all of the legitimacy, desirability, security and support that the term encompasses, without necessarily reproducing the rigid expectations of gender and sexual identities and roles.

According to Anthony Giddens, the emphasis in these family forms is on individuals making choices and negotiating responsibilities and obligations in democratic ways according to the desires and preferences of the individuals. It is for this reason that Giddens has identified same-sex couples as the vanguard of the 'pure relationship', the democratic couple relationship in which each partner remains as long as the relationship benefits them, rather than out of a sense of duty or obligation. He suggests they form the vanguard precisely because the assumptions and rules associated with the nuclear family household simply do not work for the relationships of gender- and sexually diverse people. In a non-heterosexual couple, it is not immediately clear which partner might be expected to take the role of primary carer, or which might be expected to be the primary income earner. Rather, the partners in the couple must negotiate who plays which roles, for how long, and in what ways. In this way, same-sex couples exemplify the practice of reflexivity that is presumed to be a central part of late modernity (see Chapter 1). In the absence of clear rules of interaction, they must produce their own rules and a 'life of their own' in response to their unique abilities, opportunities, constraints and preferences (Beck & Beck-Gernsheim 1995). One of the constraints they face is lack of acceptance by some members of the broader society, sometimes including within their own family of origin.

It has thus been suggested that, as a result of both choice and compulsion, gender- and sexually diverse people create their own forms of families – what have been called 'families of choice' (Weeks, Heaphy & Donovan 2001) or 'families we choose' (Weston 1991). These terms are indicative of the complexity of understanding the family beyond heteronormative sexual and gender assumptions. The saying, 'you can choose your friends, but not your family' points to some of the expectations associated with biological kin relations – that they are stable and enduring, and are a product of 'fate' rather than a matter of choice (Pahl & Spencer 2004). Friends, on the other hand, are presumed to be chosen. As a result, they are also assumed to be less stable and reliable, more fluid and flexible, and more likely to share our interests and perspectives at that particular point in time (Willmott 1986). It is thought that gender- and sexually diverse people might be more likely to find people with whom they share more in common among friends and the LGBTQIA community than within their own biological family, who are less likely to understand and appreciate their experiences of diversity.

The concept 'families' of choice suggests an effort to affirm that the relationships produced in gender and sexually diverse communities are stronger, more stable and more reliable than friendships are usually presumed to be.

Although they are not determined by biological descent or formal marriage, they are considered just as sustaining, long lasting and supportive as the sorts of relationships that are presumed to naturally come under the label of 'family'. A participant in research conducted by Weeks and colleagues (2001: 10) explained it in the following way,

> Because I have kind of, at the moment anyway, fairly negative feelings about my biological family, it [the term 'family'] maybe is not something I would actually immediately apply to my friends and the people who are important to me. Having said that, you know, I think the way I think about those people is the way that ... generally people would regard family.

What is being emphasized here is that family are expected to behave in particular ways towards each other – these include being supportive, reliable, accepting and involved. By identifying some people as 'family', even when they are not related through blood or marriage, it is this set of expectations in relation to the idea of family that is being emphasized and prioritized.

Families of choice have long been recognized as important for people who are gender and sexually diverse. However, the term has now also been extended to an understanding of *all* families in late-modern Western societies. As we have seen in earlier chapters, it is now more commonly accepted that families are not a stable institutional form. Rather, they are produced through practices, displays, negotiated obligations and choices that reproduce some bonds while allowing others to disappear or fall away. It is now more readily accepted that all families are a product of ongoing social interactions, that 'families of fate' – over which we have little choice – are increasingly being replaced by 'families of choice' (Pahl & Spencer 2004) for not only non-heterosexual but also heterosexual family units. This is in part because efforts to establish the family as a particular type of structure (Murdock 1965) or as a particular set of obligations have failed to withstand empirical scrutiny (Finch & Mason 1993), giving way to an understanding of family as produced through social interactions.

In late modernity, it is argued, traditional roles, identities, structures and expectations are in decline, being replaced by the requirement for people to cobble together their own life narrative, relationships and meaning (Giddens 1992; Beck & Beck-Gernsheim 1995). Under these conditions, the family has become more flexible. To some extent, people are able to identify who belongs and who does not belong in their own particular family group. Extended periods of co-residence or mutual interdependency help to reinforce kin-like and kin relationships, just as disengagement from others can reduce the kin-like qualities of those people who are related by marriage or biological descent. Rituals and routines of collectivity, what have been called 'family practices' (Morgan 2011) and 'family displays' (Finch 2007), help to produce and reinforce relationships that are perceived as kin-like, distinguishing them from other relationships that are perceived as more fluid and friend-like. While marriage and shared biological descent might still provide the foundations of family and kin relationships for many people, they are neither necessary to nor sufficient for the production of family or kinship.

The suffusion of families and friends

A growing body of empirical evidence is demonstrating that the presumed foundations of the family in marriage and blood are better understood as a set of symbolic resources rather than 'proof' of a family relationship. Indeed, blood and marriage are frequently adapted and transformed by people in order to make sense of their own sets of close, intimate relationships, which can include fictive kin, family-like friends and friend-like family members as well as or instead of standard family and kinship roles and relationships. Rather than family being readily identifiable as a particular set of biological and marital relations, it is probably better understood as those people with whom we have stronger, more enduring, more stable or apparently 'given' relationships that are characterized by obligation and commitment. In contrast, friends are perceived as more fluid and chosen, less reliable, more fragile and more strongly associated with pleasure, enjoyment and fun (see In Focus 8.1). However, these are ideal types. In practice, there is a great deal of suffusion between family and friends – that is, some family are perceived as having friend-like qualities such as pleasure and light-heartedness, while some friends are perceived as having family-like qualities, such as obligation and commitment, as well as being 'given' rather than chosen (Pahl & Spencer 2004).

For people who are gender and sexually diverse, the processes of distinguishing between family-like and friend-like roles and relationships have been foregrounded by their lack of access to assumed narratives of gender and sexuality in the family. Some are rejected by the people with whom they share biological descent, because of their non-normative gender or sexual identities. Others reject the assumptions and practices of heteronormativity as uncomfortable or undesirable. As a result, they are prompted to produce alternative models of family, community, solidarity and friendship that enable them to enjoy stable, supportive relationships as well as fluid, flexible, pleasurable relationships without being bound to fit heteronormative models of gender and sexuality. For some, this involves having highly significant family-like relationships with friends that replace family relationships that might otherwise be produced by shared biological descent.

What is also clear is that the identifying of relationships as more 'family-like' or more 'friend-like' changes over time. This temporal aspect of relationships was demonstrated in work by Pahl and Pevalin (2005), who used longitudinal survey data to analyse relationships with family and friends over time. What they discovered is that younger people are more likely to have friends outside of their kinship network, and older people are more likely to have their friends drawn from within their kinship network. Partners are defined as family, and also provide one of the most important sources of friendship, but so do other family members such as children, siblings and other relatives. The pessimistic argument that Bauman (2003) puts forward, suggesting that

---

In Focus 8.1 Suffusion and ideal types: family, friends and acquaintances

At first glance, the ideal types of family, friends and acquaintances seem to indicate that these are three distinct categories of relationships, with family the bonds that are imposed on us, friends the bonds that we choose, and acquaintances lacking any bonding qualities at all. The ideal types look something like this:

	Family	Friends	Acquaintances
Frequency of contact	High	Medium	Low
Sense of intimacy	High	High	Low
Source of support	High	Medium	Low
Longevity of relationship	High	Medium	Low
Capacity to choose	Low	Medium	High
Disposability	Low	Medium	High

However, the ideal types rarely stand up to scrutiny. This is captured by the idea of suffusion. In part, this is an acknowledgement that in practice we might identify the same person as friend, family or acquaintance at different times in our lives; for example, an acquaintance may become a friend over time, then become a family member through marriage, and return to an acquaintance over time after divorce. But, more importantly, it refers to the fact that we identify people as more family-like or friend-like in order to acknowledge the qualities of intimacy, contact, support and so on that we perceive in the relationship itself. Thus, some family members are also our best friends, and some friends are so close that they are considered to be family.

---

we all participate in a grand supermarket of relationships, quickly discarding some as we collect others, is not supported by this empirical research. In fact, it seems that most people, most of the time, continue to interact with the same group of friends and family over the life course, bringing some in closer than others at different times in their biography. People's personal communities are not boundless, and the people they can draw on as friends and family tend to be limited to those who share physical space, have a shared history or have interests or perspectives in common with them. That is, rather than being an infinite set of choices, the pool from which family and friends are drawn is likely to be limited, and seems to contract over the life course.

Personal life and emotion work

Rather than try to distinguish between family and friends, some scholars have suggested that it is more helpful to step outside of these terms. Rather than try to work with terms that have heteronormativity and gender ideologies embedded within them, there is an effort to seek alternative terms that enable sexual and gender identities within relationships to be analysed, rather than assumed. Thus, Pahl and Spencer (2004) talk about 'personal communities' and Carol Smart (2007a) refers to 'personal life' (see also May 2011) as a way of capturing relationships without being bound by gendered and sexual norms. These terms are meant to go beyond the institution of the family, but they are not intended to reproduce the assumptions of individualization theory. They do not place the autonomous, isolated 'individual' at the centre of analysis. Rather, the 'person' and the 'personal' are conceptualized as distinctively relational, embedded in and constructed through relationships and interactions with others.

This idea harks back to the symbolic interactionists of the mid-twentieth century, who argued that the self is constructed through our interactions with others (Mead 1934; Goffman 1959). They argued that, from infancy and throughout the life course, we come to know ourselves through the responses of others to us, and come to internalize social roles through our relationships and interactions with others. In doing so, we internalize the various symbolic cultural repertoires that shape what we perceive as possible and desirable for a person with our (gendered and sexualized) body, predispositions and abilities. That is, an account of personal life positions the individual as necessarily part of a complex system or network of interdependencies, roles and responsibilities that shape their options, opportunities and constraints throughout the life course.

This approach provides an interesting and important addition to the notion of 'choice' in late modernity, including in relation to one's biography, family and friends. Much as we seem to have choices, these choices are always necessarily constrained by the interactional experiences of socialization and the cultural models that we have internalized. This extends not only to our behaviours and practices, but also to our emotional states and the feelings that we attach to the choices available to us. Emotions are not simply 'felt', but are socially and culturally constructed (Lupton 1998). Some emotions are culturally positioned as more acceptable or more desirable, and others as signifying a problem to be solved. Furthermore, the acceptability of emotional states is gendered and classed, in what Airlie Hochschild (1979) has called sets of 'feeling rules'. Thus, for example, we learn gender-specific feeling rules as children. In many circumstances, women are discouraged from being angry, while men are discouraged from crying in front of others.

We learn to manage our emotional states in order to fit the feeling rules, by doing what Hochschild (1979) calls 'emotion work'. It is this emotion work that ensures that 'good' airline attendants suppress their own emotional states in order to present a calm, happy demeanour to their clients, and that 'good' mothers suppress their anger with a misbehaving child in order to present them with a calm, loving response to their behaviour. In some cases, there is a clash or a 'pinch' between the situation and the emotions that are felt. This is often described by gender- and sexually diverse people, who describe 'feeling different' to other people around them, sometimes resolving to suppress these feelings, and in other cases deciding to find a social context in which they can legitimately explore them. The internalization of feeling rules thus contributes to people feeling comfortable in some social spaces, and uncomfortable in others where they feel unable to fully express their sense of self.

The notions of families of choice and personal life, then, alert us to a number of points. First, that the family is an active construction, not entirely a given. Even relationships that are based on marriage and shared biological descent must be continually produced through social interactions. Second, that the distinction between family and friends is often very blurred, with some who are apparently 'family' also being labelled as friends, and some friends who do not fulfil the biological or marital dimensions of family nevertheless being labelled as 'family' or as 'family-like'. Third, this is particularly evident in the personal lives of gender- and sexually diverse people, who are less likely to find that their feelings and preferences automatically fit the gendered and sexualized assumptions of the heterosexual nuclear family model. They are instead required to construct new forms of relationality that fit the emotional expectations of secure, stable family relations while avoiding the assumptions regarding gender and sexuality that are strongly associated with cultural models of the family. Fourth, as with Fedora and Turandot, they are also required to negotiate international regimes that shape their capacity to construct satisfying personal lives, families and alternatives to family.

Queer migrations

One of the ways in which gender- and sexually diverse people manage the lack of fit between their feelings and their social context is to move away from their social context, to migrate to a place where they will feel a greater sense of belonging. Movement and migration, then, are an important part of the narrative of 'coming out' as gender or sexually diverse in a heteronormative society. There are two forms that this narrative tends to take. First is a story of men and women moving from rural to urban areas in order to explore their gender and sexual diversity. Second is an account of people moving from underdeveloped non-Western nations to developed Western nations for the same reason. That is, it is generally assumed and argued that gender and sexual diversity is more readily accepted in urban, Western contexts, and is a problem for those living in rural and non-Western contexts. Each of these movements have been identified as forms of 'queer migration' (Luibhéid & Cantú 2005; Luibhéid 2008), defined as migration that is specifically motivated by 'non-heterosexual identities, practices and performances' (Gorman-Murray 2009: 443).

Kath Weston's (1995) classic article, 'Get thee to a big city' was one of the first to identify migration as significant to gender and sexual diversity. Migration is presented in her account as a necessary part of 'coming out' and of developing a non-normative identity. It is characterized by a narrative of separation from a person's closest family and friendship network in order to explore alternative identities and experiment with new practices and behaviours. This necessarily requires meeting new people who share a sense of diversity. In some cases, it involves geographic relocation from a rural town to an urban centre, or from a non-Western to a Western nation (Smith 2012). Yet its equivalent also exists for those who grow up in Western cities known for their gay communities, who still need to create a break from their current social circle and urban space in order to seek entry into the gay community that exists in another part of the city. This could be just as daunting a journey as one that crosses national borders or involves a shift from the rural to the urban (Weston 1995).

Importantly, Weston (1995) argues that not everybody 'found' the gay community they were looking for when they migrated. Often, the community they had imagined from a distance turned out to be an illusion. Instead, they discovered people whom they did not identify as 'like them', but rather people who fulfilled a set of clichés about gay men, lesbian women and others that they rejected in their own exploration of gender and sexual identities. This insight has since been extended by a range of studies that seek to document the role of migration and mobilities in the lives of people who are gender and sexually diverse. One of the key findings is that the rural–urban migration and its equivalent are possibly best understood as 'transitions' and transitory rather than unilinear migrations (Annes & Redlin 2012). Travelling to a centre of gender and sexual diversity is an important strategy for people to find a greater concentration of diversity against which the self can be constructed and from which potential partners can be identified. However, movement after this can take multiple directions and be generated by a variety of motivations. Moreover, how migration takes place, where, and with what outcomes is historically specific, contingent on the broader context of heteronormativity within which gender- and sexually diverse people are navigating their lives (Jennings 2010; Lewis 2014; Vasquez 2014).

Migration is not a unilinear process from rural to urban, or from heterosexual to non-heterosexual communities (Gorman-Murray 2009). Previous communities and identities remain significant after the transition period. The identities and relationships within which a person grew up often retain their hold and value after migration and beyond the transition, in spite of their heteronormativity. Many rural people, for example, return to the place in which they grew up or a similar, less populous rural location at a later point in their life (Cooke & Rapino 2007; Gorman-Murray & Nash 2016). Some reject the clichés and clones of urban gay life, preferring to return to the place where they can express other parts of themselves, including their rural identities and their gender identities, more easily (Annes & Redlin 2012). Others actively seek reunion with their family of origin, in their town of origin, especially after having found a partner (Cooke & Rapino 2007; Gorman-Murray 2009; Blidon 2016).

International queer migration is typically understood to be motivated by the desire to explore identities that are not permitted in the home country, as well as to avoid discrimination and persecution in the home country (Howe, Zaraysky & Lorentzen 2008; Yue 2016). Yet, as with rural–urban migration, recent research has demonstrated a broader range of experiences in the home country, motivations for migration, and ongoing movements after the initial international migration (Adihartono 2014; Carrillo & Fontdevila 2014; Lewis & Mills 2016). Responses to the different contexts in the home country and the destination country help to shape gender and sexual identities in complex ways, contingent on opportunities that people find to have relationships, participate in employment, and maintain relationships with family and friends in the home country. For example, gay men and women from the Philippines working overseas find it difficult to find work as domestic servants, due to local rejection of their sexuality. However, they are able to fill a niche providing personal services to other workers from the Philippines, such as hairstyling and selling beauty products. Gay men report being able to adopt more feminine roles than their female equivalents, who are associated with the 'dirty work' of domestic labour (Parreñas 2001). Also, men in Mexico are able to explore (or reject) fluid models of masculinity and homosexuality in the USA in ways that vary from their experiences in the home country (Carrillo & Fontdevila 2014).

Transnational families of choice?

The focus on queer migration has not been accompanied by a sustained research focus on the role of families in the lives of migrant men and women who are gender and sexually diverse. This is part of a broader tendency to overlook the variety of motivations for migration that apply to gender- and sexually diverse people, including education, employment and life-course events (Lewis 2014; Lewis & Mills 2016). But it is possibly also because studies of queer migration tend to represent the family as something to 'escape' from (Wimark 2016a, 2016b). An alternative approach is to identify the family as a set of ongoing relationships that are negotiated and engaged with, even if that occurs at a distance. This has been explored at some length in the context of heterosexual families, but remains underexplored in the lives of people who are gender and sexually diverse (although see Vasquez 2014).

There is now a consensus that the experience of gender and sexual diversity, while informed by the global circulation of identities and consumption patterns, is also culturally specific (Altman 2001). This includes an awareness that given family relationships may seem to be more significant or more binding in some social and cultural contexts than in others. For example, Anthony Ocampo (2014) argues that the negotiation of gender and sexual diversity is particularly complex for the children of immigrants in the USA. He suggests that the children of Filipino and Latino migrants 'may feel less inclined to come out for fear of losing socio-economic or social support from family and co-ethnic backgrounds' but also 'may be concerned about how their gender presentation and sexual identity may adversely affect the status and reputation of the family within the larger immigrant community' (Ocampo 2014: 158). Similarly, attention has been drawn to the ways in which people from non-Anglo, non-Western ethnic and cultural backgrounds have coming out narratives and experiences that place a greater emphasis on protecting family relationships, reputations and expectations while also seeking to explore diverse gender and sexual identities (Wimark 2016a). Migration for employment and education has emerged as one of the legitimate strategies for protecting family relationships while creating a social and geographic distance that enables exploration and expression of diverse gender and sexual identities (Acosta 2008; Smith 2012). At the same time, globalization is rendering these strategies somewhat less effective. It is becoming increasingly difficult for a migrant to maintain a secret about their intimate life from family 'back home', who are increasingly likely to visit and to keep in continual communication.

The ongoing significance of the family for those who are gender and sexually diverse in Western as well as non-Western contexts has perhaps been too little emphasized. It is true that family are often 'left behind' in order to discover the self as a gender- or sexually diverse person. However, it is also true that 'given' family members remain important in the lives of gender- and sexually diverse people at various points in the life course. Moreover, this seems to be an increasingly significant phenomenon as social acceptance of gender and sexual diversity is becoming more widespread and new, more complex images of diversity are able to circulate through both traditional media (such as television) and the internet. Historically, participation in a gay community has been one of the few avenues available to people who wish to explore and express alternative identities and lifestyles. However, this is changing. New sources of information and a greater variety of models are now available for constructing identities (Thing 2010; Wimark 2016b). Also, more people are now able to access marriage equality and equal opportunities to have and raise children. In these circumstances, the rupture between the family of origin and the movement through the life course is significantly reduced. This might also contribute to people becoming more open to the prospect of retaining links with given family members throughout the life course (Smart 2007b; Ocampo 2014).

In spite of clear gaps in existing research, there is some work that is beginning to point to the ways in which migration and gender and sexual diversity intersect with love, family and relationships. Rebecca Jennings (2010) suggests that these intersections are particularly important for women who, more so than men, are expected to remain embedded in supportive relations of care and support with family. She describes the historical role for lesbians in family networks. As unmarried women, they were expected to be able to (and often did) contribute to the care of elderly or sick family members or young children, and to the family income. Women who resisted these roles would sometimes use migration for purposes of education or employment as a strategy for creating distance between themselves and family obligations. However, it would be wrong to limit this insight to women only. A growing range of accounts are demonstrating that men, too, are engaged in negotiating relationships as part of their narratives of migration and of gender and sexual identities over the life course.

One of the clearest examples comes from men and women who migrate to follow their partner or relocate to their partner's home country or town; that is, migration specifically for relationship reasons. In heterosexual couples, this is easily identified as spousal or partner migration (see Chapter 3), and is often made available to those in common law or de facto relationships as well as those in formal marriage relationships. However, for non-heterosexuals there are often significant obstacles to migration, including in relation to partner or family migration across national borders (Luibhéid 2002; Luibhéid & Cantú 2005). For example, in the USA there was a curious situation for many years in which a same-sex couple consisting of an American citizen and a foreign citizen could be legally married in some states, yet the foreign-born partner was not able to migrate to the USA as a family member. This was due to the Defense of Marriage Act, which defined marriage as exclusively heterosexual for all federal purposes, including immigration, overriding state-specific recognition of same-sex unions (Titshaw 2010). At the same time, it was possible for a same-sex partner to enter into the USA as a 'visitor' when they were accompanying someone who was temporarily entering the country for work or education reasons. The laws were complex and confusing, sometimes recognizing the legitimacy of same-sex relationships, and at other times denying them.

The Defense of Marriage Act has since been repealed, and same-sex couples are now able to apply for family migration. However, many couples remain caught in difficult situations as a result of past applications of the law. For example, some are now unable to take advantage of the new laws because they are residing illegally in the USA as part of an earlier strategy to maintain their relationship in spite of the previous laws (Huntley 2013). Around the world, laws still remain highly variable, with the only consistent factor being a tendency towards discriminating against or failing to fully recognize same-sex couples (Elman 2000; Tryfonidou 2014).

In Australia, it has been possible for same-sex couples to apply for a partner migration visa since 1985 (Yue 2008). However, applications must be made using the 'de facto partner' category rather than 'spouse' or 'fiancé', as Australia still does not permit or recognize same-sex marriage. Same-sex couples must also demonstrate that they have lived in a 'marriage-like' relationship, a demand that reinforces heterosexual norms of relationality and partnering (Holt 2004). In other parts of the world, the situation is also improving in uneven ways. In the UK and Canada, for example, same-sex couples have been permitted to apply for partner migration since 1997 and 2002 respectively, although requirements to demonstrate evidence of cohabitation continue to create problems for some (McGloin 1999–2000; LaViolette 2004).

The frequent challenges to these laws by couples who want to maintain their relationships indicate that, just like heterosexual couples, same-sex couples also often seek to have long-lasting relationships in which it is sometimes necessary or desirable to use migration as a means of being together. In his research, Andrew Gorman-Murray (2009) explores the intersections of love and migration for same-sex couples by documenting the moves that people make in order to be near partners or to be at a distance from ex-partners. One of the more mobile participants in his work is Sue, who explains that almost all of her migrations are motivated by her intimate and family relationships. Unlike the standard narrative, Sue's coming out experience did not require migration, as she received strong support from her family. It was not until she was ready to move in with her first significant partner that she left the family home, and it was her parents' home that she returned to when the relationship broke down a few years later. When she met a new partner, they first lived together in Sydney and then in a town where both sets of parents were living. However, as the relationship went through a turbulent period of togetherness and separation, Sue found herself moving between cities, states and towns, sometimes to live with her partner, and at other times to move away from her so as to avoid the risk of meeting her accidentally in the street. Her pattern of migration, always intranational, was also always motivated by the desire to be near to some members of her family, such as her parents and partner, and far from others, including ex-partners.

Migration and the fluidity of sexual identities

In some cases, the relationship between migration and relationships is a little more blurred. Consider, for example, the case of Karim (Fassin & Salcedo 2015). He migrated from Algeria for political reasons, aiming to seek asylum in France. While waiting for his application to be heard, he met Damien and the two later formalized their union by getting married. When his application for asylum on political grounds was rejected, he requested asylum on the basis of being gay, citing his marriage to Damien as evidence. The application was accepted and he was granted refugee status and the right to remain in France. In the process, he also relinquished his capacity to return to Algeria.

The researchers who reported Karim's narrative, Eric Fassin and Manuela Salcedo (2015), point out that it is not possible to see his migration as a 'queer migration'. His initial movement from Algeria to France was for political and safety reasons. However, the permission to remain in France was on the basis of Karim's sexuality. Moreover, it is not entirely clear that Karim identifies as 'gay'. In Algeria, Karim reports, many men have sex with men, even after having married women. But they do not identify as 'gay', this being considered normal, acceptable male behaviour. At the same time, Karim's sexuality and sexual practices in France are also more complex than his partner would like. One of the reasons Damien sought to marry Karim was in order to discourage him from having sexual encounters with women, so that he could fully embrace his gay identity. Although Karim married Damien, it is unclear whether Karim is willing to accept this limitation on his sexual behaviour. Karim has also resisted informing his mother in Algeria that he has married a man in France, preferring to leave this part of his life ambiguous and simply deflect his mother's claims that he is of an age when he should marry.

Karim's story highlights the complexities of choice in the creation and maintenance of relationships. He chooses to marry Damien, a choice that would not be possible or desirable in Algeria. In the process, he becomes identified as gay – by both his partner and by the state – even though this identity is not necessarily one that he would choose for himself, or fully accepts.

By embracing this identity in France, he is able to remain in the country, but in the process must give up any chance of returning to Algeria. He chooses to keep his marriage secret from his mother, perhaps in part because such a decision has no meaning in Algeria, except as an indicator of his assimilation of French, Western practices and identities. The story demonstrates that Karim is able to make choices, but each of these choices comes with new obligations, requirements and constraints, limiting his future options.

In some cases, it is the migration of other family members that opens the opportunity for people to express diverse gender or sexual identities. This appears to be the case for Lal, whose story is included in Michele Gamburd's (2000) account of Sri Lankan transnational families. Lal's brother Chandradasa and Chandradasa's wife Indrani both worked at a distance from their family home. Chandradasa worked in a nearby city and was able to return every few weeks, while Indrani worked overseas, able to return once a year or less. In their absence, Chandradasa's mother was nominated as the primary caregiver of their household and children. However, her arthritis made this physically difficult. In practice, it was Lal who performed the feminine tasks of caring for the household, cooking the meals and looking after the children. He suffered constant teasing and bemusement from other villagers living nearby, yet continued this work for over 12 years. Although 'there was not even the hint of rumor suggesting that Lal might be actively homosexual', his practices nevertheless raised questions about his masculinity. At times, Lal seemed to resist his feminized role. For example, he quickly accepted an opportunity for temporary masculine work on a construction site. At other times he seemed to relish his role as caregiver, taking pride in the high-quality food he prepared for the family. Migration had opened an alternative gender identity for Lal, even though he remained firmly in geographic place.

These stories of migration, relationships and gender and sexual identities confirm that it is problematic to assume that people are autonomous, isolated individuals. Wimark (2016a: 665) argues that 'to understand gay and lesbian migration, the unit of the analysis cannot rely solely on the individual but must also acknowledge the whole family'. This can be extended in two ways. First, to understand any person's migration, the unit of analysis must be larger than the individual and must include attention to the position of that individual within complex relationships of interdependency, support and affection. This is not a feature limited to the experiences of gay and lesbian migration, or to specific ethnic or cultural groups. Second, the unit of analysis should include the family, but also needs to expand to include a broader range of relationships, including friends (Wimark 2016b). In choosing to relocate, some relationships are being ended or at the very least disrupted and transformed, while others are being made possible. One insight from the families of choice research is that significant relationships are not limited to those created by marriage or shared biological descent. It is important that we do not overlook the important role that friends also play in shaping a person's opportunities, constraints and sense of self, or in creating and sustaining family-like relations of support and care.

Transnational friendships

There are two key tools for maintaining relationships at a distance and across national borders: visits and communication technologies. In descriptions of how people use these tools to keep in touch with others, there is a tendency to refer in the same breath to both 'family and friends'. This conflation of family and friends is in keeping with the accounts of families of choice and the suffusion of family and friends that were discussed earlier in this chapter. But is there also a need to distinguish between the roles of family and friends in transnational relationships? Do friends play a different role to family, and do friendships require different practices in order to maintain them?

Attention to the role and practices of transnational friendships has been relatively limited. Unlike transnational families, there have been no major studies that have explored the meanings of transnational friendships or the practices used to sustain them (but see Conradson & Latham 2005; Policarpo 2016). However, in keeping with the conceptualization of families of choice, friends are often incorporated into discussions of family relationships. This is likely to be because many of the same issues apply. For example, like families, friendships must be sustained through ongoing practices of intimacy and display (Finch 2007; Morgan 2011). Over long distances, this is usually accomplished through a combination of visits and communication technologies (Baldassar, Baldock & Wilding 2007).

Friends also play a role that is distinct from families. Indeed, it has been argued that friends have become particularly important in late-modern societies, in which the certainties of tradition and institutions such as the family can no longer be relied upon. In a society that is contingent and insecure, and in which people are required to be flexible and reflexive, friendships are arguably a more salient form of relationship. Unlike family, friendships are more capable of being multiple, allowing a person to better manage their plural interests and identities in a complex society (Allan 1989; Adams & Allan 1998). Unlike the family relationships that are given, friendships rely upon self-disclosure and the identification and assertion of similarities in values, interests and perspectives (Jamieson 1998). Friendships also enable the expansion of a social network, providing important opportunities for building social capital in a global context, considered to be particularly important for migrants (Phillips & Potter 2009). These factors all contribute to the possibility that friendship is becoming a more central form of relationship in late-modern societies (Allan 1998).

At the same time, fears have been expressed that friendships are increasingly superficial and unreliable. Zygmunt Bauman (2003), for example, talks of the disposability of relationships in late modernity, which are based on loosely knit networks rather than reliable ties to others. This is partly linked to the emergence of social media as a means of expanding social networks without ensuring their sustainability. Facebook, for example, provides the opportunity to 'friend' a limitless number of people, raising concerns that the term 'friend' has been devalued. However, it is important to recognize that there is a wide range of types of friends and that friendships perform a wide range of diverse functions (Pahl 2000). At one end of the spectrum are 'family-like' friends and fictive kin, who are embedded in dense relations of support and exchange. These are less likely to be easily discarded. At the other end are what Morgan (2009) might call 'acquaintances'. These could include people whom you would speak to when you see them, but from whom there are no particular expectations of support. They might also include people who are identified as 'friends' on social media, with whom there is ongoing communication, but who might rarely or never be physically met with. These friends will, nevertheless, be a potential or latent source of support. They might be called upon to meet or provide advice, for example, if a person is planning to travel to their location for work or tourism. Or they might provide a source of online emotional support during a period of grieving.

Communication technologies and long-distance relationships

The emergence of new online technologies has transformed the capacity and nature of friendships. New friendships can be developed online, for example, through joining online forums that support a particular personal interest (Kendall 2002). Old friendships can also be maintained. For example, in her research, Teresa Davis (2010) describes the ways in which a group of migrant and non-migrant women who attended university together use an online space to keep in touch with each other 20 years later. Their friendship is based on the shared experience at university in India. However, it is sustained through their interactions with each other in the e-group that they share, in spite of being dispersed across different locations in India, Australia, the USA and elsewhere.

Davis identifies at least three functions for this friendship group. First, it provides them with a space to share religious and cultural rituals with each other. They describe to each other the traditional dishes they are preparing for their family, recall similar events they participated in when they all lived in India, and check that they are reproducing the ritual requirements correctly. Second, it provides them with a space in which to negotiate their identities as migrants and as Indians. They critique other migrants, support each other's choices and preferences, and reinforce a sense of their collective identity in spite of dispersal. Third, they recall memories of the place they once shared together, even as they acknowledge that it no longer exists in the way it once did. In this way, they knit together the fragmentations of past, present and future identities and relationships. Through the maintaining of their friendship, these women are also able to maintain a sense of their present selves as connected to their past.

This transcending of time and place is also important for young people from migrant backgrounds. By using social media and other online tools, young people are able to transcend their local context in order to connect with friends living in their country of birth and in their parents' country of birth. In the process, they are able to practise language and cultural knowledge that helps to stitch together the different places that are significant in their lives. For example, Julia, a 15-year-old in the USA from Colombia, uses MySpace to connect with her Colombian and other friends at her US high school, as well as her friends and relatives in Colombia (McGinnis, Goodstein-Stolzenberg & Saliani 2007). She also uses it to communicate her position on political and social issues to other immigrant youth, particularly other youth from Latin America. She uses multiple languages, depending on whom she hopes to communicate with, and feels connected to a wide network of friends and acquaintances.

Friends and friendship networks clearly play an important role in providing opportunities to expand transnational networks and express cultural identities. This has emerged as particularly important for migrants and for global professionals, but also extends to the children of migrants and to youth from refugee backgrounds (Kennedy 2004; Colic-Peisker 2010; Wilding 2012; Ryan 2015; Lund et al. 2016). Yet the practice of friendship in global, mediated contexts is not necessarily easy. Online spaces for maintaining friendships, such as Facebook, require users to learn and become skilled in a whole new set of social expectations (Holmes 2011). Moreover, these expectations vary across cultural contexts, providing new opportunities for both cosmopolitanism and misunderstandings (Kraemer 2014). These are skills that people actively develop, in order to build intimate ties with others over time and space.

Conclusion

For individualization theorists, friends are arguably the model of contemporary relationships – intense while they last, but easy to dispose of when they no longer satisfy. Relationships are presumed to be equal, undemanding and disposable. However, these claims are increasingly under challenge by the empirical research. First, not all friends are disposable. Some entail significant ongoing relations of obligation and support, rendering them more 'family-like'. At the same time, given relationships within the family are also often 'friend-like' in terms of the pleasures they provide, if not in their capacity to be discarded. In both families and friendship networks, it seems that there is a wide range of qualities of relationship, some of which are relatively loose and insignificant, others of which are binding and entail significant reciprocal commitments to care and support.

Increasingly, these relationships are being shaped by a range of processes and dynamics associated with globalization. New communication technologies and access to affordable travel are transforming the disposability of relationships. Friends considered discarded many decades ago are now able to get back in touch through an online forum or quick text message. In other cases, friendships can be maintained at a loose level of vague mutual awareness for many years, without the friends ever actually meeting each other. These ties – although loose and weak – provide a form of social safety net and a mode of global connectedness. Even weak ties have the potential to be activated at some later date, when they become relevant or necessary (Wilding 2006). A wide range of relationships, including relatives but also extending beyond the family, are providing opportunities to develop a sense of belonging that extends beyond the geographic locale, and encompass a diverse range of identities and possibilities. Moreover, these loose-knit relationships are not necessarily at the expense of face-to-face relationships and personal communities. Rather, they are able to reinforce, supplement and intersect with close social networks of relationships and support. What is becoming clear is that a broad range of relationships persist and endure. This provides important evidence for contradicting arguments about the atomization of the individual in late modernity.

Families, Intimacy and Globalization: Floating Ties

The narratives of family life and relationships throughout this book help illustrate the tensions and contradictions that exist not only in the experiences and practices of intimacy, but also in the theoretical tools available to understand them. On the one hand, it seems that the family is becoming less significant as a social institution. There is ample evidence available to support claims that individuals are making choices based on their own individual preferences and desires, in the pursuit of their own life narrative, rather than slavishly reproducing the established expectations and roles that have been associated with marriage and the family. The 'traditional' family structures are under challenge from the evidence of diversity in intimate relationships, including families of choice and the wide range of household arrangements and relationship forms that people are creating. It is also clear that 'the family' is highly problematic as a conceptual tool. Its strong associations with gendered norms of behaviour, heteronormativity and co-residence provide an obstacle to being able to think about the stretching of households, relationships, intimacy and support across national and cultural borders.

At the same time, the stories throughout this book also demonstrate that the family remains very significant. People talk about following their families along migration routes, bringing families with them when they are migrating, and using a range of communication devices to connect with members of their families who are living elsewhere. Families remain a common source of social and economic support, cultural transmission and reproduction, care and intimacy. Moreover, families remain strongly associated with biological and marital connections, which are further reinforced by the laws and policies of nation-states that define particular blood and legal connections as more significant than others, and attribute to them certain enforceable rights and obligations. Even as 'the family' remains elusive and difficult to define, 'family' as an idea and an ideal is being constituted through the everyday practices with which individuals construct their own familial relationships.

John's explanation in Chapter 1, that he cares for his mum and dad from the other side of the world because they are his mum and dad, demonstrates two things. First, that the family relationship invokes obligations and expectations of care, and second, that the blood relationship also helps to explain the desire to fulfil these obligations and expectations. John cares not just because he feels he has to, but also because he wants to provide that care. He wants to express the emotions he has towards his mum and dad. These emotions are not an automatic result of the objectively evident connections through blood and marriage. Rather, these emotions are produced through the numerous culturally informed social interactions that individuals have with each other, through which we identify each other as family, as intimates, and as connected. In these social interactions we generate and reinforce not only biological and marital ties, but also shared histories of co-residence or house-holding, mutual support, and emotional terrains of love, affection, desire, care, tolerance, conflict and hostility. Thus, when the Smith family come together on Nevis for Jim's wedding (Chapter 7), they are doing so partly out of a sense of already being a family, of sharing a history of co-producing their family ties, but also partly out of the need to continually create that family.

The fact that some members of the Smith family are more involved in family events than are others is a good illustration of how families shift over time, becoming more and less significant for their various members at different moments in the life course and in response to the different actions of their members. Some people might become less involved in family activities over time, particularly when they feel that other members of the family group are displaying less involvement or less commitment towards them, or when they have diminished resources with which to display their own commitment to the family. Others might become more involved, sometimes even finding themselves at the core of family activities and identities, particularly when they hold roles or have access to resources that are recognized as being central to the production of family life and family relationships. 'Family', then, is a problematic term in part because it prompts an imagining of a fixed set of relationships, whereas family life itself is highly dynamic and changeable. The laws, policies and norms that are used to frame expectations and obligations within relationships shift over time, sometimes creating new roles or transforming existing ones within family groups. Also shifting are the particular roles that individuals fulfil within any given family. As people move through different age, employment or migration categories, their access to roles and economic resources constantly shift and change. Similarly, the capacities to partner or marry and to bear or raise children will position an individual into new roles and economic positions. These are never produced in isolation as a result of that one person's actions, opportunities and desires. Rather, these roles and positions are produced in dialogue with those of others within the family network, each person's actions, decisions, preferences and capacities being subtly adjusted by those of others, transforming what is possible, what is desired and what is required.

The experience and practice of family, intimacy and relationships changes over time, shifting in response to the demands of different stages in the life course, changing cultural models and social norms, and in accordance with the changing circumstances and life goals of individuals in a family network relative to each other. This is also illustrated by the example of Elise and Trent as they were setting out to start to create a new family of their own (Chapter 3). Their planned family began to fall apart when they failed to come to an agreement on who should care for their future children and how. Their narrative helps to illustrate how the increasing opportunities and expectations for women to participate in the paid workforce clash with simultaneous gendered models of care within the family. This was brought to a climax when Elise decided not to follow Trent overseas for his work, but it was already present in their disputes over who should do the housework, whether they should have children, and how any children they might have should be cared for. Their personal story is reflected in the broader story of increased divorce rates alongside high marriage and remarriage rates in many parts of the world, where similar renegotiations of the gendered order of paid and unpaid work are intersecting with models of how a family and its intimate relationships might be displayed and enacted.

Interpreting these changes as a crisis in the family might be tempting, but it is wholly inadequate. Family remains significant as a goal and as a practice. People continue to seek the acknowledgement of their relationships as family relationships, not just relationships of love and personal significance. This is how we explain the many years that Turandot and Fedora (Chapter 8) spent in claiming their rights for adoption from the Colombian government. They already had a set of intimate relationships. Their years spent in court battles were aimed at demanding the formal recognition of the relationships of care and support that they had already established in their family household. They sought to be recognized as a family. Yet it is reasonable to say that there has been and is a crisis in efforts to define one particular model or form of relationships or household as 'the' family. The practices, emotions and roles that people are asserting as familial are wide-ranging and diverse, responding to their changing economic, social, cultural and political circumstances and ambitions. This complex fluidity presents a challenge to states that attempt to privilege a particular form of the family in their development of laws and policies, particularly when their citizens are engaging in relationships that are stretched across national and cultural borders.

Distant love?

In their book *Distant Love*, Ulrich Beck and Elisabeth Beck-Gernsheim (2013) argue that globalization has produced what they term 'world families'. By world families, they mean 'love relationships and other forms of relationship between people living in, or coming from, different countries or continents' (Beck & Beck-Gernsheim 2013: 2). Two main forms of world families are identified: first, what they call 'multi-local families', who come from the same country of origin but are now living in different countries; and second, what they term 'multi-national families', who come from different countries of origin but are now living together as a family. These world families are argued to be distinct from the 'one-nation' families described in their earlier work (Beck & Beck-Gersheim 1995). They define world families as:

> families that live together across (national, religious, cultural or ethnic, etc.) frontiers. They are families that stick together even though they consist of elements that conventionally do not belong together. The glue provided by pre-existing traditions is replaced by *active trust*. Such families show that they can succeed even though received wisdom says they are doomed to failure; the 'alien other' becomes the nearest and dearest. (Beck & Beck-Gersheim 2013: 15, original emphasis)

What we have, then, is love relationships in which the 'glue' that holds people together is not some set of traditional rules about how to interact with each other. Indeed, world families are presented as distinctive in that they are not able to rely on the rules of tradition. Rules of tradition are necessarily produced in local social contexts, in which the bonds of convention come from continual surveillance of behaviour by others in the community or society. Because world families are stretched across multiple local social contexts, their members must negotiate the communities and social norms of multiple localities, including the ones in which they and their kin live, but also the ones that they and their kin came from. Moreover, they are forced into recognizing that some of these rules may be contradictory.

This leaves members of world families having to negotiate which rules apply in relation to which issues and relationships, when and how. The assumptions about the family are necessarily under constant negotiation. It is not possible to assume that others in the family know and understand their 'proper' place – pre-existing traditions or habits of family become the subject of reflection and adjustments. As a result of mobility, it becomes necessary to actively *produce* a shared history and a collective memory that knits together the diverse ways in which family is practised and understood by its various members, from differing backgrounds and experiences.

In the absence of the 'glue' of tradition, Beck and Beck-Gersheim (2013) suggest that 'active trust' must instead be activated by members of world families. This means that world 'families' are ultimately produced by individuals, who must make the decision to 'trust' that the others in their kin network will support and satisfy them. They must also constantly work at demonstrating their trustworthiness to the others in their family. Yet this brings families much closer to what are typically identified as 'friends' (Chapter 8). Unlike family, accounts of friends suggest that these types of relationships are much more reliant on the production and maintenance of trust in each other on the basis of some shared similarity and affection. Unlike the 'traditions' or shared histories of support and exchange that bind a family, trust must be produced through constant pleasurable interactions with each other. Trust is arguably more easily broken than the bonds of family. A friendship can be called to an end simply by refusing to interact, thereby breaching the trust in continued friendship. Family, on the other hand, continue to hold certain formal and structural roles in relation to each other, even when interactions in the relationship cease. Trust within families is reinforced by the institutions, laws and policies within which the family is produced; families, then, are produced not just by individuals, but also by the nation-states within which they live.

Underlying the production of active trust is the need or desire to protect 'love relationships and other forms of relationship'. What these other forms of relationship might be remains unspecified, but presumably it refers to relationships that are identifiable by people as somehow representing their 'family'. This raises an important question. If trust is the foundation of contemporary world families, then why use the term 'family' at all? Why not use a term such as 'personal community' or 'personal life', or more simply, 'intimacy' or 'relationships'?

Beck and Beck-Gernsheim (2013) anticipate that their notion of world families will be critiqued for its apparently anachronistic use of the term 'family', when so much research and scholarship (including their own) has moved beyond an assumption that 'family' means anything outside of its specific context and set of negotiated practices and understandings. Thus, they acknowledge:

> It may be objected that the concept of 'families' in 'world families' ignores the diversity of forms of the family that have long since been acknowledged in the field of culturally homogenous life forms and were a focus of our own study in *The Normal Chaos of Love* (1995). Is it not anachronistic to speak of world families? Would it not be essential to speak instead of world companions of the moment, world extended families, world post-divorce parenthood, world single parents, etc.? (Beck & Beck-Gernsheim 2013: 17)

Their response is to suggest that 'family' is the most appropriate term when talking about world families in the context of globalization because, outside of the West, 'family' remains a dominant term and is in active use. That is, in order to discuss world families it is necessary to use the terminology that is being used around the world, rather than applying a Eurocentric concept. Thus, they argue, 'If we wish to avoid anachronism, we must construct a concept of world families that appears anachronistic from the vantage point of Western observers' (Beck & Beck-Gernsheim 2013: 17).

The world 'family'?

Beck and Beck-Gernsheim's (2013) account does reinforce an important point: that 'family' still matters. However, they fail to address the issue of *why* it is still important. Implicit in their argument is a sense that late-modern individualization is an incomplete process in other parts of the world. In some nations, tradition and family continue to dominate and to constrain the lives of individuals. This is what Beck and Beck-Gernsheim imply produces the potential for a clash of ideologies within world families, in which at least some members will likely be exposed to Western ideals of autonomy and of the value attributed to the desires of the individual over those of some collective.

There are at least two problems with this response. First, it fails to account for the ongoing significance of 'family' in Western contexts by assuming that the term is anachronistic in Western societies – or, as Beck (in Beck & Beck-Gernsheim 2002: 204) suggests, a 'zombie category', an empty institution that is still referred to and acted upon even though it is long dead. In spite of this claim, as Gilding (2010) points out, the family as an institution and as a set of structures nevertheless continues to be reproduced and to shape the practices with which families create themselves as identifiable units of care, support and conflict. Inheritance laws are one clear example of this, in which the state reinforces the prioritizing of particular types of biological and marital relations. To this we might add particular histories of co-residence, shared biographies, householding and mutual exchanges of support and care. While the meaning of 'family' might have been extended and expanded, it retains ongoing significance as a set of privileged ties. This is evident in the great lengths that many people go to in order to stitch together the conventions of 'family' in the absence of some of its prerequisites. These include commuter couples sustaining a household across distance, same-sex couples claiming their right to marry, parents ritualizing the incorporation of international adoptees into their family structures and routines, and the ongoing provision of aged care by children to their parents even in societies in which formal paid care options are readily available.

Rather than suggesting that 'family' is a zombie category, Smart and Shipman (2004) argue that the problem with the individualization thesis is that it is 'culturally monochrome'. By this, they mean that individualization theory does not take into account the variety of models of family and relationships that are held even *within* a given nation, let alone around the world. For example, they describe the situation of young people from Pakistani and Indian backgrounds in Britain, who perceive arranged marriages as a very desirable pathway. In contrast with the assumption that ethnic communities in Western societies are becoming westernized and shifting towards valuing individual choice, the kin network remains an essential part of the self for these young people, guiding the decisions they consider possible and desirable. Rather than considering themselves as autonomous and isolated individuals, they find it difficult to imagine being satisfied with a life lived outside of their kinship and community network, or being happy with a marriage that does not take that network into account. Through their marriages within the kin network, the network itself is further reinforced – including transnationally. Thus, Smart and Shipman (2004: 503) suggest that

> the individual of the individualization thesis seems to exist without parents, without kinship ties, and with concerns only for their own psychic well-being. The lives of the individuals we interviewed were far more complex and committed than this.

That is, the family exists as an important phenomenon in Britain, for both migrants and their British-born children. It is not something that just persists 'elsewhere' or as somehow in the past.

Globalization of nuclear family ideology

This brings us to a second problem. By suggesting that 'family' is significant primarily because it is meaningful outside of the West, there is a risk of reproducing a 'denial of coevalness' (Fabian 1983) that places the West in late modernity and the 'rest' somewhere in the distant past, never quite able to catch up. Arland Thornton (2001, 2005) argues that this idea also contributes to the spread of Western models of the nuclear family around the world. The nuclear family ideology has benefited from its close association with a period of economic success and wellbeing for those who exemplified it in the middle of the twentieth century. As discussed in Chapter 1, the argument that the nuclear family is a pinnacle of modern social organization was rejected by mainstream sociology as a myth. Yet it has nevertheless remained powerful throughout the world, distributed as a cultural norm by the media, social movements and Christianity. It has also been instituted in the built forms of urbanization that emphasize the small home for a nuclear family rather than the multi-roomed spaces that are more useful for an extended family, and through the policies and programmes of developmental organizations that set gender targets for developing nations (Jayakody, Thornton & Axinn 2012). The spread of the nuclear family ideology has resulted in a strong, continuing (though not uncontested) association between non-Western family forms and the notion of 'tradition'. It is a tendency that is reproduced every time we use the term 'tradition' in relation to family and gender norms that differ from the nuclear family model (such as the extended family) or that contest individualized models of gender equality or choice in relationships.

Admittedly, referring to 'tradition' can provide a very useful shorthand, helping to create a distinction between two apparently different models of the family – the 'traditional' family that is associated with hierarchy, gender inequality, heteronormativity and predictable conservatism, and late-modern relationships, which are perceived as more democratic, egalitarian, non-heteronormative and subject to fluidity, flexibility and change as each individual constructs a life of their own. However, the use of the term 'traditional' and the association of 'family' with what is 'traditional' is not particularly helpful analytically. It risks collapsing and conflating a wide set of interlocking yet ultimately discrete issues and tensions, each of which has its own distinct impact on the maintenance and transformation of relationship dynamics. These include (but are not limited to) the distinctiveness of gender or sexual identities; gender equality as an ideal as distinct from gender equality as a practice; heteronormativity; ethnic and racial hierarchies within nations and between nations; inequalities in access to the tools of mobility and communication; age inequalities; age and life-course identities; and economic opportunities that are specific to particular locations and identities.

In order to create better understandings of contemporary relationships on a global stage, it may be necessary to discard the contrast between the 'West' and the 'non-West', and between 'tradition' and 'modernity' (or late modernity). This could help in better acknowledging the specifics of the dynamics that shape intimate and family relationships. For example, rather than contrasting traditional gender norms with modern gender arrangements, it might be better to instead speak of the parallel and intersecting dynamics of gender distinctiveness and gender equality, among other issues. Gender distinctiveness in this case refers to the claims that men and women wish to make regarding their gender identities, and the ways in which these identities are constructed in opposition to each other. By gender equality, on the other hand, we are able to refer to the extent to which both men and women have choice and autonomy over their own lives – something that needs to be understood not just in terms of gendered hierarchies, but also in terms of other hierarchies and constraints, such as those of wealth, occupation and economic opportunity.

These are separate, though linked, issues. For example, when men travel overseas for work, they and the women they leave behind are able to maintain the distinctiveness of their gendered identities, but there is arguably little opportunity for improving gender equality. On the other hand, when women travel overseas for work, they are likely to encounter improved opportunities for autonomy and economic independence, but this is often at the cost of being able to sustain the distinctive gendered identity that belongs to women from that particular place (and to the men they support from a distance). That is, improved gender equality potentially requires a relinquishing of not only local gendered norms and identities, but also a sense of being able to sustain and reproduce cultural and national identities – as a 'Vietnamese' woman, or a 'Filipino' man, for example. If we are to understand why women and men actively reproduce certain symbols of gender inequality, we may need to recognize that doing so is one of the few strategies for sustaining a valued ethnic or national identity in the context of global inequalities.

In another example, sexually diverse people might be in a position to better improve their distinctive sexual identity by moving away from their families for work or education and to come closer to a sexually diverse community, but this is at the cost of having equal access to the local identities that are associated with their families of origin, both gendered identities and also identities such as those of being rural, being from a particular region or nation, as well as identities such as those associated with being a son or daughter, or being a sibling. That is, any understanding of the practice of family under conditions of globalization requires attention to multiple forms and sources of identity, not just those associated with gender. Familial identities and roles in and of themselves remain significant, as do ethnic, national and other identities, such as geographic, religious and occupational identities.

From love to care

There is another problem with the account of world families provided by Beck and Beck-Gernsheim (2013) that needs to be acknowledged: the emphasis on 'love'. As might be expected from an account of relationships that assumes individualization, love as the foundation of family life is prioritizing a set of personal emotions, the property of an individual. Love also serves to indicate the moral behaviours that people are expected to fulfil, in that 'loved ones' are those who are determined by the state and by society to be people for whom a person has some obligations and responsibilities. They are the people whose welfare one should be concerned with and monitor, and improve where possible. Sometimes, loved ones can be people outside of the socially and culturally expected network of kin for whom one is expected to provide these supports. On occasion, 'loved ones' can refer to people who have been voluntarily brought within the network of care, within the realm of concern with welfare, on the basis of some shared interest or history, or sometimes a simple sense of affection rather than of socially constructed obligation. Yet these just serve to further reinforce the sense of obligation that is automatically associated with love. Love is not something that is freely offered to another. It is something that indicates expected pathways of support and care – whether through family ties or friendship choice – which are not easily broken.

Many of the studies and descriptions of transnational families, including many of the examples in this book, speak of the pain and anguish of being separated from 'loved ones'. The use of the term 'love' or 'loved' in this context alerts us to the emotional pain that arises from separation and migration. This is an important part of the picture, but it is not the only consideration. By referring to kin as 'loved ones', an expectation is set up that the kin relationship will correspond with and automatically produce an emotional relationship characterized by affection and intimacy. This too easily encourages overlooking the interdependencies of relationships that can rely on love, but might also be more than or beyond a concern with love. Love is a culturally specific assumption. Not all expectations and assumptions of family include an emphasis on the forms of love or intimacy associated with the pure relationship. The desirability of self-disclosure, for example, is specific to particular class and ethnic groups, rather than a global ideal. For many people around the world, such forms of intimacy are unusual or even undesirable within the family, which instead organizes the attachments and responsibilities of specific kin-based roles of care and support. The family is not necessarily reproduced by 'love' alone. Other emotions also play a role, including duty, obligation, loyalty and honour. The example of maternal ambivalence (Chapter 4) points to the fact that family relationships can motivate behaviour even when love is somewhat muted or even absent. Families are not only the people who love us, but are the people who also cause us pain, involve us in conflict, and limit our autonomy. By limiting the discussion to love, the emphasis on the individual and their emotions obscures the sense of what it means to be part of a dense set of interlocking relationships, biographies and identities, or the ways in which institutionalized obligations are rendered bearable by being positioned within emotional domains.

An alternative to conceptualizing 'love' as comprising the centre of the family is to instead consider the circulation of 'care' (Baldassar & Merla 2014). Care can be motivated by love, but it can also be motivated by obligation and entanglement in relationships of reciprocity. It is the set of family practices that 'binds members together in intergenerational networks of reciprocity and obligation, love and trust, that are simultaneously fraught with tension, contest and relations of unequal power' (Baldassar & Merla 2014: 7). By emphasizing care, it becomes possible to consider the ways in which family is produced by not only willing contributions, but also reluctant ones. This approach also helps to highlight the uneven nature of the exchanges that occur over time and place. As circumstances shift, some family members will likely receive more care than others, or more recognition for the care they provide than will others. In the context of globalization, this asymmetry is produced by at least two key factors. On the one hand, some family members (as a result of their gender, sexuality, age or skills, for example) will have greater access to the benefits and resources of global mobilities and communications, placing them in a stronger position to become the caregiver rather than the care receiver. At the same time, some family members will have greater obligations to contribute from the resources they have available to them, usually resulting from their gender, age or other identities, or structural relationship with those needing care, as well as past histories of relationship (Finch & Mason 1993; Baldassar, Baldock & Wilding 2007).

The circulation of care provides an important alternative to the emphasis on love in relationships. Yet its basis in studies of transnational families means that it also tends to imply family. This makes it potentially less useful in understanding other types of ties that extend beyond the norms of the family. The 'transnational family' is at risk of assuming the gendered, heterosexual structures or relationship and care that were identified above as problematic. It also diminishes the capacity to account for the shifts in relationships, obligations and expectations that are part of any individual's experiences of family, as discussed earlier. On the other hand, it does help in recognizing that both cultural and interpersonal expectations and assumptions associated with gender and sexuality serve to reinforce the organization of care. Culturally, women are commonly expected to be more emotionally invested in their children and parents, and so are expected to want to and actually provide more care than do men. Men, instead, are expected to fulfil 'responsibilities', something that can more easily be achieved by providing financial support or managing and delegating care from a distance, tasks that do not necessarily involve expectations of love, affection, or care in the form of emotional practical, personal or physical support.

Nation-states, institutions and the world family

By emphasizing the production of trust and the expression of love in the production of families that stretch the globe and cross borders, Beck and Beck-Gernsheim are able to articulate the sense of creative agency that is clearly one of the forces at play in the globalization of relationships and intimacy. However, alongside this sense of freedom and creativity, it is also necessary to acknowledge the constraints to agency. These are the anchors that tie individuals and social groups to particular arrangements of global householding, circulations of care and the maintenance of relationships and families across time and space. As Majella Kilkey and Laura Merla (2014) argue, in order to develop a framework for comparing diverse cross-border flows and transnational relationships, it is necessary to consider the various institutional constraints that migrants and non-migrants encounter as they display their families, produce trusting relations, and express love and affection (or not). A number of important factors must be considered when comparing the opportunities and constraints, capacities and desires of families that are stretched across time and space.

There are three key modes or sites of constraint that shape the fortunes, possibilities and obstacles for all transnational relationships (see Figure 9.1). The first of these is the policies, legislation and institutions of the nation-states within which the family is situated. This includes issues ranging from the employment and welfare context to the migration and border protection arrangements of each of the nations within which a family group is located. Factors such as the presence or absence of economic opportunities or of a minimum wage, and the degree of regulation of the labour market (including the penalties for being discovered in informal work), have a significant impact on influencing the perception that a nation is a good place to leave or a good destination for arrival. International agreements between some nations, and the absence of such agreements between other nations, help to shape the flows of migrants across particular borders and pathways. Such agreements are themselves developed out of the effects of national economic contexts, welfare settings and care regimes that produce gaps or excesses in the local labour force that are then plugged by international flows, as in the case of the European nations that are identified as the end point of global care chains from Asia (see Chapter 4). These produce additional institutional constraints on mobility, in the form of migration regulations that permit some forms of movement while constraining others, and honour some categories of migrant while stigmatizing and vilifying others.

These various legal and policy settings are important frames within which individuals and families make their decisions to move or stay, and evaluate those decisions as good or bad. However, it would be a mistake to assume that nations – powerful as they are in setting conditions for families, migration and the construction of selves – are fully in control of how people move across borders or how they live out their intimate lives of care and support.

Nation-state
- Migration policies and laws (entry, exit, residency)
- Welfare regimes
- Caregiving policies
- Legal recognition of relationship diversity
- Economic opportunities and conditions
- Employment opportunities and conditions
- International agreements for trade and migration

Social and cultural
- Definitions of social groups
- Models of the 'good' family
- Stigmatizing and honouring of social roles and identities
- Assumptions about responsibilities towards intimate or related others
- National identities, ethnic identities
- Sources of hope and despair
- Norms of gender, sexuality, age
- Distribution of knowledge
- Distribution of authority and decision making

Material
- Geographic territory
- Housing and built environment
- Communication and transport infrastructure
- Bodies as capacities and signifiers
- Economic resources (e.g. money, wealth, property)

Figure 9.1 Institutional, cultural and material constraints on perceived freedoms of the individual

While policy settings might seek to encourage or restrict certain flows or behaviours, people make their decisions within a larger social and cultural context.

Lieba Faier (2009) argues that each encounter between individuals and social groups across national and cultural borders is an articulation of other, earlier encounters across those borders. She emphasizes the contingency of each cross-border encounter, pointing to the ways in which cultural meanings and identities shape how each situation is perceived and interpreted. This helps to illuminate the fiction of not only transnationalism but also of transnational families, by pointing to the social construction of borders as diverse, shifting, renegotiated and reinterpreted sets of obstacles and opportunities in what she calls 'zones of encounter', which:

> take shape through 'power-geometries' in which places emerge as 'constellations of social relations'. They offer a different kind of geographical mapping than a nation-state or transnational space. They are filamentary networks that stretch to include those material and conceptual relationships through which people construct sense of self and live their daily lives. In this sense, zones of encounter are not cultural regions. They are areas that include people who share culture-in-relations: cultural

formations forged through relationships across difference. When we locate ourselves within such zones, we recognize these relationships so that we can learn how to become more accountable to them. (Faier 2009: 22)

Nation-states establish and reproduce the power-geometries within which intimate relations occur by establishing institutions and legal and policy settings that advantage some social positions at the expense of others. However, they do not determine how people respond to those power-geometries, or even how people interpret the borders that they encounter or the extent and boundaries of the nations in which they live. These perceptions are shaped by a much more complex set of cultural models and social subjectivities that provide the resources of hope and desire, as well as perceptions of opportunity and loss.

The social and cultural settings within which families are practised and relationships constructed include the various social and culturally specific, yet increasingly global and fluid, norms and values regarding gender, family, love, sexuality, roles, hierarchies, deviance, honour and more. The list of criteria that people draw on to evaluate the desirability of their current situations and their goals for the future might seem endless, but they nevertheless remain tied to specific expectations about what it means to be a good person and part of a family that works, and works well. The social and cultural resources are themselves unevenly distributed, depending on the authority that is accorded to different role positions (such as men and women, elders and children) and depending on the access to knowledge that each individual is able to secure. Thus, those who have encountered a wider range of social and cultural contexts have a larger set of resources to draw from in constructing their models of a good person, or a good family. However, their tendency to accept and reproduce these models will vary, depending on the extent to which they match their internalization of particular models of the good person and the good family.

Finally, it is necessary to acknowledge the role of the material context in shaping the opportunities and constraints of any given person or group of intimates. This includes resources such as income, housing and wealth that a family is able to mobilize. It also includes other features that receive less attention, but which are clearly significant to the outcomes of transnational family and intimate lives. For example, the geography of the places across which a family is distributed is significant. When the national border is a line in the sand, this creates a different transnational dynamic to a national border that is reinforced by impenetrable mountains or a large ocean. These geographic barriers also have political impacts, influencing the border policies that nations erect to manage the flows of potential migrants that their geographies have historically permitted, or that the nation is capable of imagining. Some nations are able to assert strong border protection policies in the knowledge that their borders are already difficult to cross, while others struggle with managing large numbers of people who are able to more easily make their way into the national space.

National infrastructures provide additional material constraints or potential for those who seek to live across and beyond national borders. Nations with excellent communication technology infrastructures present greater opportunities for sustaining digital or imaginary co-presence than do those at the lower end of the digital divide. Transport routes and infrastructure also contribute to the geographic materiality of nations, rendering the borders of some nations more porous than others, regardless of migration policies and legislation. Bodies, too, create limits on the capacities to choose. The visibility of some bodies in racialized societies renders them difficult to disguise, reducing the options for avoiding or negotiating migration and employment restrictions. In other cases, illness, age or disability make some bodies less mobile than others, or less amenable to reimagining and renegotiating roles and responsibilities within the family group.

Floating ties

The complexity of global population flows, national settings and geographies, and social and cultural resources of subjectivity, intimacy and care arguably require a new terminology or metaphor to help capture the transformation of social solidarity and intimacy. Having identified the problems with terms such as world families, distant love and even transnational families in the discussion above, my proposal is to speak instead of 'floating ties' (see also Chapter 1). Floating ties are relationships characterized by two apparently opposing and yet always simultaneous processes; the first is the imagining, construction and negotiation of fluid intimate lives by reflexive and responsive individuals; the second is the anchoring of those possibilities by the institutional, cultural and material factors that constrain both what is possible and what is imagined as desirable. Each of us is shaped by the contexts in which we live and by the interactions we have had with significant others throughout our lives, who inform our perceptions and practices of gender, ethnic and other identities, and shape our sense of self over the life course. Our choices are always made in the context of those identities and positions that are created in relation to others and the material and institutional contexts within which we live, have lived, and imagined living in at some point in the future. Moreover, these are not static. In the context of globalization, they are frequently subject to challenge and contestation.

'Floating ties' seeks to harness the tensions that are captured throughout this book by suggesting that they are not necessarily two competing interpretations of contemporary relationships, but rather two sides of the same coin. On the one hand, the capacity for individuals to assert individual pathways and desires in an unequal world; on the other hand, the ties that shape the decisions that those individuals make and the pathways that they desire. Accounts of individualization and the pure relationship tend to emphasize the former, by pointing to the ability and the requirement for individuals to construct a 'life of their own' within the context of an insecure world. The constraints of tradition, they argue, are no match for the global flows of capital, ideas, media and people, which disrupt all bonds and ties and instead require flexibility, fluidity and a certain lightness in being able to move through the world in the pursuit of individual self-development and economic opportunities. Yet empirical sociologists of the family and relationships provide evidence to support the latter, by identifying the ways in which ties to 'family', with all of its associations with 'tradition', continue to shape the choices that men and women make about their lives. Families and the specific forms of relationship they invoke continue to matter, continue to constrain, and continue to construct or at least shape the individual and their life project.

The terms 'transnational families' and 'transnational caregiving' have the advantage of pointing to the ways in which intimate lives are lived across borders. However, the use of the term 'transnational' is problematic in its emphasis on the nation, which implies that intimate lives are lived and negotiated across two relatively static and bounded national contexts. This overlooks the social and cultural constructions of those national contexts in the zones of encounter of intimate relationships. Distant love and world families provide an opportunity to move beyond the imagining of the nation as the natural site of analyses of the family. However, the emphasis on emotions and on choice and agency fails to account for the many constraints – national, social and cultural, and material – that continue to frame (though not necessarily determine) the options available to individuals who construct their productive and reproductive, working and family lives across national contexts. Instead, what is required is a term that refuses to place 'family' or 'love' at the centre, enabling intimate relations of care, support and contestation to be interrogated rather than assumed. As with family, so too the term 'nation' is problematic and to be avoided, in order that institutional constraints and their negotiation might be examined rather than taken for granted. Rather than 'world families' or transnational families, 'floating ties' helps to decentre the family and the nation. 'Floating' is intended to refer to the fluid, flexible, autonomous nature of relationships that is assumed and expected in so much of contemporary global society. It accounts for the individual as an agent able and required to make their own choices in order to construct a life of their own. However, this needs to be recognized as only part of the story. 'Ties' emphasizes the fact that there is no such thing as an isolated, autonomous individual who is distinct from the relationships within which their sense of self is embedded or that is free from the constraints of the institutional, cultural and material contexts within which they live.

The relationships produced and sustained by global mobilities and connectedness, whether they are commuter couples, transnational families of choice, families created by international adoption or one of the many other possible forms, help to highlight these simultaneous, yet competing tendencies in contemporary relationships. When women in the global care chain travel to work overseas and leave their children behind, they are acting both as individuals and as members of a family. Similarly, when sexually diverse people travel some distance to separate themselves from the gendered sexual identities of their families of origin, they are doing so as members of a family whose gendered structures and assumptions about sexual identities must be disrupted, though not necessarily destroyed, through that movement. Each return visit and communication interaction with significant others is an example of relationships being sustained and reproduced, creating the foundations for future reciprocal interactions of care, support and communication.

Individuals, then, float in a global ecumene, pushed and pulled by international economic and cultural forces, responding fluidly and flexibly to the conditions they encounter. But they do so within the thick stuff of their closest social relationships and the institutional, cultural and material constraints in which they live. These relationships and constraints sometimes serve to support their future mobilities, as in the case of astronaut families, and sometimes help or require them to remain in place, as in the case of the left-behind families of fly-in-fly-out (FIFO) workers. They sometimes contribute to the formation of nuclear family relationships, as in the case of commuter couples, and sometimes to the maintenance of extended kinship and ethnic networks, as in the case of Tongans and the Tongan diaspora.

By using 'floating ties', rather than 'world families', it becomes more possible to avoid immediate or automatic associations with gendered structures or expectations, sexual identities, or specific hierarchies of relationships. At the same time, it is possible to acknowledge the density of obligations and connections that encourage people to assert the significance of certain relationships in their lives, whether these are claimed as 'family', 'family-like', or some other culturally specific form, such as the ethnic community as extended kin. The term does not assume particular forms of relationship, instead allowing these to be explored and analysed for their specificities. This is necessary if we are to make sense of families, relationships and intimacy under conditions of globalization. It is not appropriate to assume that 'family' is relevant in some parts of the world and not in others, or that modern relationships are less developed in some parts of the world and more developed in others. Instead, there is a need to understand how individuals embedded in social ties make decisions about their lives and how these socially embedded individuals, through their choices, are transforming the global circulation of ideas as well as the local implementation of policies and expectations about families, relationships and individual autonomy.

Finally, it is not just transnational families or intimate lives stretched across distance and borders that are being transformed by processes of globalization. All relationships, family and otherwise, are being shaped by the political, economic, social and cultural shifts that arise from greater interconnectedness around the world, at the level of individuals, families, communities, corporations, organizations, networks, nations, and so on. The transformations are uneven and local, even as they are informed by, intersect with and impact on what happens in other parts of the world. Each individual, making their choices within the context of their families and broader personal communities, is shaping the process of globalization through their own variable preferences, strategies and tactics. It is their individual creativity towards the problems and opportunities of globalization that produces such complex outcomes at the global level and contributes to the intensification of global communications and travel that further embed individuals in social networks that float above yet intersect with local contexts and materialities. At the heart of these transformations, I suggest, is not a solitary individual, but rather the individual as relational, as caught up within the floating ties that they are constantly producing, and within which they necessarily live.

References

Abel, E (1991) *Who Cares For the Elderly? Public Policy and the Experiences of Adult Daughters*. Temple University Press, Philadelphia.

ABS (2005) *Year Book Australia, 2005*. Catalogue No. 1301.0.

ABS Census (2012a) 'Marriages and divorces, Australia', ABS Catalogue No. 3310.0.

ABS Census (2012b) 'Love me do', *Australian Social Trends* ABS Catalogue No. 4102.0.

ABS Census (2014) 'Marriages and divorces', Catalogue No. 3310.0. Available at: www.abs.gov.au/ausstats/abs@.nsf/mf/3310.0.

ABS Census (n.d.) Available at: http://abs.gov.au.

Acosta, KL (2008) 'Lesbianas in the borderlands: Shifting identities and imagined communities', *Gender and Society* vol. 22, no. 5, pp. 639–59.

Adams, R & Allan, G (eds) (1998) *Placing Friendship in Context*. Cambridge University Press, Cambridge.

Adihartono, W (2014) 'Migration and family relationships: The case of "gay Indonesia" in Paris', *Southeast Asia Research Centre Working Paper Series* No. 157, City University Hong Kong.

Akgündüz, A (2008) *Labour Migration from Turkey to Western Europe, 1960–1974: A Multidisciplinary Analysis*. Ashgate, Aldershot.

Allan, G (1989) *Friendship: Developing a Sociological Perspective*. Harvester Wheatsheaf, Hemel Hempstead.

Allan, G (1998) 'Friendship, sociology and social structure', *Journal of Social and Personal Relationships* 15, no. 5, pp. 685–702.

Altman, D (1993) *Homosexuality: Oppression and Liberation*. New York University Press, New York.

Altman, D (2001) 'Global gaze/global gays', in JC Hawley (ed.) *Postcolonial and Queer Theories: Intersections and Essays*. Greenwood Press, Westport, pp. 1–18.

Altman, D (2013) *The End of the Homosexual?* University of Queensland Press, St Lucia.

Amant, K & Olaniran, BA (2011) *Globalization and the Digital Divide*. Cambria Press, Amherst.

Anderson, EA & Spruill, JW (1993) 'The dual-career commuter family', *Marriage & Family Review* vol. 19, no. 1–2, pp. 131–47.

Angeles, L & Sunanta, S (2007) '"Exotic love at your fingertips": Intermarriage websites, gendered representation, and the transnational migration of Filipino and Thai women', *Kasarinlan: Philippine Journal of Third World Studies* vol. 22, no. 1, pp. 3–31.

Annes, A & Redlin, M (2012) 'Coming out and coming back: Rural gay migration and the city', *Journal of Rural Studies* vol. 28, pp. 56–68.

Appadurai, A (1996) *Modernity at Large: Cultural Dimensions of Globalization*. University of Minnesota Press, Minneapolis.

Appelbaum, RP & Robinson, W (eds) (2005) *Critical Globalization Studies*. Routledge, New York.

Arber, S & Attius-Donfut, C (eds) (2000) *The Myth of Generational Conflict: The Family and State in Ageing Societies*. Routledge, London.

Arber, S & Ginn, J (1995) 'Gender differences in the relationship between paid employment and informal care', *Work, Employment and Society* vol. 9, no. 3, pp. 445–71.

Aries, P (1962) *Centuries of Childhood: A Social History of Family Life*. New York, Knopf.

Asis, MMB (2005) 'Recent trends in international migration in Asia and the Pacific', *Asia-Pacific Population Journal* vol. 20, no. 3, pp. 15–38.

Asis, MMB, Huang, S & Yeoh, B (2004) 'When the light of the home is abroad: Unskilled female migration and the Filipino family', *Singapore Journal of Tropical Geography* vol. 25, no. 2, pp. 198–215.

Commonwealth of Australia (2013) *Cancer of the Bush or Salvation for our Cities? Fly-in, Fly-out and Drive-in, Drive-out Workforce Practices in Regional Australia*. Canberra, House of Representatives Standing Committee on Regional Australia, Parliament of the Commonwealth of Australia.

Baker, M (1995) *Canadian Family Policies: Cross-National Comparisons*. University of Toronto Press, Toronto.

Baldassar, L (2001) *Visits Home: Migration Experiences Between Italy and Australia*. Melbourne University Press, Melbourne.

Baldassar, L (2008) 'Missing kin and longing to be together: Emotions and the construction of co-presence in transnational relationships', *Journal of Intercultural Studies* vol. 29, no. 3, pp. 247–66.

Baldassar, L, Baldock, C & Wilding, R (2007) *Families Caring Across Borders*. Palgrave, Houndsmill.

Baldassar, L & Merla, L (eds) (2014) *Transnational Families, Migration and the Circulation of Care: Understanding Mobility and Absence in Family Life*. Routledge, London.

Baldassar, L & Merla, L (2014) 'Transnational family caregiving through the lens of circulation', in L Baldassar & L Merla (eds) *Transnational Families, Migration and the Circulation of Care: Understanding Mobility and Absence in Family Life*. Routledge, London, pp. 3–24.

Baldassar, L, Nedelcu, M, Merla, L & Wilding, R (2016) 'ICT-based co-presence in transnational families', *Global Networks* vol. 16, no. 2, pp. 133–44.

Baldassar, L, Wilding, R & Baldock, C (2007) 'Long-distance caregiving: Transnational families and the provision of aged care', in I Paoletti (ed.) *Family Caregiving for Older Disabled People*. Nova Science Publishers, New York, pp. 201–27.

Bamford, TW (1967) *Rise of the Public Schools: A Study of Boys' Public Boarding Schools in England and Wales from 1837 to the Present Day*. Nelson, London.

Banks, SP (2009) 'Intergenerational ties across borders: Grandparent narratives by expatriate retirees in Mexico', *Journal of Aging Studies* vol. 23, no. 3, pp. 178–87.

Barber, PG (2000) 'Agency in Philippine women's labour migration and provisional diaspora', *Women's Studies International Forum* vol. 23, no. 4, pp. 399–411.

Basa, C, Harcourt, W & Zarro, A (2011) 'Remittances and transnational families in Italy and The Philippines: Breaking the global care chain', *Gender and Development* vol. 19, no. 1, pp. 11–22.

Battistella, G & Conaco, MCG (1998) 'The impact of labour migration on the children left behind: A study of elementary school children in the Philippines', *Sojourn: Journal of Social Issues in Southeast Asia* vol. 13, no. 2, pp. 220–41.

Bauman, Z (2000) *Liquid Modernity*. Polity, Cambridge.

Bauman, Z (2003) *Liquid Love*. Polity, Cambridge.

Baxter, J (1997) 'Gender equality and participation in housework: A cross-national perspective', *Journal of Comparative Family Studies* vol. 28, no. 3, pp. 220–47.

Baxter, J (2002) 'Patterns of change and stability in the gender division of household labour in Australia, 1986–1997', *Journal of Sociology* vol. 38, no. 4, pp. 399–424.

Baxter, J, Hewitt, B & Haynes, M (2008) 'Life course transitions and housework: Marriage, parenthood, and time on housework', *Journal of Marriage and Family* vol. 70, no. 2, pp. 259–72.

Baxter, J, Hewitt, B & Western, M (2005) 'Post-familial families and the domestic division of labour', *Journal of Comparative Family Studies* vol. 36, no. 4, pp. 583–600.

Baxter, J & Western, M (1998) 'Satisfaction with housework: Examining the paradox', *Sociology* vol. 32, no. 1, pp. 101–20.

Beaumont, J (2011) *Households and Families*. Social Trends 41. Office for National Statistics, Newport.

Beck, U & Beck-Gernsheim, E (1995) *The Normal Chaos of Love*. Polity Press, Cambridge.

Beck, U & Beck-Gernsheim, E (2002) *Individualization*. Sage, London.

Beck, U & Beck-Gernsheim, E (2013) *Distant Love*. Polity Press, Cambridge.

Bengston, V & Achenbaum, WA (eds) (1993) *The Changing Contract Across the Generations*. Aldine de Gruyter, New York.

Bengston, VL, Biblarz, TJ & Roberts, REL (2002) *How Families Still Matter: A Longitudinal Study of Youth in Two Generations*. Cambridge University Press, Cambridge.

Bengston, V, Kim, K, Myers GC & Eun, K (eds) (2000) *Aging in East and West: Families, States, and the Elderly*. Springer Publishing Company, New York.

Bergen, KM (2010) 'Accounting for difference: Commuter wives and the master narrative of marriage'. *Journal of Applied Communication Research* vol. 38, no. 1, pp. 47–64.

Bergen, KM, Kirby, E & McBride, MC (2007) '"How do you get two houses cleaned?": Accomplishing family caregiving in commuter marriages', *Journal of Family Communication* vol. 7, no. 4, pp. 287–307.

Bernardes, J (1985) '"Family ideology": Identification and exploration', *The Sociological Review* vol. 33, no. 2, pp. 275–97.

Bernardes, J (1999) 'We must not define "the family"!', *Marriage and Family Review* vol. 28, no. 3–4, pp. 21–41.

Bittman, M, Fast, JE, Fisher, K & Thomson, C (2004) 'Making the invisible visible: The life and time(s) of informal caregivers', in N Folbre & M Bittman (eds) *Family Time: The Social Organization of Care*. Routledge, London, pp. 69–89.

Bittman, M & Pixley, J (1997) *The Double Life of the Family: Myth, Hope and Experience*. Allen & Unwin, Sydney.

Blackwell, DL & Lichter, DT (2004) 'Homogamy among dating, cohabiting and married couples', *The Sociological Quarterly* vol. 45, no. 4, pp. 719–37.

Blanchet, T (2005) 'Bangladeshi girls sold as wives in north India', *Indian Journal of Gender Studies* vol. 12, no. 2–3, pp. 305–34.

Blasco, PGY (2012) '"A wondrous adventure": Mutuality and individuality in Internet adoption narratives', *Journal of the Royal Anthropological Institute* vol. 18, pp. 330–48.

Blidon, M (2016) 'Moving to Paris! Gays and lesbians: Paths, experiences and projects', in G Brown & K Browne (eds) *The Routledge Research Companion to Geographies of Sex and Sexualities*. Routledge, London, pp. 234–46.

Bloom, DE (2011) '7 billion and counting', *Science* vol. 333, no. 6042, pp. 562–9.

Boden, S (2003) *Consumerism, Romance and the Wedding Experience*. Palgrave Macmillan, Basingstoke.

Boehm, DA (2008a) 'For my children: Constructing family and navigating the state in the U.S.-Mexico transnation', *Anthropological Quarterly* vol. 81, no. 4, pp. 777–802.

Boehm, DA (2008b) '"Now I am a man *and* a woman": Gendered moves and migrations in a transnational Mexican community', *Latin American Perspectives* vol. 35, no. 1, pp. 16–30.

Boehm, DA (2011) '*Deseos y Dolores*: Mapping desire, suffering and (dis)loyalty within transnational partnerships', *International Migration* vol. 49, no. 6, pp. 95–106.

Boehm, DA (2012) *Intimate Migrations: Gender, Family, and Illegality among Transnational Mexicans*. New York University Press, New York.

Bohr, Y & Tse, C (2009) 'Satellite babies in transnational families: A study of parents' decision to separate from their infants', *Infant Mental Health Journal* vol. 30, no. 3, pp. 265–86.

Borowski, A, Encel, S & Ozanne, E (eds) (2007) *Longevity and Social Change in Australia*. UNSW Press, Sydney.

Brand, RJ, Bonatsos, A, D'Orazio, R & DeShong, H (2012) 'What is beautiful is good, even online: Correlations between photo attractiveness and text attractiveness in men's online dating profiles', *Computers in Human Behavior* vol. 28, pp. 166–70.

Bridges, JC (2012) *The Illusion of Intimacy: Problems in the World of Online Dating*. Praeger, Santa Barbara.

Brodie, E (1981) '"Women in the middle" and family help to older people', *Gerontologist* vol. 21, no. 5, pp. 471–80.

Brodzinsky, S (2016) 'Colombia's highest court paves way for marriage equality in surprise ruling', *The Guardian*, 8 April 2016. Available at: www.theguardian.com/world/2016/apr/07/colombia-court-gay-marriage-ruling.

Brooks, R (2011) *Student Mobilities, Migration and the Internationalization of Higher Education*. Palgrave Macmillan, Basingstoke.

Brown, R (2016) 'Re-examining the transnational nanny: Migrant carework beyond the chain', *International Feminist Journal of Politics* vol. 18, no. 2, pp. 210–29.

Bryceson, D & Vuorela, U (2002), 'Transnational families in the twenty-first century', in D Bryceson & U Vuorela (eds) *The Transnational Family: New European Frontiers and Global Networks*. Berg, Oxford, pp. 3–29.

Carling, J, Menjívar, C & Schmalzbauer, L (2012) 'Central themes in the study of transnational parenthood', *Journal of Ethnic and Migration Studies* vol. 38, no. 2, pp. 191–217.

Carrillo, H & Fontdevila, J (2014) 'Border crossings and shifting sexualities among Mexican gay immigrant men: Beyond monolithic conceptions', *Sexualities* vol. 17, no. 8, pp. 919–38.

Carsten, J (2004) *After Kinship*. Cambridge University Press, Cambridge.

Cartwright, L (2003) 'Photographs of "waiting children": The transnational adoption market', *Social Text*, vol. 21, no. 1, pp. 83–109.

Castles, S, de Haas, H & Miller, MJ (2013) *The Age of Migration*. 5th edn, Palgrave Macmillan, Basingstoke.

Chamberlain, M (2006) *Family Love in the Diaspora: Migration and the Anglo-Caribbean Experience*. Transaction Publishers, New Brunswick.

Chambers, D (2012) *A Sociology of Family Life: Change and Diversity in Intimate Relations*. Polity Press, Cambridge.

Charles, N, Davies, CA & Harris, C (2008) *Families in Transition: Social Change, Family Formation and Kin Relationships*. Policy Press, Bristol.

Charsley, K (2005a) 'Vulnerable brides and transnational Ghar Damads: Gender, risk and "adjustment" among Pakistani marriage migrants to Britain', *Indian Journal of Gender Studies* vol. 12, no. 2–3, pp. 381–406.

Charsley, K (2005b) 'Unhappy husbands: Masculinity and migration in transnational Pakistani marriages', *Journal of the Royal Anthropological Institute* vol. 11, pp. 85–105.

Charsley, K & Liversage, A (2013) 'Transforming polygamy: Migration, transnationalism and multiple marriages among Muslim minorities', *Global Networks* vol. 13, no. 1, pp. 60–78.

Cheal, D (2008) *Families in Today's World: A Comparative Approach*. Routledge, London.

Chee, MWL (2003) 'Migrating for the children: Taiwanese American women in transnational families', in N Piper & M Roces (eds) *Wife or Worker? Asian Women and Migration*. Rowman and Littlefield, Lanam MD, pp. 137–56.

Cherlin, AJ (1981) *Marriage, divorce, remarriage*. Harvard University Press, Cambridge MA.

Cherlin, AJ (2004) 'The de-institutionalization of American marriage', *Journal of Marriage and Family*, vol, 66, no. 4, pp. 848–61.

Cherlin, AJ (2009) *The Marriage-Go-Round: The State of Marriage and the Family in America Today*. Alfred A Knopf, New York.

Chiang, NLH (2004) 'Middle-class Taiwanese immigrant women adapt to life in Australasia: Case studies from transnational households', *Asian Journal for Women Studies* vol. 10, no. 4, pp. 31–57.

Chiang, NLH (2008) '"Astronaut families": Transnational lives of middle-class Taiwanese married women in Canada', *Social and Cultural Geography* vol. 9, no. 5, pp. 505–18.

Clegg, A (2013) 'Tales from trailing husbands', *Financial Times*, 11 June 2013, p. 14.

Coe, C (2008) 'The structuring of feeling in Ghanaian transnational families', *City & Society* vol. 20, no. 2, pp. 222–50.

Coe, C (2011a) 'What is love? The materiality of care in Ghanaian transnational families', *International Migration* vol. 49, no. 6, pp. 7–24.

Coe, C (2011b) 'What is the impact of transnational migration on family life? Women's comparisons of internal and international migration in a small town in Ghana', *American Ethnologist* vol. 38, no. 1, pp. 148–63.

Coe, C (2014) *The Scattered Family: Parenting, African Migrants and Global Inequality*. University of Chicago Press, Chicago.

Coe, C, Reynolds, RR, Boehm, DA, Hess, JM & Rae-Espinoza, H (eds) (2011) *Everyday Ruptures: Children, Youth and Migration in Global Perspective*. Vanderbilt University Press, Nashville.

Cohen, PN (2013) *The Family: Diversity, Inequality and Social Change*. Norton, New York.

Cohen, R (1996) *Theories of Migration*. E Elgar, Cheltenham.

Colic-Peisker, V (2010) 'Free floating in the cosmopolis? Exploring the identity-belonging of transnational knowledge workers', *Global Networks* vol. 10, no. 4, pp. 467–88.

Collins, J & Gregor, T (1995) 'Boundaries of love', in W Jankowiak (ed.) *Romantic Passion: A Universal Experience?* Columbia University Press, New York, pp. 72–92.

Cong, Z. & M. Silverstein (2012) 'Parents' preferred care-givers in rural China: Gender, migration and intergenerational exchanges', *Ageing and Society* doi:10.1017/S0144686X12001237

Connell, R (1995) *Masculinities*. University of California Press, Berkeley.

Connell, R (2002) *Gender*. Polity Press, Cambridge.

Connell, R (2005) *Masculinities*. Allen & Unwin, Sydney.

Conradson, D & Latham, A (2005) 'Friendship, networks and transnationality in a world city: Antipodean transmigrants in London', *Journal of Ethnic and Migration Studies* vol. 31, no. 2, pp. 287–305.

Constable, N (2003a) *Romance on a Global Stage: Pen Pals, Virtual Ethnography, and "Mail-Order" Marriages*. University of California Press, Berkeley.

Constable, N (2003b) 'A transnational perspective on divorce and marriage: Filipino wives and workers', *Identities: Global Studies in Culture and Power*, vol. 10, no. 2, pp. 163–80.

Cooke, FL (2007) '"Husband's career first": Renegotiating career and family commitment among migrant Chinese academic couples in Britain', *Work, Employment and Society* vol. 21, no. 1, pp. 47–65.

Cooke, TJ (2001) '"Trailing wife" or "trailing mother"? The effect of parental status on the relationship between family migration and the labor-market participation of married women', *Environment and Planning A* vol. 33, pp. 419–30.

Cooke, TJ & Rapino, M (2007) 'The migration of partnered gays and lesbians between 1995 and 2000', *The Professional Geographer* vol. 59, no. 3, pp. 285–97.

Cooke, TJ & Speirs, K (2005) 'Migration and employment among the civilian spouses of military personnel', *Social Science Quarterly* vol. 86, no. 2, pp. 343–55.

Coontz, S (2005) *Marriage, a history: From obedience to intimacy or how love conquered marriage*. Viking, New York.

Cresswell, T (2010) 'Towards a politics of mobility', *Environment and Planning D: Society and Space* vol. 28, pp. 17–31.

Dalton, SE & Bielby, DD (2000) '"That's our kind of constellation": Lesbian mothers negotiate institutionalized understandings of gender within the family', *Gender and Society* vol. 14, no. 1, pp. 36–61.

Davis, T (2010) 'Third spaces or heterotopias? Recreating and negotiating migrant identity using online spaces', *Sociology* vol. 44, no. 4, pp. 661–77.

De Certeau, M (1984) *The Practice of Everyday Life*. University of California Press, Berkeley.

De Graeve, K & Bex, C (2015) 'Imageries of family and nation: A comparative analysis of transnational adoption and care for unaccompanied minors in Belgium', *Childhood*, Published online before print November 30, 2015, doi: 10.1177/0907568215613421.

De Vaus, D. (1996) 'Children's responsibilities to elderly parents', *Family Matters* vol. 45, pp. 16–21.

De Vaus, D (2004) *Diversity and Change in Australian Families: Statistical Profiles*. Australian Institute of Family Studies, Melbourne.

De Vaus, D & Qu, L (2015a) 'Demographics of living alone', *Australian Family Trends* No. 6. Australian Institute of Family Studies, Melbourne.

De Vaus, D & Qu, L (2015b) 'The nature of living alone in Australia', *Australian Family Trends* No. 9. Australian Institute of Family Studies, Melbourne.

Del Rosario, T (2005) 'Bridal diaspora: Migration and marriage among Filipino women', *Indian Journal of Gender Studies* vol. 12, no. 2–3, pp. 253–73.

Dench, G & Ogg, J (2002) *Grandparenting in Britain: A Baseline Study*. Institute of Community Studies, London.

Derluyn, I & Vervliet, M (2012) 'The well-being of unaccompanied refugee minors', in D Ingleby, A Krasnik, V Lorant & O Razum (eds) *Health Inequalities and Risk Factors Among Migrants and Ethnic Minorities*. Garant, Antwerp, pp. 95–109.

Di Leonardo, M (1987) 'The female world of cards and holidays: Women, families, and the work of kinship', *Signs* vol. 12, no. 3, pp. 440–53.

Dooghe, G. (1992) 'Informal caregivers of elderly people: A European review', *Ageing and Society* vol. 12, pp. 369–80.

Douglass, M (2006) 'Global householding in Pacific Asia', *International Development Planning Review* vol. 28, no. 4, pp. 421–45.

Douglass, M (2014) 'Afterword: Global householding and social reproduction in Asia', *Geoforum* vol. 51, pp. 313–16.

Dreby, J (2006) 'Honor and virtue: Mexican parenting in the transnational context', *Gender & Society* vol. 20, no. 1, pp. 32–59.

Duncan, S (2015) 'Women's agency in living apart together: Constraint, strategy and vulnerability', *The Sociological Review* vol. 63, no. 3, pp. 589–607.

Duncan, S, Edwards, R, Reynolds, T & Alldred, P (2003) 'Motherhood, paid work and partnering: Values and theories', *Work, Employment and Society* vol. 17, no. 2, pp. 309–30.

Duncan, S & Phillips, M (2010) 'People who live apart together (LATs) – how different are they?' *The Sociological Review* vol. 58, no. 1, pp. 112–34.

Duncan, S & Phillips, M (2011), 'People who live apart together (LATs): New family form or just a stage?', *International Review of Sociology: Revue Internationale de Sociologie* vol. 21, no. 3, pp. 513–32.

Duncombe, J & Marsden, D (1993) 'Love and intimacy: The gender division of emotion and emotion work, a neglected aspect of sociological discussion of heterosexual relationships', *Sociology* vol. 27, no. 2, pp. 221–41.

Ehrenreich, B & Hochschild, AR (2003) *Global Woman: Nannies, Maids, and Sex Workers in the New Economy*. Metropolitan Books, New York.

Ellison, N, Heino, R & Gibbs, J (2006) 'Managing impressions online: Self-presentation processes in the online dating environment', *Journal of Computer-Mediated Communication* vol. 11, no. 2, pp. 415–41.

Elman, RA (2000) 'The limits of citizenship: Migration, sex discrimination and same-sex partners in EU law', *Journal of Common Market Studies* vol. 38, no. 5, pp. 729–49.

Evandrou, M & Glaser, K (2003) 'Combining work and family life: The pension penalty of caring', *Ageing and Society*, vol. 23, no. 5, pp. 583–601.

Evans, M. (1996) 'Care of the elderly', *World-wide Attitudes* vol. 8, pp. 1–7.

Evans, M (2001) *Persistence of the Gift: Tongan Tradition in Transnational Context*. Wilfrid Laurier University Press, Waterloo Ontario.

Fabian, J (1983) *Time and the Other: How Anthropology Makes its Object*. Columbia University Press, New York.

Faier, L (2009) *Intimate Encounters: Filipina Women and the Remaking of Rural Japan*. University of California Press, Berkeley.

Fassin, E & Salcedo, M (2015) 'Becoming gay? Immigration policies and the truth of sexual identity', *Archives of Sexual Behavior* vol. 44, no. 5, pp. 1117–25.

Featherstone, M & Wernick, A (1995) *Images of Aging: Cultural Representations of Later Life*. Routledge, London.

Fiddian-Qasmiyeh, E, Loescher, G, Long, K & Sigona, N (2014) *The Oxford Handbook of Refugee & Forced Migration Studies*. Oxford University Press, Oxford.

Fildes, V (1988) *Wet Nursing: A History from Antiquity to the Present*. Blackwell, Oxford.

Finch, J (1995) 'Responsibilities, obligations and commitments', in I Allen & E Perkins (eds) *The Future of Family Care for Older People*. HMSO, London, pp. 51–64.

Finch, J (2007) 'Displaying families', *Sociology* vol. 41, no. 1, pp. 65–81.

Finch, J & Groves, D (1983) *A Labour of Love: Women, Work and Caring*. Routledge, London.

Finch, J & Kim, S-K (2012) 'Kirogi families in the US: Transnational migration and education', *Journal of Ethnic and Migration Studies* vol. 38, no. 3, pp. 485–506.

Finch, J & Mason, J (1993) *Negotiating Family Responsibilities*. Routledge, London.

Forsyth, CJ & Gramling, R (1998) 'Socio-economic factors affecting the rise of commuter marriage', *International Journal of Sociology of the Family* vol. 28, no. 2, pp. 93–106.

Freeman, C (2011) *Making and Faking Kinship: Marriage and Labour Migration between China and South Korea*. Cornell University Press, Ithaca and London.

Fu, AS & Markus, HR (2014) 'My mother and me: Why tiger mothers motivate Asian Americans but not European Americans', *Personality and Social Psychology Bulletin* vol. 40, no. 6, pp. 739–49.

Gallas, A, Herr, H, Hoffer, F & Scherrer, C (eds) (2016) *Combating Inequality: The Global North and South*. Routledge, Abingdon.

Gallegos, D (2006) *Fly-in Fly-out Employment: Managing the Parenting Transitions*. Centre for Social and Community Research, Perth WA.

Gamburd, MR (2000) *The Kitchen Spoon's Handle: Transnationalism and Sri Lanka's Migrant Housemaids*. Cornell University Press, Ithaca, NY.

Gardner, K (1995) *Global Migrants, Local Lives: Travel and Transformation in Rural Bangladesh*. Clarendon Press, London.

Gardner, K (2002) *Age, Narrative and Migration: The Life Course and Life Histories of Bengali Elders in London*. Berg, Oxford.

Gardner, K (2008) 'Keeping connected: Security, place, and social capital in a "Londoni" village in Sylhet', *Journal of the Royal Anthropological Institute* vol. 14, pp. 477–95.

Gerson, K (1994) 'A few good men: Overcoming the barriers to involved fatherhood', *American Prospect* vol. 14, pp. 78–90.

Gerstel, N & Gross, HE (1982) 'Commuter marriages', *Marriage and Family Review* vol. 5, no. 2, pp. 71–93.

Gerstel, N & Gross, HE (1984) *Commuter Marriage: A Study of Work and Family*. The Guilford Press, New York.

Giddens, A (1991) *Modernity and Self-Identity: Self and Society in the Late Modern Age*. Stanford University Press, Stanford.

Giddens, A. (1992) *The Transformation of Intimacy: Sexuality, Love and Eroticism in Modern Societies*. Polity Press, Cambridge.

Gilding, M (2010) 'Reflexivity over and above convention: The new orthodoxy in the sociology of personal life, formerly sociology of the family', *The British Journal of Sociology* vol. 61, no. 4, pp. 757–77.

Gittins, D (1985) *The Family in Question: Changing Households and Familial Ideologies*. Macmillan, Houndmills.

Glick Schiller, N, Basch, L & Blanc-Szanton, C (1992) 'Transnationalism: A new analytic framework for understanding migration', in N Glick Schiller, L Basch & C Blanc-Szanton (eds) *Towards a Transnational Perspective on Migration: Race, Class, Ethnicity and Nationalism Reconsidered*. Annals of the New York Academy of Science 645, pp. 1–24.

Goffman, E (1959) *The Presentation of Self in Everyday Life*. Doubleday, New York.

Golden, J (1996) *A Social History of Wet Nursing in America: From Breast to Bottle*. Cambridge University Press, Cambridge.

Goldstein-Gidoni, O (1997) *Packaged Japaneseness: Weddings, Business and Brides.* University of Hawai'i Press, Honolulu.

González-Pascual, JL, Ruiz-López, M, Saiz-Navarro, EM & Moreno-Preciado, M (2017) 'Exploring barriers to breastfeeding among Chinese mothers living in Madrid, Spain', *Journal of Immigrant Minority Health* vol. 19, pp. 74–79.

Goodman, C & Silverstein, M (2001) 'Grandmothers who parent their grandchildren: An exploratory study of close relations across three generations', *Journal of Family Issues* vol. 22, pp. 557–78.

Goody, J (1983) *The Development of the Family and Marriage in Europe.* Cambridge University Press, Cambridge.

Goody, J (2000) *The European Family.* Blackwell, Oxford.

Gorman-Murray, A (2009) 'Intimate mobilities: Emotional embodiment and queer migration', *Social & Cultural Geography* vol. 10, no. 4, pp. 441–60.

Gorman-Murray, A & Nash, C (2016) 'Mobile sexualities: Section introduction', in G Brown & K Browne (eds) *The Routledge Research Companion to Geographies of Sex and Sexualities.* Routledge, London, pp. 228–33.

Goulbourne, H (2002) *Caribbean Transnational Experience.* Pluto Press, London.

Goulbourne, H (2003) 'Editorial: Caribbean families and communities', *Community, Work & Family* vol. 6, no. 1, pp. 3–16.

Griffith, A & Smith, D (2005) *Mothering for Schooling.* Routledge, London.

Grimes, KM (1998) *Crossing Borders: Changing Social Identities in Southern Mexico.* University of Arizona Press, Tucson AZ.

Gubernskaya, Z & Treas, J (2016) 'Call home? Mobile phones and contacts with mother in 24 countries', *Journal of Marriage and Family* vol. 78, no. 5, pp. 1237–49.

Guo, K (2013) 'Ideals and realities in Chinese immigrant parenting: Tiger mother versus others', *Journal of Family Studies* vol. 19, no. 1, pp. 44–52.

Guo, M, Aranda, M & Silverstein, M (2009) 'The impact of out-migration on the inter-generation support and psychological wellbeing of older adults in rural China', *Ageing and Society* vol. 29, pp. 1085–1104.

Guo, M, Chi, I & Silverstein, M (2009) 'Intergenerational support of Chinese rural elders with migrant children: Do sons' or daughters' migrations make a difference?', *Journal of Gerontological Social Work* vol. 52, no. 5, pp. 534–54.

Haataja, A (2009) *Fathers' Use of Paternity Leave and Parental Leave in the Nordic Countries.* Kela/Fpa Online Working Papers 2/2009. Helsinki, The Social Insurance Institution, Research Department, Finland.

Hadi, A (2001), 'International migration and the change of women's position among the left-behind in rural Bangladesh', *International Journal of Population Geography* vol. 7, no. 1, pp. 53–61.

Haebich, A (2000) *Broken Circles: Fragmenting Indigenous Families, 1800–2000.* Fremantle Press, Fremantle.

Hannaford, D (2015) 'Technologies of the spouse: Intimate surveillance in Senegalese transnational marriages', *Global Networks* vol. 15, no. 1, pp. 43–59.

Hartley, R (ed.) (1995) *Families and Cultural Diversity in Australia.* Allen & Unwin, Sydney.

Harvey, D (1989) *The Condition of Postmodernity: An Enquiry into the Origins of Cultural Change.* Blackwell, Oxford.

Harvey, M & Weise, D (2007) 'The dual-career couple: Female expatriates and male trailing spouses', *Thunderbird International Business Review* vol. 40, no. 4, p. 359–88.

Hays, S (1996) *The Cultural Contradictions of Motherhood.* Yale University Press, New Haven.

HCCH (1993) *33: Convention of 29 May 1993 on Protection of Children and Co-Operation in Respect of Intercountry Adoption*, Hague Conference on Private International Law, The Hague. Available at: www.hcch.net/en/instruments/conventions/full-text/?cid=69.

Hebebrand, J, Anagnostopoulos, D, Eliez, S, Linse, H, Pejovic-Liovancevic, M & Klasen, H (2015) 'A first assessment of the needs of young refugees arriving in Europe: What mental health professionals need to know', *European Child and Adolescent Psychiatry* vol. 25, no. 1, pp. 1–6.

Herdt, G (1993) 'Sexual repression, social control, and gender hierarchy in Sambia culture', in BD Miller (ed.) *Sex and Gender Hierarchies*. Cambridge University Press, Cambridge, pp. 193–211.

Hernandez-Losada, C (2016) *Stories from the Closet: Gender Relations and Gender Identities of Trans Women in Bogotá, Colombia*. PhD thesis, La Trobe University.

Ho, ES (2002) 'Multi-local residence, transnational networks: Chinese "astronaut" families in New Zealand', *Asian and Pacific Migration Journal* vol. 11, no. 1, pp. 145–64.

Ho, EL-E (2008) '"Flexible citizenship" or familial ties that bind? Singaporean transmigrants in London', *International Migration* vol. 46, no. 4, pp. 145–73.

Hoang, LA & Yeoh, BS (2011) 'Breadwinning wives and "left-behind" husbands: Men and masculinities in the Vietnamese transnational family', *Gender & Society* vol. 25, no. 6, pp. 717–39.

Hochschild, A (1979) 'Emotion work, feeling rules and social structure', *The American Journal of Sociology* vol. 85, no. 3, pp. 551–75.

Hochschild, A (1983) *The Managed Heart: Commercialization of Human Feeling*. Berkeley, University of California Press.

Hochschild, A (1989) *The Second Shift: Working Parents and the Revolution at Home*. Viking Penguin, New York.

Hochschild, A (2000) 'Global care chains and emotional surplus value', in W Hutton & A Giddens (eds) *On the Edge: Living with Global Capitalism*. Jonathan Cape, London, pp. 130–46.

Hochschild, A (2012) *The Outsourced Self: Intimate Life in Market Times*. New York, Metropolitan Press.

Hochschild, A (2013) *So How's The Family?* University of California Press, Berkeley.

Hollway, W & Featherstone, B (eds) (1997) *Mothering and Ambivalence*. Routledge, London.

Holmes, M (2004) 'An equal distance? Individualisation, gender and intimacy in distance relationships', *The Sociological Review* vol. 52, no. 2, pp. 180–200.

Holmes, M (2006) 'Love lives at a distance: Distance relationships over the lifecourse', *Sociological Research Online* vol. 11, no. 3. Available at: www.socresonline.org.uk/11/3/holmes.html.

Holmes, M (2011) 'Emotional reflexivity in contemporary friendships: Understanding it using Elias and Facebook etiquette', *Sociological Research Online* vol. 16, pp. 1–11. Available at: http://www.socresonline.org.uk/16/1/11.html.

Holt, M (2004) '"Marriage-like" or married? Lesbian and gay marriage, partnership and migration', *Feminism & Psychology* vol. 14, no. 1, pp. 30–5.

Horowitz, A. (1985) 'Sons and daughters as caregivers to older parents: Differences on role performance and consequences', *Gerontologist* vol. 25, pp. 612–17.

Howe, C, Zaraysky, S & Lorentzen, L (2008) 'Transgender sex workers and sexual transmigration between Guadalajara and San Francisco', *Latin American Perspectives* vol. 35, no. 1, pp. 31–50.

Howell, S (2003) 'Kinning: The creation of life trajectories in transnational adoptive families', *Journal of the Royal Anthropological Institute* vol. 9, pp. 465–84.

Howell, S (2006) *The Kinning of Foreigners: Transnational Adoption in a Global Perspective*. Bergahn Books, New York.

Huang, S & Yeoh, BSA (2005) 'Transnational families and their children's education: China's "study mothers" in Singapore', *Global Networks* vol. 5, no. 4, pp. 379–400.

Hughes, D. (2000) 'The Internet and sex industries: Partners in global sexual exploitation', *IEEE Technology and Society Magazine* Spring, pp. 35–42.

Hughes, J (2013) 'A logical response to the demands of the labour market? Young people living alone in Australia', *Current Sociology* vol. 61, no. 7, pp. 966–83.

Hughes, J (2015) 'The decentring of couple relationships? An examination of young adults living alone', *Journal of Sociology* vol. 51, no. 3, pp. 707–21.

Hugo, G (2001) 'A century of population change in Australia', *Year Book Australia, 2001*. ABS Catalogue no. 1301.0

Huntley, S (2013) 'International love and unlawful presence: A new challenge for same-sex binational couples after the repeal of the Defense of Marriage Act', *Southwestern Journal of International Law* vol. 20, pp. 201–25.

Ikels, C (1993) 'Chinese kinship and the state: Shaping of policy for the elderly', in G Maddox & M Powell Lawton (eds) *Annual Review of Gerontology and Geriatrics. Volume 13 Kinship, Aging and Social Change*. Springer, New York, pp. 123–46.

Illouz, E (1997) *Consuming the Romantic Utopia: Love and the Cultural Contradictions of Capitalism*. University of California Press, Berkeley.

Illouz, E (2007) *Cold Intimacies: The Making of Emotional Capitalism*. Polity Press, Cambridge.

Insight (2010) *Family*. SBS One, March 16 2010. Available at: www.sbs.com.au/news/insight/tvepisode/family.

Ip, M (2002) 'Chinese female migration: From exclusion to transnationalism', in L Fraser & K Pickles (eds) *Shifting Centers: Women and Migration in New Zealand History*. Otago University Press, Dunedin, pp. 149–65.

Isaksen, LW, Devi, SU & Hochschild, AR (2008) 'Global care crisis: A problem of capital, care chain, or commons?' *American Behavioral Scientist* vol. 52, no. 3, pp. 405–25.

Jacobs, SE, Thomas, W & Lang, S (1997) *Two-Spirit People: Native American Gender Identity, Sexuality and Spirituality*. University of Illinois Press, Urbana.

Jagganath, G (2015) 'Migration experiences of the "trailing wives" of professional and highly skilled NRIs in Durban, KwaZulu Natal', *The Oriental Anthropologist* vol. 15, no. 2, pp. 405–17.

Jagger, E (2001) 'Marketing Molly and Melville: Dating in a postmodern, consumer society', *Sociology* vol. 35, no. 1, pp. 39–57.

James, K (1997) 'Reading the leaves: The role of Tongan women's traditional wealth and other "contraflows" in the processes of modern migration and remittance', *Pacific Studies* vol. 20, no. 1, pp. 1–27.

Jamieson, L (1998) *Intimacy: Personal Relationships in Modern Societies*. Polity Press, Cambridge.

Jankowiak, W (ed.) (1995) *Romantic Passion: A Universal Experience?* Columbia University Press, New York.

Jayakody, R, Thornton, A & Axinn, WG (2012) *International Family Change: Ideational Perspectives*. Taylor and Francis, New York.

Jennings, R (2010) '"It was a hot climate and it was a hot time"', *Australian Feminist Studies* vol. 25, no. 63, pp. 31–45.

Jones, G (2005) 'The "flight from marriage" in South-East and East Asia', *Journal of Comparative Family Studies* vol. 36, no. 1, pp. 93–119.

Jones, G (2010) 'Changing marriage patterns in Asia', *Asia Research Institute Working Paper Series* No. 131, January 2010. Asia Research Institute, National University of Singapore, Singapore.

Jones, G (2012a) 'International marriage in Asia: What do we know, and what do we need to know?' *Asia Research Institute Working Paper Series*, No. 174, January 2012, www.ari.nus.edu.sg/pub/wps.htm. Asia Research Institute, National University of Singapore, Singapore.

Jones, G (2012b) 'Late marriage and low fertility in Singapore: The limits of policy', *The Japanese Journal of Population* vol. 10, no. 1, pp. 89–101.

Jones, G & Yeung, WJ (2014) 'Marriage in Asia', *Journal of Family Issues* vol. 35, no. 12, pp. 1567–83.

Jordan, M (2001) 'Your career matters: Have husband, will travel – world of the trailing spouse isn't wives-only anymore; "It's the best job I ever had"', *Wall Street Journal*, 13 February 2001, B.1

Jurgens, J (2001) 'Shifting spaces: Complex identities in Turkish-German migration', in L Pries (ed.) *New Transnational Social Spaces: International Migration and Transnational Companies in the Early Twenty-First Century*. Routledge, London, pp. 94–113.

Kabeer, N (2007) *Marriage, Motherhood and Masculinity in the Global Economy: Reconfigurations of Personal and Economic Life*. IDS Working Paper 290. Institute of Development Studies, University of Sussex.

Kaczmarek, E & Sibbel, A (2008) 'The psychosocial well-being of children from Australian military and fly-in/fly-out (FIFO) mining families'. *Community, Work & Family* vol. 11, no. 3, pp. 297–312.

Ka'ili, T (2005) 'Tauhi vā: Nurturing Tongan sociospatial ties in Maui and beyond', *The Contemporary Pacific* vol. 17, no. 1, pp. 83–114.

Kalpagam, U (2005) '"American varan" marriages among Tamil Brahmans: Preferences, strategies and outcomes', *Indian Journal of Gender Studies* vol. 12, no. 2–3, pp. 189–215.

Kendall, L (2002) *Hanging Out in the Virtual Pub: Masculinities and Relationships Online*. University of California Press, Berkeley.

Kennedy, P (2004) 'Making global society: Friendship networks among transnational professionals in the building design industry', *Global Networks* vol. 4, no. 2, pp. 157–79.

Khoo, SE, McDonald, P, Giorgas, D & Birrell, B (2002) *Second Generation Australians: Report for the Department of Immigration and Multicultural and Indigenous Affairs*. DIMIA, Canberra.

Kilkey, M (2014) 'Polish male migrants in London: The circulation of fatherly care', in L Baldassar & L Merla (eds) *Transnational Families, Migration and the Circulation of Care: Understanding Mobility and Absence in Family Life*. Routledge, London, pp. 185–99.

Kilkey, M & Merla, L (2014) 'Situating transnational families' care-giving arrangements: The role of institutional contexts', *Global Networks* vol. 14, no. 2, pp. 210–47.

Kim, E (2005) 'Wedding citizenship and culture: Korean adoptees and the global family of Korea', in TA Volkman (ed.) *Cultures of Transnational Adoption*. Duke University Press, Durham, pp. 49–80.

King, R (2010) *People on the Move: An Atlas of Migration*. University of California Press, Berkeley.

King, R & Vullnetari, J (2006) 'Orphan pensioners and migrating grandparents: The impact of mass migration on older people in rural Albania', *Ageing and Society* vol. 26, pp. 783–816.

King, R, Cela, E, Fokkema, T & Vullnetari, J (2014) 'The migration and well-being of the zero generation: Transgenerational care, grandparenting and loneliness amongst Albanian older people', *Population, Space and Place* vol. 20, no. 8, pp. 728–38.

Kinsella, K (2000) 'Demographic dimensions of global aging', *Journal of Family Issues* vol. 21, no. 5, pp. 541–58.

Kjeldstad, R (2001) 'Gender politics and gender equality', in M Kautto, J Fritzell, B Hvinden, J Kvist & H Uusitalo (eds) *Nordic Welfare States in the European Context*. Routledge, London, pp. 66–97.

Knodel, J, Kespichayawattana, J, Saengtienchai, C & Wiwatwanich, S (2010) 'How left behind are rural parents of migrant children? Evidence from Thailand', *Ageing and Society* vol. 30, pp. 811–41.

Kofman, E (2012) 'Rethinking care through social reproduction: Articulating circuits of migration', *Social Politics* vol. 19, no. 1, pp. 142–62.

Kofman, E & Raghuram, P (2012) 'Women, migration and care: Explorations of diversity and dynamism in the global south', *Social Politics* vol. 19, no. 3, pp. 408–32.

Kohli, R (2011) 'Working to ensure safety, belonging and success for unaccompanied asylum-seeking children', *Child Abuse Review* vol. 20, no. 5, pp. 311–23.

Kojima, Y (2001) 'In the business of cultural reproduction: Theoretical implications of the mail-order bride phenomenon', *Women's Studies International Forum*, vol. 24, pp. 199–209.

Kraemer, J (2014) 'Friend or freund: Social media and transnational connections in Berlin', *Human-Computer Interaction* vol. 29, no. 1, pp. 53–77.

Krasovitsky, M, Zaballa, A, Purcell, D, Mitchell, A, Davidson, T, Gebicki, C, Drakopoulos, L, Gunn, L, Wadhera, M, La, W, Barrett, D & Garrick, L (2016) *Willing to Work: National Inquiry into Employment Discrimination Against Older Australians and Australians with Disability*. Australian Human Rights Commission, Sydney. Available at: http://hdl.voced.edu.au/10707/403097.

Kreager, P (2006) 'Migration, social structure and old-age support networks: A comparison of three Indonesian communities', *Ageing and Society* vol. 26, pp. 37–60.

Künemund, H (2006) 'Changing welfare states and the "sandwich generation": Increasing burden for the next generation?', *International Journal of Ageing and Later Life* vol. 1, no. 2, pp. 11–29.

Kwok, H (2006) 'The son also acts as major caregiver to elderly parents', *Current Sociology* vol. 54, no. 2, pp. 257–72.

Lam, RC (2006) 'Contradictions between traditional Chinese values and the actual performance: A study of the caregiving roles of the modern sandwich generation in Hong Kong', *Journal of Comparative Family Studies* vol. 37, no. 2, pp. 299–313.

Lang, G & Smart, J (2002) 'Migration and the "second wife" in south China: Toward cross-border polygyny', *International Migration Review* vol. 36, no. 2, pp. 546–69.

Lareau, A (2002) 'Invisible inequality: Social class and childrearing in black and white families', *American Sociological Review* vol. 67, pp. 747–76.

Lareau, A (2003) *Unequal Childhoods: Class, Race and Family Life*. University of California Press, Berkeley.

Lasch, C (1979) *The Culture of Narcissism*. Norton, New York.

LaViolette, N (2004) 'Coming out to Canada: The immigration of same-sex couples under the Immigration and Refugee Protection Act', *McGill Law Journal* vol. 49, pp. 969–1003.

Lee, H (2003) *Tongans Overseas: Between Two Shores*. University of Hawai'i Press, Honolulu.

Lee, H (2004a) '"Second generation" Tongan transnationalism: Hope for the future?', *Asian Pacific Viewpoint* vol. 45, no. 2, pp. 235–54.

Lee, H (2004b) 'All Tongans are connected: Tongan transnationalism', in V Lockwood (ed.) *Globalization and Culture Change in the Pacific Islands*, Prentice Hall, Englewood Cliffs NJ, pp. 133–48.

Lee, H (2006) '"Tonga only wants our money": The children of Tongan migrants', in S Firth (ed.) *Globalisation, Governance and the Pacific Islands*. ANU E-Press, Canberra.

Lee, H (2007) 'Transforming transnationalism: Second generation Tongans overseas', *Asian and Pacific Migration Journal* vol. 16, no. 2, pp. 157–78.

Lee, H (2009) 'The ambivalence of return: Second-generation Tongan returnees', in D Conway & RB Potter (eds) *Return Migration of the Next Generations: 21ˢᵗ Century Transnational Mobility*. Ashgate, Surrey, pp. 41–58.

Lee, H (2011) 'Rethinking transnationalism through the second generation', *The Australian Journal of Anthropology* vol. 22, pp. 295–313.

Levin, I (2004) 'Living apart together: A new family form', *Current Sociology* vol. 52, no. 2, pp. 223–40.

Levin, I & Trost, J (1999) 'Living apart together', *Community, Work and Family* vol. 2, no. 3, pp. 279–94.

Levitt, P (2001) *The Transnational Villagers*. University of California Press, Berkeley.

Lewis, NM (2014) 'Moving "out", moving on: Gay men's migrations through the life course', *Annals of the Association of American Geographers* vol. 104, no. 2, pp. 225–33.

Lewis, NM & Mills, S (2016) 'Seeking security: Gay labour migration and uneven landscapes of work', *Environment & Planning A*, doi: 10.1177/0308518X16659773

Ley, D & Kobayashi, A (2005) 'Back to Hong Kong: Return migration or transnational sojourn?' *Global Networks* vol. 5, no. 2, pp. 111–27.

Lichter, DT, Anderson, RN & Hayward, MD (1995) 'Marriage markets and marital choice', *Journal of Family Issues* vol. 16, no. 4, pp. 412–31.

Lie, MLS (2010) 'Across the oceans: Childcare and grandparenting in UK Chinese and Bangladeshi households', *Journal of Ethnic and Migration Studies* vol. 36, no. 9, pp. 1425–43.

Lindholm, C (1995) 'Love as an experience of transcendence', in W Jankowiak (ed.) *Romantic Passion: A Universal Experience?* Columbia University Press, New York, pp. 57–71.

Lindsay, J (1999) 'Diversity but not equality: Domestic labour in cohabiting relationships', *The Australian Journal of Social Issues* vol. 34, no. 3, pp. 267–83.

Litwak E (1960a) 'Occupational mobility and extended family cohesion', *American Sociological Review* vol. 25, no. 1, pp. 9–21.

Litwak, E (1960b) 'Geographic mobility and extended family cohesion', *American Sociological Review* vol. 25, no. 3, pp. 385–94.

Litwak, E & Kulis S (1987) 'Technology, proximity, and measures of kin support'. *Journal of Marriage and the Family* vol. 49, pp. 649–61.

Liu, Y & Erwin, L (2015) 'Divided motherhood: Rural-to-urban migration of married women in contemporary China', *Journal of Comparative Family Studies* vol. 46, no. 2, pp. 241–63.

Luibhéid, E (2002) *Entry Denied: Controlling Sexuality at the Border*. University of Minnesota Press, Minneapolis.

Luibhéid, E (2008) 'Queer/migration: An unruly body of scholarship', *GLQ: A Journal of Lesbian and Gay Studies* vol. 4, no. 2, pp. 169–90.

Luibhéid, E & Cantú, L (eds) (2005) *Queer Migrations: Sexuality, US Citizenship and Border Crossings.* University of Minnesota Press, Minneapolis.

Lund, R, Kusakabe, K, Panda, SM & Wang, Y (2016) 'Building knowledge across transnational boundaries: Collaboration and friendship in research', *Emotion, Space and Society* vol. 20, pp. 18–24.

Lupton, D (1998) *The Emotional Self: A Sociocultural Exploration.* Sage, London.

Luster, T, Qin, D, Bates, L, Rana, M & Lee, JA (2010) 'Successful adaptation among Sudanese unaccompanied minors: Perspectives of youth and foster parents', *Childhood* vol. 17, no. 2, pp. 197–211.

Lutz, H & Palenga-Möllenbeck, E (2012) 'Care workers, care drains and care chains: Reflecting on care, migration and citizenship', *Social Politics* vol. 19, no. 1, pp. 15–37.

Madianou, M (2012) 'Migration and the accentuated ambivalence of motherhood: the role of ICTs in Filipino transnational families', *Global Networks* vol. 12, no. 3, pp. 277–95.

Madianou, M & Miller, D (2012) *Migration and New Media: Transnational Families and Polymedia.* Routledge, Abingdon.

Mahler, S (2001) 'Transnational relationships: The struggle to communicate across borders', *Identities: Global Studies in Culture and Power* vol. 7, no. 4, pp. 583–619.

Makela, L, Suutari, V & Mayerhofer, H (2011) 'Lives of female expatriates: Work-life balance concerns', *Gender in Management: An International Journal* vol. 26, no. 4, pp. 256–74.

Manalansan, MF (2008), 'Queering the chain of care paradigm', *S&F Online* vol. 6, no. 3 Available at: http://sfonline.barnard.edu/immigration/manalansan_01.htm.

Mandel, R (1990) 'Shifting centres and emergent identities: Turkey and Germany in the lives of Turkish gastarbeiter', in DF Eickelman & JP Piscatori (eds) *Muslim Travellers: Pilgrimage, Migration and the Religious Imagination.* Routledge, London, pp. 153–70.

Mandel, R (2008) *Cosmopolitan Anxieties: Turkish Challenges to Citizenship and Belonging in Germany.* Duke University Press, Durham.

Mason, J (1999) 'Living away from relatives: Kinship and geographical reasoning', in S McRae (ed.) *Changing Britain Families and Households in the 1990s.* Oxford University Press, Oxford, pp. 156–75.

Mason, J (2004) 'Managing kinship over long distances: The significance of "the visit"', *Social Policy and Society* vol. 3, no. 4, pp. 421–29.

Mason, J (2008) 'Tangible affinities and the real life fascination of kinship', *Sociology* vol. 42, no. 1, pp. 29–45.

May, V (ed.) (2011) *Sociology of Personal Life.* Palgrave Macmillan, Houndmills.

McBride, MC & Bergen, KM (2014) 'Voices of women in commuter marriages: A site of discursive struggle', *Journal of Social and Personal Relationships* vol. 31, no. 4, pp. 554–72.

Macdonald, CL (1998) 'Manufacturing Motherhood: The Shadow Work of Nannies and Au Pairs', *Qualitative Sociology*, vol. 21, no. 1, pp. 25–53.

McDonald, P (1995) *Families in Australia: A Socio-Demographic Perspective.* Australian Institute of Family Studies, Melbourne.

McGinnis, T, Goodstein-Stolzenberg, A & Saliani, EC (2007) '"indnpride": Online spaces of transnational youth as sites of creative and sophisticated literacy and identity work', *Linguistics and Education*, vol. 18, pp. 283–304.

McGloin, B (1999–2000) 'Diverse families with parallel needs: A proposal for same-sex immigration benefits', *California Western International Law Journal* vol. 30, pp. 159–74.

McKay, S (2010) '"So they remember me when I'm gone": Remittances, fatherhood and gender relations of Filipino migrant men', in LA Hoang & B Yeoh (eds) *Transnational Labour Migration, Remittances and the Changing Family in Asia*. Palgrave, Houndmills, pp. 111–35.

Mclean, K (2012) 'Mental health and well-being in resident mine workers: Out of the fly-in fly-out box', *Australian Journal of Rural Health* vol. 20, pp. 126–30.

McNulty, Y (2012) '"Being dumped in to sink or swim: An empirical study of organizational support for the trailing spouse', *Human Resource Development International* vol. 15, no. 4, pp. 417–34.

McRae, S (ed.) (1999) *Changing Britain: Families and Households in the 1990s.* Oxford University Press, Oxford.

Mead, GH (1934) *Mind, Self and Society from the Standpoint of a Social Behaviorist.* The University of Chicago Press, Chicago.

Menjivar, C (2002) 'Living in two worlds? Guatemalan-origin children in the United States and emerging transnationalism', *Journal of Ethnic and Migration Studies* vol. 28, no. 3, pp. 531–52.

Menjivar, C & Abrego, L (2009) 'Parents and children across borders: Legal instability and intergenerational relations in Guatemalan and Salvadoran families', in N Foner (ed.) *Across Generations: Immigrant Families in America*, New York University Press, New York, pp. 160–89.

Miller, D (1981) 'The "sandwich" generation: Adult children of the aging', *Social Work* vol. 26, no. 5, pp. 419–423.

Miller, R (2013) *Wife and Baggage to Follow.* Halstead Press, Braddon ACT.

Miller, T (2011) 'Falling back into gender? Men's narratives and practices around first-time fatherhood', *Sociology* vol. 45, no. 6, pp. 1094–1109.

Miltiades, HB (2002) 'The social and psychological effect of an adult child's emigration on non-immigrant Asian Indian elderly parents', *Journal of Cross-Cultural Gerontology* vol. 17, pp. 33–55.

Minervini, BP & McAndrew, FT (2006) 'The mating strategies and mate preferences of mail order brides', *Cross-Cultural Research* vol. 40, no. 2, pp. 111–29.

Moran-Taylor, MJ (2008) 'When mothers and fathers migrate north: Caretakers, children, and child-rearing in Guatemala', *Latin American Perspectives* vol. 35, no. 4, pp. 79–95.

Morgan, D (1996) *Family Connections.* Polity Press, Cambridge MA.

Morgan, D (2009) *Acquaintances: The Space Between Intimates and Strangers.* Open University Press.

Morgan, D (2011) *Rethinking Family Practices.* Palgrave, Basingstoke.

Murdock, G (1965) [1949] *Social Structure.* The Free Press, New York.

Murphy, B, Schofield, H, Nankervis, J, Bloch, S, Herrman, H & Singh, B (1997) 'Women with multiple roles: The emotional impact of caring for ageing parents', *Ageing and Society* vol. 17, no. 3, pp. 277–91.

Myers, GC & Nathanson CA (1982) 'Aging and the family', *World Health Statistics Quarterly* vol. 35, no. 3–4, pp. 225–38.

Nagle, LE (2012) 'Giving shelter from the storm: Colombians fleeing persecution based on sexual orientation', *Tulsa Law Review* vol. 48, no. 1, pp. 1–26. Available at: http://digitalcommons.law.utulsa.edu/tlr/vol48/iss1/1.

Nanda, S (1996) *Neither Man Nor Woman: The Hijras of India.* Wadsworth, Belmont.

Nava, M (1983) 'From utopian to scientific feminism: Early feminist critique of the family', in L Segal (ed.) *What is to be done about the family?* Penguin, Harmondsworth, pp. 65–105.

Neidomysl, T, Osth, J & van Ham, M (2010) 'The globalisation of marriage fields: The Swedish case', *Journal of Ethnic and Migration Studies* vol. 36, no. 7, pp. 1119–38.

Nelson, M (2010) *Parenting Out of Control: Anxious Parents in Uncertain Times.* New York University Press, New York.

Neumayer, E (2006) 'Unequal access to foreign spaces: How states use visa restrictions to regulate mobility in a globalized world', *Transactions of the Institute of British Geographers* vol. 31, no. 1, pp. 72–84.

Neysmith, SM & Zhou, YR (2013) 'Mapping another dimension of a feminist ethics of care: Family-based transnational care', *International Journal of Feminist Approaches to Bioethics* vol. 6, no. 2, pp. 141–59.

Nishitani, M (2014) 'Kinship, gender, and communication technologies: Family dramas in the Tongan diaspora', *The Australian Journal of Anthropology* vol. 25, pp. 207–22.

Nolan, C (2006) *Transnational Ruptures: Gender and Forced Migration.* Ashgate, Aldershot.

Nukaga, M (2013) 'Planning for a successful return home: Transnational habitus and education strategies among Japanese expatriate mothers in Los Angeles', *International Sociology* vol. 28, no. 1, pp. 66–83.

Oakley, A (1974) *Women's Work: The Housewife, Past and Present.* Random House, New York.

Ocampo, AC (2014) 'The gay second generation: Sexual identity and family relations of Filipino and Latino gay men', *Journal of Ethnic and Migration Studies* vol. 40, no. 1, pp. 155–73.

Office for National Statistics (n.d.) Available at: www.ons.gov.uk.

Office for National Statistics (2012) 'Divorces in England and Wales, 2011'. Available at: www.ons.gov.uk/ons/rel/vsob1/divorces-in-england-and-wales/2011/index.html.

Office for National Statistics (2015), 'Families and Households: 2015'. Available at: www.ons.gov.uk/peoplepopulationandcommunity/birthsdeathsandmarriages/families/bulletins/familiesandhouseholds/2015-11-05.

Oishi, N (2005) *Women in Motion: Globalization, State Policies, and Labor Migration in Asia.* Stanford University Press, Stanford.

Olwig, KF (1999) 'Narratives of the children left behind: Home and identity in globalised Caribbean families', *Journal of Ethnic and Migration Studies* vol. 25, no. 2, pp. 267–84.

Olwig, KF (2002) 'A wedding in the family: Home making in a global kin network', *Global Networks* vol. 2, no. 3, pp. 205–18.

Olwig, KF (2007) *Caribbean Journeys: An Ethnography of Migration and Home in Three Family Networks.* Duke University Press, Durham.

Olwig, KF (2012) 'The "successful" return: Caribbean narratives of migration, family, and gender', *Journal of the Royal Anthropological Institute* vol. 18, pp. 828–45.

Olwig, KF (2014) 'Migration and care: Intimately related aspects of Caribbean family and kinship', in L Baldassar & L Merla (eds) *Transnational Families, Migration and the Circulation of Care: Understanding Mobility and Absence in Family Life.* Routledge, London, pp. 133–48.

Ong, A (1999) *Flexible Citizenship: The Cultural Logics of Transnationality.* Duke University Press, Durham.

Otnes, C & Pleck, E (2003) *Cinderella Dreams: The Allure of the Lavish Wedding.* University of California Press, Berkeley.

Pahl, R (2000) *On Friendship.* Polity Press, Cambridge.

Pahl, R & Pevalin, DJ (2005) 'Between family and friends: A longitudinal study of friendship choice', *The British Journal of Sociology* vol. 56, no. 3, pp. 433–50.

Pahl, R & Spencer, L (2004) 'Personal communities: Not simply families of "fate" or "choice"', *Current Sociology* vol. 52, no. 2, pp. 199–221.

Palenga-Möllenbeck, E (2013) 'Care chains in Eastern and Central Europe: Male and female domestic work at the intersections of gender, class and ethnicity', *Journal of Immigrant and Refugee Studies* vol. 1, no. 3, pp. 364–83.

Palriwala, R & Uberoi, P (2005) 'Marriage and migration in Asia: Gender issues', *Indian Journal of Gender Studies* vol. 12, no. 2–3, pp. 5–29.

Pananakhonsab, W (2016) *Cross-Cultural Relationships and Cyberspace: The Work of Thai Women's Imagination in Intermarriage Online Dating.* Palgrave Macmillan.

Pantea, MC (2012) 'Grandmothers as main caregivers in the context of parental migration', *European Journal of Social Work* vol. 15, no. 1, pp. 63–80.

Papastergiardis, N (2000) *The Turbulence of Migration: Globalization, Deterritorialization and Hybridity.* Polity Press, Cambridge.

Parkes, K, Carnell, SC & Farmer, EL (2005) 'Living two lives', *Community, Work & Family* vol. 8, no. 4, pp. 413–37.

Parreñas, RS (2000) 'Migrant Filipina domestic workers and the international division of reproductive labor', *Gender & Society* vol. 14, no. 4, pp. 560–81.

Parreñas, RS (2001) *Servants of Globalization: Women, Migration and Domestic Work.* Stanford University Press, Stanford CA.

Parreñas, RS (2005) *Children of Global Migration: Transnational Families and Gendered Woes.* Stanford University Press, Stanford CA.

Parreñas, RS (2008) 'Transnational fathering: Gendered conflicts, distant disciplining and emotional gaps', *Journal of Ethnic and Migration Studies* vol. 34, no. 7, pp. 1057–72.

Parsons, T (1943) 'The kinship system of the contemporary United States', *American Anthropologist* vol. 45, no. 1, pp. 22–38.

Parsons, T (1955) 'The American family: Its relations to personality and to the social structure', in T Parsons & R Bales, *Family, Socialization and Interaction Process,* Free Press, New York.

Paz Cruz, V (1987) *Seasonal Orphans and Solo Parents: The Impact of Overseas Migration.* Scalabrini Migration Center, Quezon City.

Pe Pua, R, Mitchell, C, Iredale, R & Castles, S (1996) *Astronaut Families and Parachute Children: The Cycle of Migration Between Hong Kong and Australia.* Bureau of Immigration, Multicultural and Population Research, Canberra.

Phillips, J & Potter, RB (2009) 'Questions of friendship and degrees of transnationality among second-generation return migrants to Barbados', *Journal of Ethnic and Migration Studies* vol. 35, no. 4, pp. 669–88.

Phillipson, C, Bernard, M, Phillips, J & Ogg, J (2001) *The Family and Community Life of Older People.* Routledge, London.

Phu, T (2014) 'Diasporic Vietnamese family photographs, orphan images, and the art of recollection', *Trans Asia Photography Review* vol. 5, no. 1. Available at: http://hdl.handle.net/2027/spo.7977573.0005.102.

Pingol, AT (2001) *Remaking Masculinities: Identity, Power and Gender Dynamics in Families with Migrant Wives and Househusbands.* University of the Philippines, Manila.

Pini, B & Mayes, R (2012) 'Gender, emotions and fly-in fly-out work', *Australian Journal of Social Issues* vol. 47, no. 1, pp. 71–86.

Piper, N (2003) 'Feminization of labor migration as violence against women: International, regional and local nongovernmental organization responses in Asia', *Violence Against Women* vol. 9, no. 6, pp. 723–45.

Piper, N (2013) 'International migration and gendered axes of stratification', in N Piper (ed.) *New Perspectives on Gender and Migration: Livelihood, Rights and Entitlements.* Taylor and Francis, New York/London, pp. 17–51.

Pocock, B (2003) *The Work/Life Collision – What work is doing to Australians and what to do about it.* Federation Press, Annandale.

Pocock, B (2005) 'Mothers: The more things change, the more they stay the same', in M Poole (ed.) *Family: Changing Families, Changing Times.* Allen & Unwin, Sydney, pp. 113–34.

Policarpo, V (2016) '"The real deal": Managing intimacy within friendship at a distance', *Qualitative Sociology Review* vol. 12, no. 2, pp. 22–42.

Portes, A & Rumbaut, RG (2001) *Legacies: The Story of the Immigrant Second Generation.* University of California Press.

Posthuma, RA, Wagstaff, MF & Campion, MA (2012) 'Age stereotypes and workplace age discrimination', in J W Hedge & WC Borman (eds) *The Oxford Handbook of Work and Aging.* Oxford University Press, Oxford, pp. 298–312.

Pribilsky, J (2001) 'Nervios and "modern childhood": Migration and shifting contexts of child life in the Ecuadorian Andes', *Childhood* vol. 8, no. 2, pp. 251–73.

Purkayastha, B (2005) 'Skilled migration and cumulative disadvantage: The case of highly qualified Asian Indian immigrant women in the US', *Geoforum* vol. 36, pp. 181–96.

Pyper, W (2006) 'Balancing career and care', *Perspectives on Labour and Income* vol. 7, no. 11, pp. 5–15.

Quiroz, PA (2012) 'Cultural tourism in transnational adoption: "Staged authenticity" and its implications for adopted children', *Journal of Family Issues* vol. 33, no. 4, pp. 527–55.

Rechel, B, Grundy, E, Robine, JM, Cylus, J, Mackenbach, JP, Knai, C & McKee, M (2013) 'Ageing and the European Union', *The Lancet* vol. 381, no. 9874, pp. 1312–22.

Reiger, K (1985) *The Disenchantment of the Home: Modernizing the Australian Family 1880–1940.* Oxford University Press, Melbourne.

Reimondos, A, Evans, A & Gray, E (2011) 'Living-apart-together (LAT) relationships in Australia', *Family Matters* no. 87, pp. 43–55.

Reynolds, T (2011) 'Caribbean second-generation return migration: Transnational family relationships with "left-behind" kin in Britain', *Mobilities* vol. 6, no. 4, pp. 535–51.

Ritzer, G (1993) *The McDonaldization of Society: An Investigation of the Changing Character of Contemporary Social Life.* Pine Forge Press, Newbury Park, California.

Roberts, A (1976) 'Mothers and babies: The wetnurse and her employer in mid-nineteenth century England', *Women's Studies* vol. 3, pp. 279–93.

Robertson, R (1995) 'Glocalization: Time-Space and Homogeneity-Heterogeneity', in M Featherstone, S Lash & R Robertson (eds) *Global Modernities.* Sage, Thousand Oaks, pp. 25–44.

Robertson, Z, Wilding, R & Gifford, A (2016) 'Mediating the family imaginary: Young people negotiating absence in transnational refugee families', *Global Networks* vol. 16, no. 2, pp. 219–36.

Robinson, K (2007) 'Marriage migration, gender transformations, and family values in the 'global ecumene', *Gender, Place and Culture* vol. 14, no. 4, pp. 483–97.

Rose, N (1999) *Governing the Soul: The Shaping of the Private Self.* 2nd ed. Routledge, London.

Rossi, AS & Rossi, PH (1990) *Of Human Bonding: Parent-Child Relations Across the Life-Course.* Aldine de Gruyter, New York.

Ruggles, S (1994) 'The origins of African-American family structure', *American Sociological Review* vol. 59, no. 1, pp. 136–51.

Ryan, L (2015) 'Friendship-making: Exploring network formations through the narratives of Irish highly qualified migrants in Britain', *Journal of Ethnic and Migration Studies* vol. 41, no. 10, pp. 1664–83.

Ryan, L & Mulholland, J (2014) '"Wives are the route to social life": An analysis of family life and networking amongst highly skilled migrants in London', *Sociology* vol. 48, no. 2, pp. 251–67.

Ryan, L, Sales, R, Tilki, M & Siara, B (2009) 'Family strategies and transnational migration: Recent polish migrants in London', *Journal of Ethnic and Migration Studies* vol. 35, no. 1, pp. 61–77.

Santos, A (2016) 'Stuck with lousy spouses for now; divorce is still illegal in the Philippines, but groups are working hard to change that', *Los Angeles Times*, 24 August 2016, p. A3(1).

Sciachitano, M (2000) '"MOBS" on the net: Critiquing the gaze of the "cyber" bride industry', *Race, Gender & Class* vol. 7, no. 1, pp. 57–69.

Scharlach, AE, Kellam, R, Ong, N, Baskin, A, Goldstein, C & Fox, PJ (2008) 'Cultural attitudes and caregiver service use: Lessons from focus groups with racially and ethnically diverse family caregivers', *Journal of Gerontological Social Work* vol. 47, no. 1–2, pp. 133–56.

Schwartz, C (2013) 'Trends and variation in assortative mating: Causes and consequences', *Annual Review of Sociology* vol. 39, pp. 451–70.

Seligman, L (2013) *Broken Links, Enduring Ties.* Stanford University Press.

Shaibu, S & Wallhagen, MI (2002) 'Family caregiving of the elderly in Botswana: Boundaries of culturally acceptable options and resources', *Journal of Cross-Cultural Gerontology* vol. 17, pp. 139–54.

Shaw, A (2000) *Kinship and Continuity: Pakistani Families in Britain.* Harwood Academic, Amsterdam.

Sheller, M & Urry, J (2006) 'The new mobilities paradigm', *Environment and Planning A*, vol. 38, pp. 207–26.

Sigad, LI & Eisikovits, RA (2013) 'Grandparenting across borders: American grandparents and their Israeli grandchildren in a transnational reality', *Journal of Aging Studies* vol. 27, pp. 308–16.

Singh, S (2006) 'Towards a sociology of money and family in the Indian diaspora', *Contributions to Indian Sociology* vol. 40, no. 3, pp. 375–98.

Singh, S (2016) *Money, Migration and Family.* Palgrave Macmillan, New York.

Singh, S & Bhandari, M (2012) 'Money management and control in the Indian joint family across generations', *The Sociological Review* vol. 60, no. 1, pp. 46–67.

Singh, S, Cabraal, A & Robertson, S (2010) 'Remittances as a currency of care: A focus on "twice migrants" among the Indian diaspora in Australia', *Journal of Comparative Family Studies* vol. 41, no. 2, pp. 245–63.

Singh, S, Robertson, S & Cabraal, A (2012) 'Transnational family money: Remittances, gifts and inheritance', *Journal of Intercultural Studies* vol. 33, no. 5, pp. 475–92.

Skeggs, B (2004) *Class, Self, Culture.* Routledge, London.

Skolnick, AS & Skolnick, JH (1974) *Intimacy, Family and Society*. Little Brown, Boston.

Small, C (1997) *Voyages: From Tongan Villages to American Suburbs*. Cornell University Press, Ithaca.

Smart, C (2007a) *Personal Life: New Directions in Sociological Thinking*. Polity, Cambridge.

Smart, C (2007b) 'Same sex couples and marriage: Negotiating relational landscapes with families and friends', *The Sociological Review* vol. 55, no. 4, pp. 671–86.

Smart, C & Neale, B (1999) *Family Fragments?* Polity, Cambridge.

Smart, C & Shipman, B (2004) 'Visions in monochrome: Families, marriage and the individualization thesis', *The British Journal of Sociology* vol. 55, no. 4, pp. 491–509.

Smith, G (2012) 'Sexuality, space and migration: South Asian gay men in Australia', *New Zealand Geographer* vol. 68, pp. 92–100.

Smith, RC (2006) *Mexican New York: Transnational Lives of New Immigrants*. University of California Press, Berkeley CA.

Storey, K (2001) 'Fly-in/fly-out and fly-over: Mining and regional development in Western Australia', *Australian Geographer* vol. 32, no. 2, pp. 133–48.

Storey, K & Shrimpton, M (1989) *Impacts on Labour of Long Distance Commuting in the Canadian Mining Industry*. ISER Report No. 3. Institute for Social & Economic Research, Memorial University of Newfoundland, St John's.

Strathern, M (2005) *Kinship, Law and the Unexpected: Relatives are Always a Surprise*. Cambridge University Press, Cambridge.

Summers, A (2003) *The End of Equality: Work, Babies and Women's Choices in 21ˢᵗ Century Australia*. Random House, Sydney.

Suwannapat, N (2014) *Self in Marriage, Marriage in the Self: Negotiating 'Modern' and 'Traditional' Values in Thai Newlywed Marriages*. PhD Thesis, Sociology, La Trobe University.

Tacoli, C (1999) 'International migration and the restructuring of gender asymmetries: Continuity and change among Filipino labor migrants in Rome', *International Migration Review* vol. 33, no. 3, pp. 658–82.

Tan, BAL & Yeoh, BSA (2011) 'Translocal family relations among the Lahu in Northern Thailand', in K Brickell & A Datta (eds) *Translocal Geographies: Spaces, Places, Connections*. Ashgate, Surrey, pp. 39–54.

Taylor, J & Simmonds, J (2009) 'Family stress and coping in the fly-in fly-out workforce', *The Australian Community Psychologist* vol. 21, no. 2, pp. 23–36.

Thing, J (2010) 'Gay, Mexican and immigrant: Intersecting identities among gay men in Los Angeles', *Social Identities* vol. 16, no. 6, pp. 809–31.

Thomas, M (1999) *Dreams in the Shadows: Vietnamese-Australian Lives in Transition*. Allen and Unwin, Sydney.

Thornton, A (2001) 'The developmental paradigm, reading history sideways, and family change', *Demography* vol. 38, no. 4, pp. 449–65.

Thornton, A (2005) *Reading History Sideways: The Fallacy and Enduring Impact of the Developmental Paradigm on Family Life*. University of Chicago Press.

Titshaw, S (2010) 'The meaning of marriage: Immigration rules and their implications for same-sex spouses in a world without DOMA', *William & Mary Journal of Women and the Law* vol. 16, pp. 537–611.

Tolentino, RB (1996) 'Bodies, letters, catalogs: Filipinas in transnational space', *Social Text* vol. 48, pp. 49–76.

Torkington, A, Larkins, S & Gupta, TS (2011) 'The psychosocial impacts of fly-in fly-out and drive-in drive-out mining on mining employees: A qualitative study', *Australian Journal of Rural Health* vol. 19, pp. 135–41.

Torpey, JC (2000) *The Invention of the Passport: Surveillance, Citizenship and the State*. Cambridge University Press, Melbourne.

Treas, J (2008) 'Transnational older adults and their families', *Family Relations* vol. 57, pp. 468–78.

Treas, J (2009) 'Four myths about older adults in America's immigrant families', *Generations* vol. 32, no. 4, pp. 40–5.

Treas, J & Mazumdar, S (2002) 'Older people in America's immigrant families: Dilemmas of dependence, integration, and isolation', *Journal of Aging Studies* vol. 16, no. 3, pp. 243–58.

Treas, J & Mazumdar, S (2004) 'Kinkeeping and caregiving: Contributions of older people in immigrant families', *Journal of Comparative Family Studies* vol. 35, no. 1, pp. 105–22.

Trotzig, A (1996) *Blod ar Tjockare an Vatten* [Blood is Thicker than Water]. Bonniers, Stockholm.

Tryfonidou, A (2014) 'EU free movement law and the legal recognition of same-sex relationships: The case for mutual recognition', *Columbia Journal of European Law* vol. 21, pp. 195–248.

United Nations (2002) *Report of the Second World Assembly on Ageing*. Madrid, 8–12 April 2002. A/CONF.197/9. United Nations, New York.

United Nations (2015) *World Population Ageing 2015*. Department of Economic and Social Affairs, Population Division, United Nations, New York.

Upton-Davis, K (2012) 'Living apart together relationships (LAT): Severing intimacy from obligation', *Gender Issues* vol. 29, no. 1–4, pp. 25–38.

Upton-Davis, K (2013) 'Subverting gendered norms of cohabitation: living apart together for women over 45', *Journal of Gender Studies* vol. 24, no. 1, pp. 104–16.

Urrieta, L & Martínez, S (2011) 'Diasporic community knowledge and school absenteeism: Mexican immigrant pueblo parents' and grandparents' postcolonial ways of educating', *Interventions: International Journal of Postcolonial Studies* vol. 13, no. 2, pp. 256–77.

Urry, J (2000) *Sociology Beyond Societies: Mobilities for the Twenty-first Century*. Routledge, London.

Urry, J (2007) *Mobilities*. Polity Press, Cambridge.

Vaittinen, T (2014) 'Reading global care chains as migrant trajectories: A theoretical framework for the understanding of structural change', *Women's Studies International Forum* vol. 47, pp. 191–202.

Van der Klis, M (2008) 'Continuity and change in commuter partnerships: Avoiding or postponing family migration', *Geojournal* vol. 71, pp. 233–47.

Van der Klis, M & Karsten, L (2009a) 'The commuter family as a geographical adaptive strategy for the work-family balance', *Community, Work and Family* vol. 12, no. 3, pp. 339–54.

Van der Klis, M & Karsten, L (2009b) 'Stories of belonging: Commuting partners, dual residences and the meaning of home', *Journal of Environmental Psychology* vol. 29, no. 2, pp. 235–45.

Van der Klis, M & Mulder, CH (2008) 'Beyond the trailing spouse: The commuter partnership as an alternative to family migration', *Journal of Housing and the Built Environment* vol. 23, pp. 1–19.

Vasquez, DAE (2014) *Being a Man in a Transnational World: The Masculinity and Sexuality of Migration*. Routledge, New York.

Vervliet, M, Vanobbergen, B, Broekaert, E & Derluyn, I (2015) 'The aspirations of Afghan unaccompanied refugee minors before departure and on arrival in the host country', *Childhood* vol. 22, no. 3, pp. 330–45.

Vespa, J, Lewis, JM & Kreider, RM (2013) 'America's families and living arrangements: 2012. Population characteristics'. United States Census Bureau P20-570. Available at: https://www.census.gov/prod/2013pubs/p20-570.pdf.

Vincent, C & Ball, S (2006) *Childcare, Choice and Class Practices: Middle-Class Parents and their Children*. Routledge, London.

Vogl, G & Kell, P (2010) *Global Student Mobility in the Asia Pacific*. Cambridge Scholars Publishing.

Voigt-Graf, C (2004) 'Towards a geography of transnational spaces: Indian transnational communities in Australia', *Global Networks* vol. 4, no. 1, pp. 25–49.

Voigt-Graf, C (2005) 'The construction of transnational spaces by Indian migrants in Australia', *Journal of Ethnic and Migration Studies* vol. 31, no. 2, pp. 365–84.

Volkman, TA (2005) 'Introduction: New geographies of kinship', in TA Volkman (ed.) *Cultures of Transnational Adoption*, Duke University Press, Durham, pp. 1–22.

Wade J, Mitchell F & Baylis G (2005) *Unaccompanied Asylum Seeking Children. The Response of Social Work Services*. British Association for Adoption and Fostering, London.

Wakeford, J (1969) *The Cloistered Elite: A Sociological Analysis of the English Public Boarding School*. Macmillan, London.

Walker, I (2012) 'Marrying at home, marrying away: Customary marriages and legal marriages in Ngazidja and in the diaspora', in K Charsley (ed.) *Transnational Marriage*. Routledge, London, pp. 105–26.

Wall, K & Bolzman, C (2014) 'Mapping the new plurality of transnational families', in L Baldassar & L Merla (eds) *Transnational Families, Migration and the Circulation of Care: Understanding Mobility and Absence in Family Life*. Routledge, London, pp. 61–77.

Wallerstein, I (1974) 'The rise and future demise of the world capitalist system: Concepts for comparative analysis', *Comparative Studies in Society and History* vol. 16, no. 4, pp. 387–415.

Wallin, AM & Ahlstrom, GI (2006) 'Unaccompanied young adult refugees in Sweden, experiences of their life situation and well-being: A qualitative follow-up study', *Ethnicity & Health* vol. 10, no. 2, pp. 129–44.

Waring, M (1988) *Counting for Nothing: What Men Value and What Women are Worth*. Allen & Unwin and Port Nicholson Press, Wellington.

Waters, J (2003) '"Satellite kids" in Vancouver: Transnational migration, education and the experiences of lone-children', in MW Charney, BSA Yeoh & TC Kiong (eds) *Asian Migrants and Education: The Tensions of Education in Immigrant Societies and Among Migrant Groups*. Kluwer Academic Publishers, Dordrecht, pp. 165–84.

Waters, JL (2010) 'Becoming a father, missing a wife: Chinese transnational families and the male experience of lone parenting in Canada', *Population, Space and Place* vol. 16, pp. 63–74.

Watts, JL (2004) *Best of Both Worlds? Fly In Fly Out Research Project Final Report*. Pilbara Regional Council, Karratha.

Weeks, J (1991) 'Pretended family relationships', in D Clark (ed.) *Marriage, Domestic Life and Social Change*. Routledge, London, pp. 178–94.

Weeks, J, Heaphy, B & Donovan, C (2001) *Same Sex Intimacies: Families of Choice and Other Life Experiments*. Routledge, London.

West, C & Zimmerman, D (1987) 'Doing gender', *Gender & Society* vol. 1, no. 2, pp. 125–51.

Weston, K (1991) *Families We Choose: Lesbians, Gays, Kinship*. Columbia University Press, New York.

Weston, K (1995) 'Get thee to ab big city: Sexual imaginary and the great gay migration', *GLQ: A Journal of Lesbian and Gay Studies* vol. 2, pp. 253–77.

Wetzel, JR (1990) 'American families: 75 years of change', *Monthly Labor Review* March 1990, pp. 4–13.

Whitehouse, B (2009) 'Transnational childrearing and the preservation of transnational identity in Brazzaville, Congo', *Global Networks* vol. 9, no. 1, pp. 82–99.

Williams, L (2010) *Global Marriage: Cross-Border Marriage Migration in Global Context*. Palgrave Macmillan, Houndmills.

Williams, S (2008) 'What is fatherhood? Searching for the reflexive father', *Sociology* vol. 42, no. 3, pp. 487–502.

Willmott, P (1986) *Social Networks, Informal Care and Public Policy*. Policy Studies Institute, London.

Wilding, R (2003) 'Romantic love and "getting married": Narratives of the wedding in and out of cinema texts', *Journal of Sociology* vol. 39, no. 4, pp. 373–89.

Wilding, R (2006) '"Virtual" intimacies? Families communicating across transnational contexts', *Global Networks* vol. 6, no. 2, pp. 125–42.

Wilding, R (2012) 'Mediating culture in transnational spaces: An example of young people from refugee backgrounds', *Continuum* vol. 26, no. 3, pp. 501–11.

Wilding, R & Baldassar, L (2009) 'Transnational family-work balance: Experiences of Australian migrants caring for ageing parents and young children across distance and borders', *Journal of Family Studies* vol. 15 no. 2, pp. 177–87.

Wilding, R & Gifford, S (2013) 'Introduction: Forced displacement, refugees and ICTs', *Journal of Refugee Studies* vol. 26, no. 4, pp. 495–504.

Williams, L (2010) *Global Marriage: Cross-Border Marriage Migration in Global Context*. Palgrave Macmillan, Houndmills.

Wimark, T (2016a) 'The impact of family ties on the mobility decisions of gay men and lesbians', *Gender, Place & Culture: A Journal of Feminist Geography* vol. 23, no. 5, pp. 659–76.

Wimark, T (2016b) 'Migration motives of gay men in the new acceptance era: A cohort study from Malmo, Sweden', *Social & Cultural Geography* vol. 17, no. 5, pp. 605–22.

Yasuike, A (2011) 'The impact of Japanese corporate transnationalism on men's involvement in family life and relationships', *Journal of Family Issues* vol. 32, no. 12, pp. 1700–25.

Yeates, N (2004) 'A dialogue with "global care chain" analysis: Nurse migration in the Irish context', *Feminist Review* vol. 77, pp. 79–95.

Yeates, N (2005) 'A global political economy of care', *Social Policy and Society* vol. 4, no. 2, pp. 227–34.

Yeates, N (2009) 'Production for export: The role of the state in the development and operation of global care chains', *Population, Space and Place* vol. 15, no. 2, pp. 175–87.

Yeates, N (2012) 'Global care chains: A state-of-the-art review and future directions in care transnationalization research', *Global networks* vol. 12, no. 2, pp. 135–54.

Yeoh, BS, Chee, HL & Vu, TKD (2013) 'Global householding and the negotiation of intimate labour in commercially-matched international marriages between Vietnamese women and Singaporean men', *Geoforum* vol. 51, pp. 284–93.

Yngvesson, B (2010) *Belonging in an Adopted World*. University of Chicago Press, Chicago.

Yngvesson, B (2013) 'The child who was left behind: "Dynamic temporality" and interpretations of history in transnational adoption', *Childhood* vol. 20, no. 3, pp. 354–67.

Yue, A (2008) 'Same-sex migration in Australia: From interdependency to intimacy', *GLQ: A Journal of Lesbian and Gay Studies* vol. 14, no. 2–3, pp. 239–62.

Yue, A (2016) 'Queer migration: Going south from China to Australia', in G Brown & K Browne (eds) *The Routledge Research Companion to Geographies of Sex and Sexualities*. Routledge, London, pp. 247–55.

Zechner, M (2004) 'Family commitments under negotiation: Dual carers in Finland and Italy', *Social Policy and Administration* vol. 38, no. 6, pp. 640–53.

Zelizer, VA (1994) *Pricing the Priceless Child: The Changing Social Value of Children*. Princeton University, New Jersey.

Zetter, R (2007) 'More labels, fewer refugees: Remaking the refugee label in an era of globalization', *Journal of Refugee Studies* vol. 20, no. 2, pp. 172–92.

Zhan, HJ & Montgomery, RJV (2003) 'Gender and elder care in China: The influence of filial piety and structural constraints', *Gender & Society* vol. 17, no. 2, pp. 209–29.

Index

Adoption   3, 5, 78–80, 92–95, 118, 120,
    137–138, 157, 160, 169
Aged care   2, 7, 26, 68, 97–115, 119, 160
Aged care, cultural norms   107–108, 111
Aged care, transnational   108–113
Ageing populations   96–104
Albania   104–108, 114
Algeria   149–150
Appadurai, A   13
Astronaut family   77, 86–88, 170
Asylum seekers   15, 29, 89, 137, 149
Australia   2–4, 6–7, 11, 14, 25, 29, 50–51,
    61, 78, 90–92, 97–100, 109–113, 128,
    130, 132, 148, 152

Baldassar, L   7, 14, 16, 90, 101–103,
    109–113, 151, 164
Baldock, C   7, 14, 16, 101–103,
    109–113, 151, 164
Bangladesh   30–33, 37, 39, 54, 92
Bauman, Z   9–10, 44, 117, 141, 151
Beck, U   8–9, 24, 39–40, 42, 100, 117,
    139–140, 157–160, 163, 165
Beck-Gernsheim, E   8–9, 24, 39–40, 42, 100,
    117, 139–140, 157–160, 163, 165
Birth mother   5, 94
Boehm, D   15, 52–54, 74–75, 90
Britain, United Kingdom   4, 7, 11, 25, 28–33,
    39, 53, 61, 66, 73, 92, 102–103, 126,
    134, 148, 160–161
Bryceson, D   120, 122

Canada   14, 50, 76, 86, 114, 148
Care   65–77, 163–164
    aged care   7, 19, 26, 68, 97–115, 119, 160
    care work   58, 65–66, 68–69
    child care   4, 38, 42, 45, 56–57, 60,
        63–65, 74–76, 79–88, 90, 99, 101,
        114, 119, 126, 129
    circulation   102, 124, 131, 164–165
    contributions of elderly   101
    crisis of   97–104
    culturally specific   6–7, 111, 129
    deficit   42, 66, 77
    emotional support   3, 5, 45, 58, 63,
        71–72, 75, 99, 102–103, 109–110,
        119, 122, 152, 156, 164

financial support   36–37, 62–64, 68–69,
    72–73, 99, 102, 106, 109. 119, 122,
    130–133, 164
global care chains   59, 65–70, 78, 81–86,
    165
informal support   97, 100–106,
    109–111
personal care   63, 103, 110–111,
    164
practical support   102, 109–111, 119,
    164
Caribbean   100, 123–128, 130, 134
Castles, S   14–16, 67
Chamberlain, M   123, 125
Childcare   4, 38, 42, 45, 56–57, 60, 63–65,
    74–76, 79–88, 90, 99, 101, 114, 119,
    126, 129
Childhood   78–96
    agency   85–86, 88
    cultural constructions of   77, 79–80,
        85
    cultural maintenance   80, 84, 88, 90, 102,
        114, 129
    education   80–81, 86–87, 129
    forced migration   88–91
    identity   91–95
    international adoption   92–95
    satellite babies   84
    sense of abandonment   60, 81, 88
    state regulation of   80
    transformation of   79–81
Chile   61
China   21, 25, 29, 31–32, 44–45, 61, 84,
    86–87, 92, 113–114
Coe, C   64, 79–80
Cohabitation   4, 49, 148
Colombia   136–137, 153, 157
Communication technologies   2, 13,
    16–17, 24, 28, 30, 37, 44, 47, 54–55,
    71–77, 83–85, 102, 108–112, 117,
    120–121, 126, 129–131, 133, 135,
    147, 151–153, 155, 161, 164, 166,
    168, 170
Commuter couples   44, 46–48, 50, 52, 160,
    169–170
Connell, R   5, 43
Constable, N   6, 35, 38

Co-presence 64, 84, 95, 97, 120–122, 130, 168,
Croatia 25
Cultural logics of desire 38
Culture 21–22, 24, 28, 30, 33, 36, 45–46, 56, 62, 67, 77, 79, 84, 91, 104, 106, 118, 123, 129, 131, 157, 160, 167
   birth culture 94
   consumer culture 24
   cultural capital 33, 76, 80, 86, 168
   cultural change 1, 6, 16, 27, 35, 48
   cultural diversity 1, 11, 29, 43, 118, 131,
   cultural maintenance 5, 53, 88, 90, 94, 109, 114, 122, 129, 155, 162
   cultural models 6–7, 18, 31, 34, 38, 43, 54, 58, 64, 67, 76, 79–80, 82, 85, 100, 103, 123, 143–144, 157, 167
Czech Republic 25

Dating
   cross-cultural 33, 35–38
   online 24, 27, 35–38
   television shows 21–23
   transnational 24, 28, 37–38
Denmark 25, 29
Desire 10, 23, 28, 35, 37, 59, 120
   cultural logics of 38–39
Detraditionalization 8–9, 24, 63
Diaspora 90, 129–131, 170
Digital divide 13, 168
Divorce 3, 7–8, 10, 25–26, 29, 35–36, 49, 53, 56, 63, 118–121, 142, 157
Doing gender 43

Education 15, 24, 26–27, 33–35, 42, 54, 56, 59–62, 66, 71, 80–81, 84–90, 97, 99, 105, 107, 113, 127, 129, 133, 146–148, 162
Egypt 25
El Salvador 55, 74–76, 83–84
Emotion 3, 6–10, 21, 23, 51, 62–64, 69, 80, 85–86, 88, 105, 119, 124
Emotion work 43, 49, 51, 58, 70, 73, 93, 142–144
Emotional abuse 4
Emotional costs 60, 67,
Emotional pain 60, 67, 69, 107–108, 133, 163
Emotional support 3, 5, 45, 58, 63, 71–72, 75, 99, 102–103, 109–110, 119, 122, 152, 156, 164
Extended family 16, 21, 30, 36, 45, 53, 56, 60, 64, 75, 78, 80, 83, 91, 99, 105, 116–136, 159, 161, 170
   modified 102, 119

Faier, L 166–167
Family
   astronaut 86–88, 170

crisis of 4, 7, 31, 62, 157
definitions 3
deviant 29, 47, 118, 123
display 120–121, 126–127, 134, 140, 151, 156–157, 165
diversity 4, 11, 80, 92, 118, 136–141
dual career 42–47
extended 16, 21, 30, 36, 45, 53, 56, 60, 64, 75, 78, 80, 83, 91, 99, 105, 116–136, 159, 161, 170
gender roles 34, 36, 47, 53–54, 56–57, 65, 81–82, 101
ideology 5, 12, 17–18, 22, 61, 118, 161–162
nuclear 3–11, 16–19, 42, 45–47, 52, 55, 61–62, 65, 72–73, 79–82, 85, 92, 117–119, 123–125, 128, 131, 138–139, 144, 161–162, 170
obligations 6–7, 9, 11, 17, 26, 48, 66–67, 100, 102, 104–105, 109, 119–120, 124–127, 130, 140–141, 147, 150, 155–156, 163–164, 170
policies 4, 6–7, 12, 17–18, 29, 33, 36, 66, 109, 118, 123, 137, 155, 159, 161, 165–166
practices 5, 11–12, 17, 64, 118, 120–122, 125, 140, 164
reputation 30, 130–131, 135, 146
roles 5–8, 11, 17, 22, 26, 31, 33–34, 36, 42–43, 47, 52–54, 56–57, 62, 65, 67, 72, 76–77, 81–82, 84, 97, 99, 106, 113–114, 121, 123–124, 134, 136, 138–141, 147
transnational 30, 80, 85, 98, 109, 111, 120–135, 146–149, 150, 163–164, 166–167, 169–170
Families of choice 22, 93, 138–141, 144
   transnational 146–149
Fassin, E 149
Fatherhood 4–6, 46, 56, 62–63, 72–74, 82
   absent fathers 63
   economic support 72
   from a distance 72–74, 82
   primary caregivers 56, 63
Femininity 5, 7, 18, 35–36, 38, 43, 46, 53–54, 71–73
Fertility rates 61, 65, 98, 124
FIFO 49–52, 170
Finch, J 7, 86, 88, 101–102, 104, 109, 111, 119–121, 140, 151, 164
Finland 100, 112
Floating ties 16, 168–171
Fly-In-Fly-Out 49–52, 170
France 53, 61, 149–150
Friends 11, 16, 19, 47, 49, 89, 120, 139–144, 150–153, 158, 163

Gamburd, M 56, 68–70, 150
Gardner, K 30–31, 54, 92

Gender inequalities   6, 33. 52, 61, 65, 67, 161–162
Gender roles   34, 36, 47, 52–54, 56–57, 65, 73, 81–82, 101
Gendered subjectivities   36, 43, 55, 57–58, 167–168
Germany   15, 25–26, 100, 136–137
Ghana   64
Giddens, A   8–12, 22, 24, 43, 62, 73, 117, 139–140
Gifts   60, 69–71, 75, 81, 83, 98, 110, 121, 127, 129, 133
Gilding, M   120, 160
Global care chains   59, 65–70, 78, 81–86, 165
Global householding   123–124, 165
Global hypergamy   35
Global inequalities   13, 33, 37, 65–67, 162
Global nanny   67–70
Glocalization   13
Goody, J   4, 11, 24
Gorman-Murray, A   144–145, 148
Grandparents   57, 64, 75, 79, 84, 86, 99, 110, 113–114, 119, 126
    transnational   113–114

Hannaford, D   54
Heteronormativity   22–23, 136–153, 155, 161
Heterosexuality   22, 40, 55, 57, 81, 118, 138–140, 144–148, 164
Ho, E   87, 122
Hochschild, A   15, 51, 65–67, 69, 100, 143
Holmes, M   49, 58, 153
Home   14–15, 33, 42, 45–46, 48–49, 51–55, 61–62, 64, 72, 75, 82, 87–88, 92, 108–114, 121, 126, 133, 161
Hong Kong   27, 29, 55, 86, 88, 99
Households
    family   3–4, 6–7, 10, 14, 33, 42–43, 45, 47, 52–57, 62, 64, 68, 72, 79, 85, 87, 99, 117–119, 124, 126, 131
    LAT   48–49
    single person   10–11
Huang, S   55–56, 62, 77, 86–88

Identities   5, 8, 11, 22, 24, 30, 43, 47, 53, 62, 71, 81, 91–95, 113, 123–125, 131, 138–139, 140–152
Illouz, E   9, 24, 37–38
India   14, 31, 44, 45, 61, 78–79, 92, 105–107, 131–134, 152, 160
Individualization   7–11, 22, 24, 26, 43, 60, 80, 95, 100, 117–118, 136, 143, 153–161, 163, 168
Inheritance   120, 125, 127, 133–134, 137, 160
International adoption   78, 92–95
Intimacy   9–11, 48, 51, 54, 70–75, 114, 151, 167

Ireland   2, 16, 25, 66, 97–98, 109–113
Italy   14, 16, 25, 55, 68, 76, 100, 109–114

Japan   25, 27, 46, 99
Jennings, R   145, 147

Ka'ili, T   128–129
Kilkey, M   72–73, 165
King, R   107–108
Kinning   93, 122
Kofman, E   67, 124
Korea   31–32, 86, 88, 92, 94

Labour export   66
LAT   48–49
Lee, H   90–91, 128–131
Left-behind children   81–86
Left-behind elderly   104–108
Left-behind husbands   55–57
Left-behind wives   52–55
Levin, I   48
Licence to leave   103
Litwak, E   102–103, 108, 119
Living alone   10, 118
Living Apart Together   48–49
Loneliness   10, 47, 51, 60, 85, 105
Love   5, 9–10, 18, 21–26, 28, 33–34, 36–39, 41, 57, 64, 69, 72–73, 75–76, 83, 93, 111, 114, 147, 157–159, 163
Love and money   36–37
Luibheid, E   144, 148

Madianou, M   17, 68, 71, 75, 83
Mahler, S   54–55, 73
Malaysia   61, 86, 132
Marriage   4–10, 22, 24–39, 40–58, 149–150
    arranged   26, 28–31
    brokers   32
    choice   26
    commercial   33
    cousin   29–31
    cross-cultural   33
    global hypergamy   35
    homogamy   26–27
    hypergamy   26–27, 35
    international   29
    market   26–28
    matchmakers   32
    policies   29
    polygamy   29
    rates   27
    risk   31–34
    squeeze   27
    tours   33
    transnational   28–33, 52–57
Masculinity   5, 18, 31, 35, 38, 43–44, 46, 53–54, 56–57, 72–73, 82, 146, 150
Mason, J   7, 101–104, 111, 119, 140, 164
Mcdonaldization   12

Merla, L   102, 164, 165
Mexico   15, 25, 52–54, 74–76, 146
Migration   12–16, 29, 43, 52–53, 103–108,
        113, 130, 132, 163–167
    borders   14–15, 74
    chain   14, 132
    child   64, 80–81, 86–88
    complexity   14, 16, 145
    contract labour   15, 66
    economic   14, 29–30, 55, 81–83, 89, 107,
        123–124, 133
    family   48, 64, 86–87, 124–126,
        133, 150
    father   67, 72, 82, 85
    female   14, 16, 55–56, 68, 70–72, 82
    forced   15, 88–91, 122
    informal   15, 74
    labour   13, 29–30, 55–56, 66, 68,
        70–72, 90
    licence to leave   103
    male   14, 54, 82–83
    marriage   29–33
    mother   67–68, 70–72, 82–84
    policies   15, 29, 66, 70, 89, 108, 123,
        126, 148
    queer   144–146, 149–150
    resettlement   16, 88, 116
    rural-urban   24, 31–33, 104, 107,
        144–146
    settlement   14–15, 66
    skilled   15, 45
    spousal   29–31
    student   15, 86–87, 107
    unaccompanied minors   89
Miller, Daniel   17, 68, 71, 75, 83
Miller, Dorothy   99
Miller, M   14–15, 67
Miller, T   6, 63
Miltiades, H   104–106
Mobilities   43–52, 145, 164, 169–170
Modified extended family   102, 119
Morgan, D   5, 11–12, 120–122, 140, 151–152
Motherhood   5–6, 35–36, 56, 60–63, 65–67,
        70–72, 75, 79, 80–84, 86–87, 94, 98,
        113, 131, 143
    absent mother   80–83
    displaced mothering   65
    from a distance   60, 70–72, 82
    intensive   6, 62, 71, 83, 86
    myth of   6, 61–62, 67, 94
    and paid work   6, 56, 62, 71
    shadow mothering   70
Multiculturalism   16
Murdock, G   3, 5, 140

Nannies   32, 59, 60–70, 75
Nation
    state   122–124, 136–141, 155, 159,
        165–168

Nervios   85–86
Netherlands   22, 47–48, 109–113
New Zealand   3, 13–14, 25, 61, 78, 90,
        109–113, 128, 130
Nishitani, M   130

Ocampo, A   146–147
Olwig, KF   64, 125–128
Online communications   19, 24, 27–28, 30,
        37–38, 130, 152–153

Pahl, R   139–143, 152
Pakistan   28–31, 33, 160
Pananakhonsab, W   35–37
Parenting   6, 43, 48, 50–51, 59–77
    contradictory pressures   59–62
    fatherhood   4–6, 46, 56, 62–63, 72–74, 82
    from a distance   50–51, 81–86
    intensive   62, 76, 86
    motherhood   5–6, 35–36, 56, 60–63,
        65–67, 70–72, 75, 79, 80–84, 86–87,
        94, 98, 113, 131, 143
    paid parental leave   6
    rights   137
    trailing parents   45
    transformation of   60–65
Parrenas, R   56, 65, 68–70, 72–73, 82–83, 146,
Parsons, T   3, 9–10, 42–43, 117, 119, 138
Patrilineal joint family   131
Personal life   142–144, 159
Peru   25
Philippines   6, 14, 34, 55–56, 60–61, 66,
        68–69, 71–73, 76, 82–83, 86, 123,
        134, 146, 162
Photographs   79, 107, 115, 121–122
Place   52–53
Poland   73
Polymedia   17, 71, 130,
Pribilsky, J   85–86
Pure relationship   9, 22–25, 139, 163, 168

Reflexive self   8–10, 24
Relativising   122
Remittances   14–15, 56, 64, 66, 68, 72, 76,
        82–83, 89–90, 107, 109, 123,
        126–128, 132, 134
Robertson, R   13
Robertson, Z   122
Robinson, K   35–36
Romantic love   21–25, 36–39
Rural   14–15, 24–27, 31–32, 65, 104,
        107–108, 144–145, 162

Salcedo, M   149
Same-sex parents   6, 137
Same-sex relationships   22, 40, 138–139,
        148, 160
Sandwich generation   97–99
Satellite babies   84

Second generation migrants   28, 88–91, 95, 127, 130
Senegal   54–55
Shipman, B   160
Singapore   25, 27, 33–35, 55–56, 109–113, 122
Singh, S   131–133
Smart, C   29, 119, 143, 147, 160
Social media   21, 23, 83, 122, 130, 151–152
Social mobility   133
Spain   84
Spencer, L   139, 140–143
Sri Lanka   56, 61, 66, 68–70, 150
Suffusion   141–142, 151

Thailand   27, 34–36, 66, 117, 121
Tonga   90–91, 128–131, 170
Tradition   18, 22, 26, 30–32, 34–36, 38, 43, 47, 64, 84, 90, 106, 118, 129–130, 152, 158–159, 161–162, 168
Trailing parent   45
Trailing spouse   44–46, 48–49
Transnational adoption   92–95
Transnational aged care   108–113
Transnational couples   52–57
Transnational families   30, 80, 85, 98, 109, 120–134, 146–150, 163–170
Transnational grandparents   113–114
Treas, J   17, 101–102
Trost, J   48
Trust   30, 34, 74–75, 133–134, 158–159, 164–165
Turkey   15, 25, 29, 90

Unaccompanied minors   89
United Kingdom, Britain   3–4, 6–7, 11, 25, 28–33, 39, 53, 61, 66, 68, 71, 73, 92, 102–103, 126, 134, 148, 160–161
United States of America   3, 6, 14, 15, 25, 31, 46, 52, 61, 69, 74–76, 92, 105–107, 113, 128, 148
Urry, J   44
Uruguay   61

Vietnam   55–56, 90, 92, 162
Visits   2, 15, 30, 32, 48, 57, 68, 76, 79, 83, 87, 90, 98, 105, 108–117, 121, 129, 147, 151, 170
Vullnetari, J   104, 107–108
Vuorela, U   120, 122

Weeks, J   22, 138–141
Weston, K   22, 139, 144–146
Work
    paid   6, 42, 47, 49, 61, 84
    unpaid   6, 42–43, 61
    women's double burden   42, 51, 99–101, 112
World families   158–159

Yeates, N   13, 65–67
Yeoh, B   34, 55–56, 62, 77, 86–88, 122

Zones of encounter   166

Printed in Great Britain
by Amazon